# DISTANT
# SKIES

# DISTANT
# SKIES

## An American Journey on Horseback

Melissa A. Priblo Chapman

TRAFALGAR SQUARE
North Pomfret, Vermont

First published in 2020 by
Trafalgar Square Books
North Pomfret, Vermont 05053

Some names and identifying details have been changed to protect the privacy of individuals.

**Disclaimer of Liability**
The author and publisher shall have neither liability nor responsibility to any person or entity with respect to any loss or damage caused or alleged to be caused directly or indirectly by the information contained in this book. While the book is as accurate as the author can make it, there may be errors, omissions, and inaccuracies.

The author and publisher have made every effort to obtain a release from photographers whose images appear in this book. In some cases, however, the photographers were not known or could not be contacted. Should additional photographers be identified, they will be credited in future editions of this book.

Trafalgar Square Books encourages the use of approved safety helmets in all equestrian sports and activities.

**Library of Congress Cataloging-in-Publication Data**
Names: Chapman, Melissa A. Priblo, author.
Title: Distant skies : an American journey on horseback / Melissa A. Priblo
   Chapman.
Description: North Pomfret, Vermont : Trafalgar Square Books, 2020. |
   Summary: "Melissa Chapman was 23 years old and part of a happy, healthy,
   loving family. She had a decent job, a boyfriend she cared about, and
   friends she enjoyed. Yet on the first of May in 1982, she said good-bye
   to all of it. Carrying a puppy named Gypsy, she climbed aboard a horse
   and rode away from everything, heading west. With no cell phone, no GPS,
   no support team or truck following with supplies, Chapman quickly
   learned that the reality of a cross-country horseback journey was quite
   different from the fantasy. Her solo adventure would immediately test
   her mental, physical, and emotional resources as she and her four-legged
   companions were forced to adapt to the dangers and loneliness of a trek
   that would span over 2600 miles, beginning in New York State and
   reaching its end on the other side of the country, in California"--
   Provided by publisher.
Identifiers: LCCN 2020001560 (print) | LCCN 2020001561 (ebook) | ISBN
   9781570769603 (paperback) | ISBN 9781646010240 (epub)
Subjects: LCSH: Chapman, Melissa A. Priblo--Travel. | Horsemen and
   horsewomen--United States--Biography. | Endurance riding
   (Horsemanship)--United States--Biography. | Overland journeys to the
   Pacific. | Human-animal relationships.
Classification: LCC SF284.52 .C43 2020 (print) | LCC SF284.52 (ebook) |
   DDC 798.092 [B]--dc23
LC record available at https://lccn.loc.gov/2020001560
LC ebook record available at https://lccn.loc.gov/2020001561

Photos courtesy of the author unless otherwise noted.

Book design by Tim Holtz
Cover design by RM Didier
Typefaces: Sabon, Orpheus

Printed in the United States of America
10 9 8 7 6 5 4 3 2 1

For Rainy, Gypsy, and Amanda.
*Every road is a story.*

# CONTENTS

PROLOGUE    XIII

PART ONE
## Before    I
Rainy    5
The Dream    6
Conditioning, Training    7
A Guy and a Dog    8
Gypsy    12
48 Hours until Departure    13

PART TWO
## On Our Way    17
Leaving    21
Longest Day    22
Different Day    28
Ghosts    29
Old Toys, Country Roads    30
Meshoppen    33
Crying to Singing    35

The Bridge          36

Too Long, Too Far          37

Traveler's Spring          38

Welcome to Hughesville          40

House of Guys          40

Along the River          43

Unexpected Friendship          43

Just People          48

Funhouse Faces          49

Penn State          50

Grier School          52

Louie's Lounge          56

Storm on the Mountain          59

Tunnel          62

Rainy's Twin...and the News          64

Dead Head          66

Animal Rights          67

Country Club          69

A Sign          72

PART THREE

**On the Road**          75

Locusts          79

Brad          80

Danger on the Road          82

Goodmans          84

Jump Aboard          88

Ice Cream Shop          88

On Saddles          89

Cowboys for Christ          91

Shadows          92

Welcome to Indiana          93

Golden Boy     96

Construction Site     97

Sundays     99

Revival     100

Land of Lincoln     103

Carlyle     105

Big River     108

A Mystery     110

Diamond Jim     111

Soothing Sunsets     113

Luxenhaus Farm     113

Good Dog, Bad Dog     117

Serendipity     119

Copperhead     120

Inside Horse     123

My Rainy     125

Nannie and Anthis     126

Deerfield     128

Delays     129

Vet Call     133

Oh No     135

The Worried Walk     137

Twists and Turns     138

Tom and Barb     141

Haying     143

Days     146

Kansas Time     148

Phone Call     149

Three Simple Words     151

A Meeting     153

Getting to Know Her     155

Time Is Ours     156

Gone Down the Road     157
Morning Star     158

PART FOUR
# The Road West     161
Amanda, Gypsy     165
Flint Hills     166
Little Guardian     167
Diamond Day     168
Round House, Round Moon     169
Wide Open Lonesome     170
Reunion Road     171
Heat and Sweetness     173
State Line     175
Winning Over the Mule     175
Borders     176
Texas     178
Nowhere     180
Along the Tracks     182
Signs     184
The Darkest Night     185
Full Circle     192
Antelope     195
West     196
Tucumcari     198
Hitchhiker     199
Cuervo     201
What Gypsy Uncovered     203
Goodbye Road     205
Skins     207
Cold Night Near Grants     208
An Old Man, His Cowboy Hat, and His Son     209

The Great Divide        211
Lines (Cattle Guard)        213
Unplanned        216
Fort Wingate        217
Feelings for New Mexico        219
East of Gallup        220
Sidewalks of Gallup        221
Navajo Woman        225
Kindred Spirit        227
Here and Now        229
Near Lupton, Arizona        229
A Different View        232
Douglas Sky        233
Friend Amanda        235
Sunsets, Seasons        236

PART FIVE

# The Road Is Ours        239

Chambers, Arizona        243
The Only Direction        244
Rest Stop: You Never Know        245
Rest Stop West: Circle the Wagons        249
Literal        251
Canteen        252
Highway        254
Winslow        256
Teepee Rock Ranch/Turquoise Ranch        258
Moonrise at Two Guns        259
Truck Stop Diner, Twin Arrows        261
Nuts…and Grateful        263
Gold in the Day        266
Trust        267

Beauty Large and Small        270
Saddle Tramp        272
On the Wild Trail        275
Cheers, Peace        278
The Road Is Ours        279
Hualapai Diner        280
Hilltop Honkytonk        282
Closeness        285
Camera-Conscious        287
Decision        288
Kingman        289
Haunted        291
Black Mountains        295
Wild Watchers        296
Davis Dam        297
Casino Night, Laughlin        298
Nevada Silver        301
Sign in the Desert        302
Near        304
Needles, California        306
About Ending...        310
At "Home," in Kansas        313

PART SIX
After        315
        Love Goes On        319

ACKNOWLEDGMENTS        325

ABOUT THE AUTHOR        329

# PROLOGUE

---

I can't tell you exactly how the dream of riding a horse across the country started. I can tell you how it flourished.

As a young child, I was known in my family as "spacey." I'd sit in school, and instead of paying attention, I'd be lost in my own fantasy world, looking out the window, imagining riding through some distant town on a trustworthy horse.

From the back seat of the family car, no dirt road or shady trail escaped my notice. They beckoned to me, making me wish I could follow as they led me somewhere green and wild. I could almost feel the swing of a horse's stride beneath me and the breeze at my back as my horse and I discovered where those roads and trails might take us.

Time passes and daydreamy kids grow up. But as a young adult, every time I stood in line for too long at the department of motor vehicles or struggled to pay bills, the fantasies reemerged. I still dreamed of living like a gypsy on the road, spending every day riding and free.

I had my own horse—a lovely older gelding my dad helped me buy—and as I was nearing the end of my teens I acquired a second mount: a four-year-old Quarter Horse I called Rainy. This horse proved to be remarkable, and by the time I was twenty-three and

Rainy was seven, I knew I had the right horse for the journey I'd dreamed of. Rainy and I were in good health and good shape. I couldn't think of a reason *not* to try to make it happen.

I wasn't trying to escape a troubled life. Just the opposite was true. I was part of a happy family. I had a job, a boyfriend, and friends I cared about. Yet in the spring of my twenty-third year, I said goodbye to all of that. Carrying a puppy named Gypsy, I climbed up on Rainy, the horse I loved so dearly, and we walked away from everything, heading west.

This is the story of our journey.

# PART ONE

———

# BEFORE

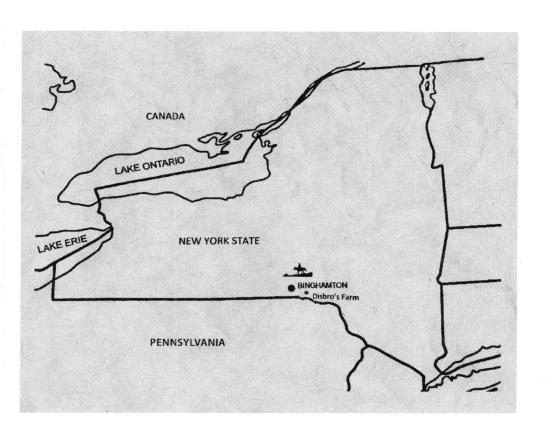

CANADA

LAKE ONTARIO

LAKE ERIE

NEW YORK STATE

● BINGHAMTON
* Disbro's Farm

PENNSYLVANIA

## RAINY

A secret quest brought me to a winding country road, a folded newspaper with one small, circled classified ad on the seat beside me. I knew when I found the place I was looking for: a barn, and down the hill, horses grazing in a grassy field. The owner of the farm came out as I pulled in, and together, we walked toward the pasture.

I noticed a buckskin horse standing out amongst the sorrels and bays. He looked up from his grazing, walked up to us, and stopped in front of me. His coat was a light golden color, his mane and tail, midnight black. His muzzle and ears were a soft charcoal, like shadows. I took in every detail of this horse with deep clarity—his velvety coat and deep brown eyes. I held out my hand and the young horse met it with his muzzle, blowing a soft puff of air onto my palm. Right then, I knew he was my horse.

I asked my veterinarian to visit the buckskin and check him over, make sure he was healthy and sound. My vet took a liking to him, too, confirming my belief that I'd found an exceptional horse. This was important, because I was keeping something to myself: I was searching for a horse that could carry me a long distance. A *very* long distance—like across the whole United States.

Some might have said I should've been looking for an older and more experienced horse. An older and wiser person would not have succumbed to love at first sight. But I was nineteen years old. I wasn't listening to common sense the day I met the buckskin. I was listening to an impulse deep inside me.

The young horse I named Raindance came home to live with me and my old gelding, Bo. The first sight of the buckskin across that green field, how he walked over and stood with me, felt like fate. We were never apart again.

## THE DREAM

There's an old horseman's saying that it takes six months to know if you bought the right horse and a year to really bond with him. Horses are creatures of flight, hardwired as prey animals to flee at the first sign of trouble. They're peaceful animals, but they walk through life warily. Teaching them to accept what we humans ask of them takes time, patience, knowledge, and skill.

But Rainy and I started right out as if we had been together a long time. We didn't have experience, but we had what I believed was an almost mystical connection. In my heart, that mattered more than all the training in the world.

Now that I had the right horse, my dream of a cross-country journey began to find form. In my mind, it combined all I loved: I would be outdoors, riding the horse I felt so connected to, traveling somewhere new each day, and seeing the country. I didn't mind being alone; in fact, I liked it. At the same time, I enjoyed meeting people and hearing their stories. What could be more perfect than a horseback trip across the United States?

I researched other adventurers who had traveled long distances by horseback. I studied equine conditioning and training. But mostly, I rode. It was autumn when Rainy came to me, and we roamed the countryside all season, first through the farm fields as leaves fell. By the time the snow blew in flakes around us, we had wandered many back roads and trails. The trust was there and the idea of walking away together had taken on a life of its own.

The late teens and early twenties are a funny age; you are legally an adult but oh so young. It's easy to get confused by conflicting desires: the yearning for a sense of belonging and a need to strike out on our own; the natural instinct to love and care for something, clashing with the thirst for independence. For me, Rainy fulfilled all those mixed up emotions. Having him allowed me to pursue my dream, while at the same time teaching me to be responsible and put his care above my own. The young buckskin could be counted on to go forward willingly, and he seemed to enjoy our meanderings as much as I did. We spent so much time exploring those first few months, I believe he came to trust that I'd never ask him to do anything frightening or harmful, and I began to trust him to carry me through anything.

The journey became something more than just, "Ride a horse across the USA." It became, "Ride across the USA on *this* horse." It was about a unique experience that Rainy and I would share as a team. There would be no other horse and no other way.

## CONDITIONING, TRAINING

Early on, before I had a real idea of when we would actually start the trip, I got serious about preparations and developing a conditioning program to get ready for our long ride. The advice available was a mixed bag, further diluted by the fact that no one I could contact had done exactly what I was planning to do. I searched for any nugget of wisdom that might help: My veterinarian researched vaccinations that Rainy might need in other parts of the country. I learned to read topographical maps. I studied articles about endurance riding, which taught me about electrolytes, hydration, and the horse's pulse and respiration rates—how they should be at rest and how these numbers should change as Rainy's fitness improved. My dad, though not a horseman, was a marathon runner with lots of training experience, and his advice added to the disparate collection of information I used to prepare my horse and myself to walk approximately twenty-five miles a day for many months over varying terrain in changeable weather.

The mental training you give a horse is as important as the physical. There are many varied personalities in the horse world, and certain horses are better suited to certain activities than others. Along with his willingness, Rainy proved to be quite unflappable. I rode him on bridges, past livestock, and through water. I practiced camping with the buckskin tied near my tent at night.

As we prepared for the adventure I'd wished for my entire life, I dated, I went out with friends, and I had several jobs. Twice, I chose a date to begin our journey, and twice, I postponed it, not feeling anywhere near ready to leave. Then one winter day, it dawned on me that Rainy was now seven, a prime age for a horse. And I was twenty-three, a prime age for a human. We were in as good a shape as we ever would be.

I picked a date for the following spring, the first of May, 1982, which would take advantage of the longest stretch of good weather along my planned route, from my hometown in New York State to California. The timing would give us three seasons to cross the country before snow came again.

The first of May. It felt right.


## A GUY AND A DOG

I had a departure date and new saddle packs. The local newspaper ran a story about the trip, followed by features on local television. The publicity brought me an unexpected offer of sponsorship from Eureka! Camping, a business based in Binghamton, New York. They would provide all the camping gear I needed if they could sew an extra logo or two on the tent, and I agreed to wear their tee shirts once in a while, during my travels. Of course I agreed. My budget was not nearly as grand as my dreams.

I heard from old friends, even people I barely knew, and received letters and cards wishing us luck. I was touched by these gestures, but they also made me feel my first bit of nervousness. Now, with a professional business giving us a sponsorship and people I knew (and didn't know) rooting for me, some hidden doubt surfaced. I didn't want to let anyone down.

Then, about six weeks before Rainy and I were scheduled to leave, two things happened that changed everything.

At a time when all I could think about was the upcoming journey and riding my horse, and the least practical thing I could do was meet someone, I fell in love.

Leaving a work party in late March, I said my goodbyes and went to cross a busy street to where I'd parked my car. A guy I recognized from another department at my company was waiting at the curb, too. Every time it seemed safe to cross, another car would whip around the curve, making us step back. After the third attempt, we looked at each other and laughed. Then he reached out his hand, I took it, and together we dashed across the street.

It was a bold move, but sweet, too. We stood talking by our cars, and it started right there. His name was Mike. He was funny, self-confident, and respectful. He knew about my trip and how soon I'd be leaving, but we started dating anyway. My attachment to him grew quickly.

The second event affected my journey deeply, in ways I could not have imagined.

The first time I practiced camping with Rainy was at the edge of some woods just over the border in Pennsylvania. A stream bubbled comfortingly nearby and the stars were out. It was lovely, and being there alone, the pleasant scene made me feel strong and capable.

Then, during the night, I heard a noise in the woods—the crackle of twigs as something moved nearby. When I looked over at Rainy, his ears and head were up, looking toward the trees. I told myself it was nothing, but the sound came closer, and it really put me on edge.

From the darkness at the boundary of the tree line, a whitetail doe came, stepping carefully toward the small stream. Seeing her, I took some deep breaths to try to calm myself after the adrenaline rush of fear. In that moment, I suddenly wished I had a dog with me. Rainy was my stalwart companion, but he could not curl up in the tent with me. A dog could be a guard and protector, or just sit with me and observe the natural world in peace.

A few days after that camping trip, I was officially in search of the perfect dog. But I felt torn. Could a dog be ready for such a long trip in such a short time? Would a dog be an asset and not a liability? I decided I would look at different dogs and see if the right thing to do would come to me.

My sister, Jan, and I made several trips to meet dogs at the pound, and we visited a dog breeder or two, but none of them felt right. Then one day, as puppies of all colors and sizes clambered on cage doors and barked for attention at a shelter, one small, mongrel pup sat watching us with bright and curious eyes. A Collie-German-Shepherd mix, she had a golden coat with white markings on her chest and paws like a collie and the ears of a German Shepherd. She was not timid, but calm, quietly observing things around her. She had a look that conveyed intelligence and a special light from within. Rainy had that look, too.

Yet I walked away.

I was plagued with doubt. As a rider, I should always be in control of Rainy. He needed to be my focus on this journey. But in a tense situation, would I be able to keep control with *two* animals to watch out for? I was drawn to that puppy, but I fought the feeling, and we left her there.

Two days later, I woke from a deep sleep knowing I had to get that dog.

It was a restless couple of hours, waiting for nine o'clock when the shelter opened. My fear now was that she would be gone. I bit my nails and paced, checking the clock every few minutes. Well before the doors were unlocked, I was parked outside the shelter office in my old Chevy Nova, waiting anxiously. An employee pulled up, and I jumped out and approached her. "We open at nine," she said, briskly walking by me, fumbling with the keys.

"I know," I answered with an apologetic look. "I'm just anxious to see if the puppy I want is still here." She shrugged, but as she opened the door, she tipped her head at me, indicating it was okay to follow her in.

Behind her, I waited, fidgeting nervously, while she found another key to open the puppy area. I kept silently repeating, *Please let that puppy be here.*

As we finally stepped into the area where I'd seen the pup, my eyes did a quick, apprehensive search. There were black puppies and spotted puppies and beagle-looking puppies and then…there she was.

She sat alert, looking at me. I flew over and knelt near her kennel, sticking my fingers through the wire. The pup stood up and began to lick my fingers, her whole body wagging from head to tail.

When I picked her up and held her in my arms, a feeling of happiness came over me. It felt like the last piece of a puzzle had just fit, and I had a sense of having done something wise.

The puppy licked my ear, and I whispered to her, "I've come to take you with me."

And I did.

## GYPSY

My mother thought of calling the puppy Gypsy. No other name was ever considered.

Gypsy was small and even-tempered; it was easy to take her everywhere with me. Despite how well she handled herself, I found it nerve-racking to bring her to the farm for the first time. I carried her as I walked down the barn aisle between the cow stanchions on one side and horse stalls on the other. When I finally set her down, Gypsy put her nose to the ground, sniffing and exploring. She was intrigued by the cows in the stanchions but kept a respectful distance from their hooves.

I saddled Rainy and walked outside with him, mindful of the puppy trotting along with us. I picked Gypsy up, but it was awkward trying to mount while holding her. The only way I could swing up into the saddle was to zip her into my jacket. That's how we rode off together for the first time: Rainy walking in his steady pace, Gypsy peeking out from my jacket, and me with a happy grin on my face.

In the field of the farm's hilly pasture, I stopped Rainy and dismounted, setting Gypsy on the ground. After a minute, I got back on, leaving the puppy on her own, and asked Rainy to walk on. Gypsy trotted over to keep up with us. She found "her spot," behind and a little to the side of Rainy, and she stayed with us in her roly-poly puppy way. The dog showed an innate sense of how to act around a horse. I couldn't have asked for more.

In the coming days Gypsy learned to "heel" with a horse: We'd ride along a dirt road, and if I heard a car coming, I'd say, "Over," and she'd move right into the heel position behind Rainy. She made the association so well that before long, if she heard a car before I did, she'd move over all by herself.

Gypsy was content to ride along with me, too. When the warmer days came later in the spring, and I no longer had a jacket to tuck her into, the puppy would lie across the saddle in front of me. Rainy was not bothered by her, whether on board or running behind him. There were three of us now, and we were a good team.

## 48 HOURS UNTIL DEPARTURE

As departure drew near, it seemed everyone in my life had something to say about my upcoming adventure. Most expressed support but admitted to skepticism. My parents tried to convince me to ride out for a few days and "get it out of my system," then come home. Friends with horse trailers told me they'd be glad to hitch up their rigs and come fetch Rainy, Gypsy, and me when I "got tired of it." Friends, cousins, coworkers...so many people sent cards and called, wishing us luck. I would have liked for someone, *anyone*, to say they *knew* we could do it, that they *knew* I really was going to ride my horse all the way to California. But I don't think anyone in my life thought that. They were supportive but not necessarily believers. I had to settle for their good wishes.

It was only when the last days before leaving could be counted in hours that the enormity of what I was planning got to me.

My aunts and uncles came to see me before I left. "You won't believe some of the mountains you're going to hit, just in western Pennsylvania," my Uncle Mack warned. I envisioned myself and Rainy and Gyspy, dwarfed like tiny specks in a land of towering peaks, looming far, far away. It made me feel small and vulnerable, and a lump formed in my throat.

The rush of emotion came again when my farrier's truck pulled up to the curb at my parents' house—an unusual sight. Larry got out of his truck and walked his distinctive bow-legged walk up the walkway, his old worn cowboy hat on his head. I tried to get him to sit on the porch, but he stood, fidgeting, twisting and untwisting a bag in his hands.

Larry handed me a folded up paper. "Here's the name of a horse family right outside Montrose. I just did their horses, and they'll have a stall ready and a place for you to stay on your first night."

Better still, there were more names and addresses and phone numbers on the paper. Larry had been shoeing and working with horses his whole life, and he knew people everywhere. "I made a few calls," he explained. "I got a place for you guys at my uncle's near Forksville, and then at a big Arabian barn with a tack shop on the grounds. If you make it out past Williamsport, that'll be a good place to stop. They'll help you if you need anything."

I was relieved more than I expected to be, knowing we had a few specific destinations to ride toward and people watching for us.

"And I made this for you," Larry went on, pulling a coiled rope from the paper bag. "It's a neck rope. You just put this part over Rainy's head." He held up the rope to demonstrate.

I took the rope and looked it over. All of a sudden I felt short of breath. I was starting to feel a little scared.

I consciously pushed the feeling away. We would be fine. This trip, the trip I'd been planning for as long as I could remember, was going to be great.

It took my mom a while to finally accept that I was going to try to ride my horse, alone, across the country. She did not want me to, and I think she expected it to be a short-lived adventure. To show her support, my mom went shopping, picking up things she thought I'd need. She came home with a bag. "I got these things for your trip," she said.

I poured out the contents on the bed where I was packing. There was makeup. And nail files. And moisturizer and other things a girl uses—a girl who is maybe going out on a date or something. There was even an electric hair dryer.

Maybe my mom was not quite accepting what I was about to do, after all.

Even though her choices seemed like a sort of denial, my mother was subtly reminding me to remember to be, as she would always say, "a lady." It didn't matter what I was doing or where I was, it was how I conducted myself that mattered.

And you know what? The moisturizer and the nail files were actually pretty smart. There were times later, on the road, I was glad to have them.

In dreaming about my journey across the country, it seemed like a free-spirited adventure, a lark on a grand scale. I never thought about how different alone is when it's every night, or how different goodbye feels when it means for a very long time. Or what a huge responsibility it was to care for the horse who was giving his all, and the dog, so full of trust, who joined us.

On the day we set out, my lack of emotional preparation made me wonder if following my dream was a big mistake and if I was going to regret starting the whole thing.

# PART TWO

---

# ON OUR WAY

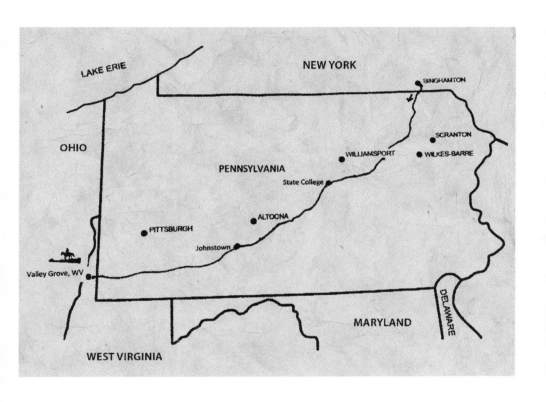

## LEAVING

My father asked, "You have enough money, don't you?"

Money was something he could control. Daughters who dreamed of sleeping under the stars? Out of his hands.

So he asked again. I nodded my head yes. Who knew how much money I should have? I'd never lived off the back of a horse before. My mom had a crumpled tissue in her hand. My younger brother Vince was on his knees, playing with Gypsy. He looked at me for a minute, and we both smiled, but he avoided my eyes after that.

I'd been waiting for the moment I'd ride off and "be free" for years. But there I was, checking the packs I'd already checked, tightening the saddle I'd already tightened. The feelings inside were not nearly as simple as I thought they would be. I couldn't believe I was really doing it.

Then, I swung up in the saddle. Vince handed me Gypsy. I leaned in to hug him as tears formed, and my mom and my dad got in there, too, holding me tight. Rainy stood quietly within my family's embrace.

When they stepped back, my mom dabbed at her eyes with the tissue as my dad said, "You're going to call us tonight, right?" I nodded, wiping my own eyes, saying I love you, letting Rainy walk away.

We followed the farm drive, the dirt under Rainy's feet still soft and damp with morning dew. When we reached the main road, I turned back in the saddle, looking for them, huddled together up by the barn. I raised my arm and waved. Then, I faced forward.

Rainy turned left off the driveway. His horseshoes rang out a hollow sound on the pavement. I brushed the tears that remained from my eyes. With so many unknowns before me, I needed to see clearly.

## LONGEST DAY

We crossed over a creek rushing with spring runoff. A late-season snowstorm had hit the area, and where we were riding had been buried in snow just a few weeks before. Now the sun was shining. Trees lined the road in a lacy shade of light green.

I'd imagined this moment many times. I never imagined I'd feel unsure and confused.

Rainy, Gypsy, and I rode past the farm where my old horse Bo was staying while I was gone. Bo paced back and forth by the fence, whinnying to Rainy. The buckskin gave a little nicker back. It sounded as sad to me as Bo's frantic calling. The horses knew something unusual was happening.

Seeing Bo in such a state was the last straw in an emotional morning, and the tears started again. I kept Rainy going up the road until I couldn't hear Bo's whinnies anymore. We rode on until the road turned from paved to dirt. A small stone monument, old and tilted with age, marked the border between New York and Pennsylvania. We weren't far from home, but we'd crossed our first state line.

We were making poor time. By midday, we were at Quaker Lake, not nearly as far as I thought we'd be. I considered pressing on and skipping lunch with the friends who'd invited us to stop in. Then I reminded myself what the trip was about, how I'd said there'd be no strict schedule. The stop would give Rainy a break, and seeing friendly faces might help me get some of my confidence back and shake the doubt I was feeling.

Mary Larabee offered hot soup and cold drinks. Gypsy curled up to nap on the cool tile floor. Mary and her husband Byron seemed happy to be part of our first day, and I felt better spending a little time with them. As I saddled up to leave, Mary offered her hand to me.

"We want you to have this," she said, depositing something in my palm. "It's the Saint Christopher medal I gave Byron when we were first married. Saint Christopher is the patron saint of traveling people." Mary wrapped my hand around the medal. I promised to carry it with me and tucked it in my pocket for safekeeping as Rainy, Gypsy, and I got on our way.

After a while, Rainy's pace slowed. Gypsy looked uncomfortable, panting in the unseasonable heat. I had no idea why this first day was so hard on all of us.

As we crossed a little bridge that spanned the neck of Laurel Lake, Gypsy decided she'd had enough. My young pup plopped down in the middle of the road. She wouldn't get up. I coaxed, I made kissy noises, I pleaded. I tugged on the leash, but she just rolled around. Finally, I scooped her up into my arms, which made it hard to get back in the saddle. I began to walk on foot.

That's when Rainy decided *he'd* come far enough.

I tried to lead him forward but the buckskin planted his feet, refusing to budge. I set Gypsy down in order to take the horse's reins in both hands, and my dog took the opportunity to lie down again, flat on the road.

The sun was burning my nose and cheeks enough to hurt. Gnats had been bothering us all day. There by the lake, mosquitoes stung my arms and the back of my neck. I couldn't swat at them because my hands were busy trying to pull Rainy and Gypsy forward. In the midst of this, I heard a chuckle. Teenage boys were fishing on the shore near the bridge and were watching us, laughing at our struggle.

My dream never seemed more impossible than it did at that moment.

My face grew hot with embarrassment. Those boys would never believe I was on my way across the country with these two animals. No one who could see us at that moment would take a bet that we'd make it thirty miles, much less three thousand.

After a moment's reflection, I knew what was wrong. Rainy and Gypsy were extremely capable of reading emotions. Stories abound of horses and dogs sensing danger, grief, fear, and other feelings. They pick up on and react to what they sense around them. My horse and dog were acting out what *I* felt inside: balking and scared, daunted by the task I'd set us out to accomplish.

I stopped all the tugging. I took a deep breath and let my animals stay right where they were. I scratched Rainy's neck and patted him, and he relaxed and lowered his head. I rubbed Gypsy's belly, earning a tail wag. Thank goodness animal friends forgive us our mistakes so easily. I started to walk once more, and this time both Rainy and Gypsy moved along with me.

Not long after the tussle on the bridge, a car passed and did a U-turn, coming back to pull up beside us. I recognized an older gentleman, a neighbor who lived near the farm where I boarded Rainy and Bo.

"Hey!" he called out. "I heard you were going on a long trip! Which way are you heading?" I told him we were aiming to reach Montrose by the end of the day. "Well, what're you doing going this way?" he asked. "I know a better way."

For some reason, after thinking about my trip and planning it for *years*, I changed my plan. I let the man convince me that a different route was *easier, better, shorter*. With my confidence slipping away, those words tempted me. But soon his "better way" had us climbing steep hills, and I didn't see any familiar landmarks.

In the many hours I'd spent riding alone, I'd never had an encounter that made me feel I was in danger. I told my mom and dad you didn't have to worry out in the country. So it unnerved me when a car slowed, coming dangerously close to Rainy, and an obviously drunk man leaned his head out the window, calling out really raunchy things. I tried to avoid eye contact as I urged Rainy around the car.

"Hey! I'm talking to you!" he shouted angrily. He pulled the car up close to us again. I could see his red-rimmed eyes and greasy dark hair. I was not at all sure what to do with him blocking the road and no one else anywhere around. "Are you ignoring me?" he slurred, followed by, "Bitch."

Then as suddenly as he arrived, he sped away.

I was truly shaken by the encounter. How could this happen *now?*

I had to admit to myself that on our first day, on the trip I'd planned for years, we were lost. I slumped in the saddle, completely beaten down. Rainy's head drooped before me. Gypsy panted in the heat. I felt stiff and tired. I deeply regretted changing my route, but there was nothing to do about it but keep going and hope that soon I'd come to a road I recognized. When we finally did, I felt a rush of relief, followed by dismay. We were still about six miles from our planned destination, and even as we rode forward, I knew we wouldn't make it by dark.

The woods thinned out ahead and a neat yellow house came into view on the side of the road. A large shade tree stood in the middle of a sprawling lawn. Knowing I shouldn't push the animals any farther, I envisioned Rainy tied to the tree and my tent right near it.

A man and a woman carrying a baby came out of the house. The family paused near their car when they saw us, and I rode toward them with a shaky smile and a hello.

"Can I tie my horse to that tree and set my tent up in your yard for the night?" I asked after quickly explaining who I was and what I was doing. My voice trembled with fatigue and emotion. The strain of the day had taken its toll; there was no hiding my feelings.

The couple looked at me with kind expressions. The baby cooed from his mother's shoulder. I was embarrassed by how fragile I probably seemed. I knew none of us looked like we could go another mile, never mind across the whole country.

"Well, sure," said the man, "but you might be happier with our neighbors who have a barn and pasture. Let me give them a call."

I nodded wearily, thankful to have help.

We ended the first day of the great adventure not at all where I expected to be: Rainy safely stabled in a barn; Gypsy and I visiting with new friends, the Rennees. We sat around their kitchen table, and as I shared the trials of our day, it started to sound a tiny bit more like a funny story than a complete disaster. I told them about the Larabees, and the Saint Christopher medal they'd given me, and reached into my pocket to pull it out.

My pockets were empty. I searched frantically in all my clothing, but the medal was gone. Mary Larabee thought Saint Christopher would keep us safe, and I'd lost him the first day on the road. It was not a good sign at all. I looked at my hosts, with dismay. Mr. and Mrs. Rennee tried to comfort me, but there was nothing anyone could do. I felt horrible.

After a few awkward moments, the Rennees gently reminded me to call my mom and dad. I think they hoped it would make me feel better about the loss of the medal, but when I reached my parents, they were upset and worried because it was so late. I heard the doubt and concern in my mom's voice. *Yes, I'm in the home of complete strangers,* I told her. *No, nothing today worked out the way we planned.*

How could I make my mom and dad feel better when my own idea of what to expect from this trip had already been shaken to the core? I couldn't help but wonder if the whole journey was going to be like the first day: frustrating, intimidating, and lonely.

I also called the family in Montrose who had been expecting us that night and told them we were not going to make it. They had a new name and phone number for me, which I jotted down: A 4-H family down in Springville, who they knew, had said they were more than happy to meet me the following day and have Rainy stay in their barn for the night. I didn't know it then, but it was the beginning of a chain of families and horse people who would help us on our way.

The Rennees graciously invited me and Gypsy to stay inside their small home, but I declined. I wanted to sleep outside in my tent. I clung desperately to the image I had of how this trip would be, of me and my animals, part of the wild outdoor world.

I set up my tent alongside the stream that ran behind the Rennees' house. Daffodils grew all around and the stream made a bubbly, cheerful sound. Branches of a weeping willow gently swept the water's surface. As I laid my things out, the evening air began to be a comfort, a warm shawl laid across my shoulders. The soothing surroundings worked their magic, somehow making the end of the difficult day seem not quite so bad.

Gypsy crawled into the tent as soon as it was ready, curling up on the sleeping bag. I wasn't ready to close my eyes, instead lying awake, mentally cataloging all my mistakes. I'd gotten lost, sunburned, bitten by bugs, scared by a drunk. I'd wildly misjudged time and distance, cried in front of total strangers, seen my animals try to quit on me, and lost a precious gift.

Back when the trip was just something I just talked about, people always asked why I wanted to do such a thing, and I would casually toss off phrases like, "I want to see our country," "I love to travel, to ride, to be outdoors." The reasons I'd always given now seemed overly simplistic. I thought about the goodbye party my friends had given me, and the cards and letters of encouragement I'd received after our story was in the news. I thought about the humiliation I'd feel if I were to give up too easily.

Pride can be a great motivator.

I looked out at the starry sky, and listened to the sound of spring peepers and the gurgling stream. We made it through the first day. We were okay. And we were fifteen miles closer to California.

## DIFFERENT DAY

With the morning sun heating up our tent I woke with a start, anxious to check on Rainy. He gave a friendly nicker when he saw me. I ran my hands along his back and down his legs. Nothing seemed sore, and I breathed a sigh of relief that he'd handled the previous day's ride well. I felt stronger just being around him, and I rubbed his neck and told him so.

I adjusted the packs while Rainy stood patiently. Mrs. Rennee approached with a kind smile.

"I have something I'd like to give you," she stated. She held out her hand, showing me a small cross. "I'd really like it if you'd take this with you. I made it for you late last night. It's from two palm leaves that were blessed at my church on Palm Sunday."

I picked up the delicate cross. "Oh, thank you so much!" I smiled at Mrs. Rennee. My belief in the "bad omen" of having lost the Saint Christopher medal was quieted with the gesture. Hope and faith sprang up from somewhere inside me as Gypsy found her position at Rainy's heels and we set out.

After the solitude of the previous day, it was fun passing through downtown Montrose, Pennsylvania. We walked down the main street, and people stopped to watch. By afternoon, we were heading south on Route 29—a busy road for a horse, but the drivers were mostly considerate, and not much bothered Rainy.

About halfway to Springville, a light breeze picked up, bringing an unexpected cloudburst. As the first drops plopped heavily on the pavement, I twisted around and fumbled for my rain poncho in the packs. By the time I found it and pulled it out of its plastic sleeve and over my head, the rain ended. I was drenched, my horse and dog were drenched, and so were the saddle and our packs.

The brief rain brought humidity. Gnats hovered around us. The rain poncho had visible lines on it from being folded in its protective sleeve, but that didn't mean I could fold it back up again. It was now a bright yellow jumbled mess, half in and half out of the packs behind me. I swatted at insects, Gypsy whined, and Rainy kept dropping his head down to rub his wet, itchy ears on his legs. My jeans were soaked and hot, and we moved down the road in a slow and heavy way. *Well,* I thought. *The well-oiled machine is at it again.*

## GHOSTS

We approached a crossroads, a Little League field on one side and an ice cream stand on the other. Behind the ice cream stand, a board fence enclosed a small area with grass, trees, and a picnic table. I tied Rainy to the fence, loosened his girth, and walked around to the ice cream window.

My chocolate ice cream was dripping down the cone by the time I returned to my animals. I sat on the edge of the picnic table, my legs swinging, Gypsy watching. Her eyes never left the cone in my hand. She looked so serious; it made me laugh.

The edge of the outfield across the road was visible from where we rested, and I listened to the Sunday afternoon baseball game: the crack of the bat, families cheering, kids yelling. The sounds seemed to float on the air.

No one saw the three of us, tucked away in this shady spot. No one knew we were there. It was almost like invisibility, sitting alone, observing the small town goings-on. It occurred to me that we were on the outskirts of things now. We were on the edges, the way a ghost would be—hovering around loved ones, harmless, undiscovered.

We found the two big blue Harvestore silos that identified the Hietsmans' farm—the 4-H family who'd promised us a place to stay the night—by late afternoon. When I met Mr. and Mrs. Hietsman and their children, Doug and Julie, I liked them right away.

"You've ridden for two days. Maybe you should come home now?" my dad tried when I called to say I'd made it to our Day Two Destination.

"I'll come and meet you there," Mike promised when I told him the next town we planned to ride to was Meshoppen.

After a simple breakfast with the family the next morning, Mr. Hietsman shared some advice.

"Be careful of crossing Route 6," he warned. "And there's one road you should avoid that's steep and has no shoulder. Watch out for the P&G factory you'll come to...oh, and you should know there's a big high bridge out that way, too." But he had some good news, as well. Mr. and Mrs. Hietsman told me they'd allowed Julie to take the day off from school so she could ride along with me the entire way to Meshoppen.

"I'd really like that," I said as I helped clear the breakfast dishes. It was an understatement. I was afraid I'd look desperate if I let them know how happy the news made me. I'd only been on the road a few days, and it had been a shock to discover how lonesome I was.

We saddled the horses together and set out early. Julie and her horse Van led the way on old logging trails, fire roads, and hunt-camp tracks. The wooded dirt roads were perfect for riding. We never saw traffic of any kind. The soft, damp soil muffled the sound of the steady footfalls from the horses walking side by side.

We came to a break in the dense forest where a tiny cabin hid in the shadows of tall evergreens. On the weathered porch sat an ancient and frail old man. My eyes widened as the man smiled a toothless grin, and, without a word, held up a painstakingly repainted toy Tonka truck for us to see, a proud look on his face.

Julie, who didn't seem surprised by the scene, shook her head at him.

"No, thank you, Mr. Troy!" she called out in a loud voice as we walked past several more restored toys, scattered about the yard. I noticed a worn sign nailed to a tree with "TROY'S TOYS" scrawled crookedly across the board.

"Does he live here in the woods all by himself?" I asked Julie. "Can he possibly sell *any* of those toys?" I looked around at the dense forest and the narrow dirt lane we were riding on. We hadn't seen a car or another human being all morning!

Julie shrugged, as if the old man was just part of the landscape.

"Old Mr. Troy has been in his cabin as long as I remember," she said.

To me, it was like an illusion, as if, were I to go back and try to find that old cabin and the little spots of brightly painted toys in the woods, I would find no sign of them at all.

It felt like it was too soon when Julie and Van brought us to the edge of a paved road, and we traded the deep forest for sunlit farm roads that wound through Pennsylvania's Endless Mountains. Signs of spring in the country were everywhere. Black-and-white dairy cows in green fields turned their heads as we passed. Farmhouse gardens overflowed with daffodils and tulips. Carpets of bright pink phlox covered the banks, sloping up from the roadsides.

We rode up to a little cluster of homes and a general store—a place called Lynn. "I've always wanted to tie a horse here, like they did in the old days!" Julie announced, pointing to an old hitching post outside the store.

It was obvious the woman in the store was curious about us—we could see her face, pressed up against the window of the door. She surely knew that Julie was supposed to be in school, and I was a stranger, which was kind of unusual for this tiny crossroads.

"Before I get home tonight, I guarantee my parents will have gotten a phone call, telling them about us being here today," Julie said with a laugh.

This was my introduction to the country grapevine.

Our horses were well matched in their gaits and temperaments, and it made for an easy rapport between us as we rode. Gypsy explored the ditches and sniffed the fence posts. The leaves on the trees were just beginning to open, making everything around us seem green and full of life. We stopped to watch a trio of golden draft horses lope across a meadow, the Endless Mountains in layers of purple and blue in the distance.

Our day's destination was Slumber Valley Campground in Meshoppen. Julie's grandma had called the Jennings family, the owners of Slumber Valley, and arranged for me to stay, with special permission granted for my horse and dog. When we arrived we were shown to a spot along a creek with a grassy area where Rainy could graze. It couldn't have been better.

Julie and I unsaddled the horses, and soon they were munching grass contentedly. It was easy work for two of us to prepare my tent for the night. Together, we collected twigs for tinder. The campsite was homey and friendly looking in the twilight. We sat at the picnic table, chatting about the day and eating crackers. Gypsy slept a sound, tired, puppy sleep at our feet.

Lulled by the peace of the setting and the quiet company, it was a jolt when Julie suddenly said, "There's my dad." I saw a pickup truck coming across the grounds, an empty horse trailer rattling behind it. We'd had so much fun that day, I actually got a sick feeling in my stomach with the reminder that Julie and Van would be leaving, and I'd be on my own again.

After parking the truck, Mr. Hietsman joined us at the table and asked about our day. Julie looked around wistfully at the horses and the campsite.

"I wish I could stay here and camp with you tonight," she said to me, though her eyes watched her dad to gauge his reaction. She knew, and I knew, she'd already missed one day of school and had to go back.

Bob Hietsman looked somewhat dismayed at the prospect of leaving me. Even after Julie's horse was loaded in the trailer, he asked again if I was all right and if I needed anything. I must have looked more fragile and lonely than ever. I fought back tears as they pulled away. I noticed for the first time how empty the campground was around us. The last rays of sun disappeared as the truck and trailer grew smaller and smaller, until they were gone.

## ▰▰ MESHOPPEN

Twilight deepened. I was a little unsettled, but also a tiny bit excited. This was the first real camping of our trip. I called Gypsy to me, and we explored along the creek.

Purple violets dotted the grass on the path where we walked. In clear pools, minnows darted from side to side. On the opposite bank, the woods already had the look of nighttime, dark and full, now that the sun was behind the hills.

Back at our campsite, I lit the little teepee of twigs that Julie and I had prepared, and watched the edges turn electric orange and begin to curl and burn. Soon a fire crackled gently, warming me and taking the edge off being alone. I watched my animals and listened to the twilight sounds. Rainy slowly lowered his weight to the ground, stretched out, and slumbered. Gypsy was long asleep in the tent. The mosquitoes, so prevalent in the day, were gone now as the night air chilled my skin at the same time the day's sunburn heated it.

I'd made calls home and to Mike earlier from the campground office. If Mike could get out of work early (he worked the third shift, usually from midnight to eight in the morning) he'd drive down to see us. I vowed not to sleep so I could watch for him.

The campfire dwindled to a warm glow. Despite my vow, I drifted off, waking sometime in the wee hours to the sound of a car on the gravel campground road, and feeling ridiculous that I felt so elated when I recognized Mike's Buick.

After a jubilant greeting from me, and one from a wiggling Gypsy, Mike and I sat at the picnic table to eat the breakfast he'd brought. As the sun grew stronger, we walked to the waterfalls, talking nonstop.

"How is everyone at work?" I wanted to know. I teased him when he admitted he'd been playing the albums I'd left at his house. And then I asked, "Will you be able to come and see me on the road again at some point?"

"You've only been gone a few days!" Mike laughed.

I was startled to realize he was right. It felt like so much longer to me!

Mike helped groom Rainy, and the morning passed in a companionable way, one of us on each side of the buckskin, brushing his sun-warmed coat.

Mike knelt down by my packs and dug around until he found the sunscreen, buried deep within.

"Here, let me do this," he said, holding my face with one broad hand while he applied the lotion to my sunburned cheeks with the other. We had been talking all morning, but now I stood silently. We both knew it was time to go. He was going one way, and Rainy, Gypsy, and I were going another.

I loaded my carefully arranged saddlebags onto my horse as Mike awarded Gypsy one last scratch. With a nod from me, he gave me a leg up into the saddle.

Rainy, Gypsy, and I walked away from the quiet campsite, and the beautiful creek, and Mike, standing there by his car. Saying goodbye made me sad, but there was something else that morning... an unwanted gut feeling that rose deep inside—a weird and sudden belief that I would never see him again.

## CRYING TO SINGING

I rode along, worrying. So far, the trip had been so different from what I expected. I'd been mostly consumed by negative emotions. Instead of a sense of adventure and excitement, I felt lonesome and anxious. *Maybe I'm not cut out for this. Will we all be all right? What lies ahead?*

Insecure thoughts ran their course as Rainy, Gypsy, and I made our way up the mountain road. I'd never know what awaited us on the road ahead, yet something kept me going. No one made me do this. *This was my dream.*

The road was steep. Occasionally a big logging truck blew by with a load of timber. There was little shoulder to ride on, but Rainy wasn't rattled by the monsters passing so close to us. I shook my head, dislodging my gloomy musings. I needed to pay attention. I focused on Rainy—this good horse on this bad road, making his steady way, up and up.

We hugged the guardrail on the right side, and I tried to ignore the steep dropoff. The left side was sheer rock face where the road had been cut, and the mountain appeared alive with layers of stone, dripping spring water everywhere. It seeped from the very earth, helping graceful ferns grow all along our path. Tall evergreen trees kept us in dappled shade.

I had been sniffling when we started up this road. Little by little, the bubbling springs, the birds, and the breeze began to bring me a sense of gratitude. I became aware of something surprising: I was singing. The goodbyes and the worries had fallen aside as I became engrossed in a remarkable May day. I was singing!

## ■■■ THE BRIDGE

As we worked our way down another steep road, I caught glimpses of silver through the trees. At first I thought there was a body of water below us. As we descended, the bright flashes came more clearly into focus.

I stopped Rainy and sat, staring. Before us was the largest industrial spread I'd ever seen. Metal buildings covered the land for acres. Smokestacks billowed white smoke upward, and a multitude of parking lots and structures extended almost as far as I could see in one direction. The Hietsmans had mentioned the Procter & Gamble Company plant I would come upon in Mehoopany, but its size in this rural place was as unexpected as finding an iceberg in the desert.

Despite the vastness of the massive factory, it was mostly quiet, and after the initial shock of seeing it, there was not much to look at. We headed toward a bridge I could see ahead.

Mr. Hietsman had warned me to avoid reaching P&G around three o'clock. At the time, I couldn't imagine how huge the place was, and the schedule of "some factory" had little meaning to me. As I guided Rainy onto the long, high bridge that spanned the Susquehanna River far below, I heard a long whistle wail, like a fire alarm, behind me. My grip on the reins and the dog on the saddle in front of me reflexively tightened.

In only minutes, a wave of traffic from the plant poured from the parking lots like a dam had burst open. Vehicles came toward us, then swarmed around us like a horde of angry hornets.

The bridge was a long expanse of roadway, framed by concrete walls on each side. There were no sidewalks or shoulders; there was no way to escape. We were like a rock in a stream as the sudden traffic parted around us, its flow unbroken. Not just cars—trucks, too, blowing diesel fumes and hissing air brakes. Gypsy hunched in front of me, frightened by the surge of motion and noise.

Rainy walked on. My horse, a creature of flight, didn't hesitate; he didn't spook. The factory whistle wailed again, but he kept his steady rhythm, getting us safely through the onslaught of workers blinded by their hurry to get home. Shaken, I felt both awe and relief in the presence of Rainy's nerves of steel and sense of responsibility as he got us across.

A white Cadillac passed and pulled over just in front of us. A woman stepped out of the car, dressed top to bottom in studded denim, dark sunglasses covering half her face.

"I'll give you five thousand dollars for that horse," she announced as we approached.

I just shook my head and laughed.

We turned up Route 87, on our way, my five-hundred-dollar horse, my dog-pound dog, and me.

## TOO LONG, TOO FAR

The momentum from the bridge and the first little hint of optimism I felt carried us through the next days. My uncertainty was quelled by Rainy; I saw strength in his shoulders as he carried us up the hilly back roads.

It was supposed to be a twenty-mile day but as evening neared, I knew I'd miscalculated, and we were riding farther and longer than I'd planned. I kept thinking we'd come to Higley Park Campground, where we were expected, around the next bend in the road. Twilight turned to darkness. I pushed on, knowing that someone was watching for us.

It was late when we reached our destination, and I finally tended to my animals and made camp. As I sat outside my tent, watching Rainy eat, I berated myself for the day's schedule, worrying that I'd pushed my horse and dog too hard, all for my own sense of security. *I must become more adaptable and learn to improvise*, I thought. I had to always put Rainy first, as I'd sworn I would.

As I watched Rainy lower himself down and lie flat on the grass to sleep, I wondered if it was normal behavior for him. It made me realize there were holes in what even the most devoted horse owners knew about their equines. I was now living with Rainy every day and every night. We would be eating together, sleeping right near each other, and watching every hour pass together. I'd be able to observe firsthand how my horse adapted to the variables that this trip would bring: changes in feed, climate, and terrain. I'd see how he used his different senses in each new situation. How would he act when he was introduced to new horses? Would the long and steady walking every day build him up or run him down? I'd be monitoring his physical condition, and as we traveled, I'd share daily life with my horse in a way that was not common in the modern world. Would Rainy, separate now from his equine family back home, transfer his strong herd association to me and Gypsy? As my animals and I came to depend on each other for all that we needed, I'd have a unique opportunity to learn how deep our bond could get.

Assuring myself that my horse was tired but seemed okay, I crawled into the tent, where Gypsy was already asleep. Exhausted by the long hours in the saddle and worry, I vowed to make the next day short and easy.

## TRAVELER'S SPRING

The first thing I saw when I crawled from the tent in the morning was Rainy's perfect black hooves and his charcoal muzzle as he steadily worked his way through thick bunches of grass. I ran my hands over his body, checking for heat and soreness, talking to him while he grazed. He twitched an ear and swung his head around to look at me.

The sun hadn't been up long when Rainy, Gypsy, and I were off again, back down the mountain road we'd climbed wearily in the dark the night before. The sky was a vibrant blue. Hemlocks rose majestically on both sides of the narrow lane of pavement, keeping the air refreshingly cool.

At the village of Forksville we rode across the wooden planks of a covered bridge one hundred and fifty feet long and built in 1850, but still in use for everyday traffic. Rainy's hoof beats echoed a sound from the past, and we stopped in the middle to look out over the beauty of the flowing creek and forested hills beyond.

Outside town again, Rainy walked along steadily, Gypsy trotting beside us. I was lulled by the familiar creak of saddle leather, the rhythm of Rainy's stride, and the birdsong. It was only a few miles before we rounded a bend and came upon an artesian spring. The water bubbled up cleanly, dampening the ground under Gypsy's paws. An old milk can sat nearby, a tin cup on top, and a ladle hung from a nail on a tree.

I got off Rainy, and because it seemed right, I filled the ladle and gave Gypsy a drink, then I drank, too, splashing the icy spring water on my face like the blessing it was before we moved on.

Like the covered bridge, the mountain spring invited us to stop for a moment and reflect. It was a message saying, *Slow down, traveler.* Just a day after I'd pushed my horse too hard, just as I was telling myself to look around and be grateful, here were real reminders of the reasons why I wanted to travel across the country on horseback: The belief that there were beautiful little forgotten things out in the world, waiting for those of us in the slow lane to discover them.

## WELCOME TO HUGHESVILLE

On the other side of the Endless Mountains, I rode into the town of Hughesville with the notion of camping at the fairgrounds. Dignified, well-kept Victorian homes lined Main Street, their lawns neat and trim, shaded by old oak trees.

Though a small and quaint-looking place, it was not "normal" for a horse to be passing through the middle of this town. Rainy, Gypsy, and I began to attract attention, and soon we were like the Pied Piper with a growing crowd of children walking along with us. The kids peppered me with questions:

"What's your horse's name?"

"How come your dog can ride a horse?"

"Can I have a ride on your horse?" (All of them asked this one.)

The ringleader was a bright young girl named Mindy. She kept up an intelligent chatter, filling me in on who in our entourage was not allowed to go farther than the corner, and that she, Mindy, happened to *love* horses.

"We all know where the fairgrounds are," she also said. "You better let us show you the way."

I jumped down to walk along beside the girl, lifting the children up one by one, so they could take turns riding horseback through their neighborhood. They held on to the saddle horn and looked around, beaming, their friends on the ground, skipping and talking all at once. Rainy walked on, with his usual patience.

## HOUSE OF GUYS

I'd been looking forward to our stop at Callenberger's Arabian Horse Farm, one of the connections made via my farrier Larry. Because I'd known ahead of time that we'd stay there one night, I'd designated it my first mail pickup. I'd told friends and Mike, and now a few of the people we'd met during the first week of our trip, to write to me care of my mom at my home address. She'd taken the letters and packaged them all in a manila envelope, forwarding them on to this farm in Montgomery, Pennsylvania.

Whenever we arrived at a destination, I asked for nothing but a safe spot for me and my animals to spend the night off the road. I was happy to sleep in the barn or camp in my tent. But many people invited me and Gypsy into their homes. Bob Callenberger, of Callenberger's Arabian Horse Farm, and his friend Rudy, were no exception, offering me a spare bedroom. I struggled with the decision at first, feeling like I should be outside, but I was also starting to realize that I was the designer of my own journey. It was not about whether there was a roof or stars over my head. It was about doing what felt right in each moment and being safe.

I gratefully accepted.

I wanted to get a professional assessment of how Rainy was handling the ride so far, so Bob helped me schedule a vet check. When the veterinarian arrived, I found him to be an outgoing, funny character, tall and broad. "What a wonderful idea!" he exclaimed when told about our trip. I laughed as he described his four buffalo: Marlene, Charlene, Darlene, and Big Al.

After a thorough examination, the vet praised Rainy's feet and legs and his condition. We passed with flying colors. And when the time came to pay the bill, there wasn't one. Another kindness sent our way.

By the time Rainy's appointment was over, it was already late in the day. I helped with barn chores. Bob and Rudy were expecting company from New York City that evening, and three men arrived as I set the long table in Bob's kitchen. One of the guys, a lean blonde with a buzz cut, stared at me, then immediately marched over and started sorting through strands of my hair, examining them.

"Oh. My. God." He sighed dramatically. "You are *not* riding out in the sun all day without something on your hair, are you? Look at these ends!" He lifted a strand of my brown hair between one forefinger and thumb. "It's so dry! You *have* to do leave-in conditioner. Do you hear me? Oh my God!" He shook his head in disbelief at my lack of hair care. I smiled, thinking my mother would approve of his advice.

In no time, I was completely comfortable with Bob and Rudy's crew. We were like a loud boisterous family gathered around the dinner table, eating spaghetti, buttering rolls, and passing dishes as we joked and laughed, Gypsy curled at my feet. They asked about my trip; we debated whether people are mostly good or bad, discussed movies old and new, and compared notes on New York City. We made a strange bunch, the five guys and I.

Gypsy and I headed for bed right after dinner. I'd already read my mail, almost as soon as Bob handed it to me, but I read through each letter one more time before falling into a tired sleep. It hadn't been long when I woke with a start, realizing I'd gotten my period. I swore softly to myself as I went through my gear—nothing. How had I forgotten something as basic as tampons? It was another reminder of how woefully unprepared in some aspects I really was. I'd thought of every little thing that Rainy and Gypsy would need, but basic supplies for myself? I was so focused on the beginning of our journey that I'd overlooked something I'd obviously need down the road.

I had no choice but to walk downstairs where the men were still visiting and drinking wine.

"Can someone, uh, bring me to town?" I asked awkwardly. They all stared at me.

"Do you need something for the trip?" Bob queried, setting down his wine glass. "I bet we have everything you need right here!"

"No..." I replied, cheeks burning. "Not everything..."

For the first time that night, none of the guys had anything to say. Then Rudy, blushing, offered to take me to a store.

## ALONG THE RIVER

Bob planned to accompany me for a stretch of the ride toward White Deer. His Arabian horses hung their delicate heads out over their stall doors, watching us leave, unencumbered by packs and gear.

Bob rode his gray stallion, who got along surprisingly well with Rainy. The stud was a little skittish at first and let Rainy take the lead, but he settled right in. Arabian horses are smart, and this one learned quickly.

We rode on a grassy stretch along the Susquehanna River. The trees in bloom created dappled pathways as we walked beneath their branches. From the saddle, Bob reached up and broke off a piece from the limbs overhead.

"Here," he said, handing me the twig. "Chew on this a little bit; see what it tastes like."

I chewed for a minute, savoring the familiar flavor. I tried to place it, but Bob couldn't hold back the answer for long.

"It's birch beer! Doesn't it taste just like birch beer?"

I laughed and nodded, and contentedly we rode on, chewing twigs.

## UNEXPECTED FRIENDSHIP

As we traveled my "chain of people" kept on growing. It seemed to work out that at the end of each day, there was usually a place to stay or someone watching out for us. This chain brought us to Route 192, one of the most beautiful roads in Pennsylvania.

Acres of vivid green farm fields rolled away from both sides of the highway. To the south, looming in the hazy sunshine, was the dark green presence of Nittany Mountain, part of the Appalachian Mountain Range.

We'd stayed with the Hare Chambers, a 4-H family in Mifflinberg the night before, and Tracy Hare and her horse were riding with me. We walked along, talking at first, but grew quiet once we recognized the sights, sounds, and scents of Amish farmland. Approaching a square, whitewashed building, we stopped our horses. Amish children dressed in black, white, and navy blue filed outside the one-room schoolhouse and made their way toward a nearby grove to eat lunch in the shade of the trees. We watched the children hold hands and skip together, the dark colors of their clothing standing out in the bright sunshine and green growing fields.

Dave, Tracy's stepdad, collected horse-drawn vehicles and often traded with the Amish. He had made arrangements for me to stay with an Amish family on their farm—a kind gesture, which of course I appreciated. Curious, I'd asked if he'd stayed with them himself.

"No!" he'd answered adamantly, "Of course not! Very few non-Amish ever stay with them!"

His answer left me feeling a little nervous. Now that we were in the heart of their community, I was even more intimidated. I tried to recall what I knew about Amish people, and all I could remember hearing was that they lived a strict and austere lifestyle and were very religious. And here I was, in my jeans, roaming the countryside alone on a horse. I was afraid we were too different. I was afraid they would preach at me. I knew it wasn't very worldly or open-minded, but I didn't want to spend a night with people who probably didn't want me there. I rode along with growing apprehension.

Tracy and I dilly-dallied at a general store, drinking Cokes on the steps while we gave the horses a break. By mid-afternoon, near the little town of Rebersburg, we came to the long farm drive with the name "Melvin Stoltzfus" on the mailbox. We started down the dirt path, and I felt I was surely leaving behind the world as I knew it. I realized that Tracy must have been worried about fitting in, too.

"I wonder where my dad is with the trailer?" she mused as she looked back at the road.

A small girl in a plain blue dress and braids watched us from outside the house I could see at the end of the lane. As we approached, she ran inside and reappeared, pulling a woman by the hand, closely followed by another woman, both dressed in similar fashion—long dresses and aprons.

I smiled nervously and called out a hello. *What if Dave never reached them to make the arrangements? They didn't use phones, right?* Then a new thought occurred to me as they walked toward us, looking somewhat nervous themselves. *What if they are worried about meeting me, like I'm worried about meeting them?*

As I was shown where I could care for Rainy in the big white barn to the right of the farmhouse, Dave Chambers arrived with the trailer to take Tracy and her horse home. I waved as they drove away. Then, I joined the women who had gone inside the house and were preparing cold drinks for the men who were out working in the field. I watched quietly as the little girl, Katie, led a small pony to a hitching post, fastened a complex arrangement of buckles and straps, then climbed aboard a cart. She took up the reins and drove off by herself, across the fields, to deliver the drinks. She wasn't more than six years old!

That was my first lesson about the Amish—everybody on the farm had a job, from the littlest child right up to the elderly aunts I met later in the second house on the farm, piecing together fabric in bright, startling colors, making quilts to sell.

Evening on the farm brought the sound of harnesses jingling and horse snorts and hoof beats as neighbors came by to find out *what's going on at the Stoltzfus place.* It wasn't long before several wagons and horses were parked around the yard. My animals and I were the subject of quite a bit of curiosity! After a few introductions, I sat on the lawn, where most of the young children were gathered, happily fielding their questions:

"Do you have parents?"

"How far away is New York?"

"Do you have a car or only just that horse?" (I answered that I'd had a car, but I got rid of it to ride my horse on the trip I was taking. This produced much giggling for some reason.)

A couple of the older girls whispered in the background, until one of them stepped forward, announcing that her name was Naomi, and she, too, had a question: Had I ever been on a buggy ride?

My "no" produced more giggling, and Naomi appeared to decide then to take me under her wing.

"Come with me," she said, leading me to a small horse-drawn carriage. We climbed aboard, and Naomi casually gave the reins a little shake as she clucked to the ginger-colored horse in front of us. He began a precise and careful backing and turning around.

"Thank you for the ride," I offered shyly.

"I figured you might be needing a girl to talk to," was her wise response.

Her words caused me to choke up for a moment, as they touched upon a loneliness inside me. She sensed right: I did crave a girlfriend to talk to. I'd shared surface chatter with Tracy and had friendly conversations with various mother figures over dinner tables in the past week. But we mostly talked about horses, and I answered questions about my journey. Naomi and I were able to connect in a different way. As the little horse trotted along, the conversation flowed easily between us, and cultural differences and lifestyles and religion didn't matter.

We passed several young Amish men out driving their buggies, and they smiled and waved at Naomi, who smiled back in acknowledgment. I thought she might be enjoying their surprise at seeing me with her as much as I was now enjoying her world.

On our way back to the main house, Naomi asked, "Would you like to try driving?" and handed me the reins. I'd been a rider most of my life, but holding the double leathers of the harness was a whole new experience. The horse knew a rookie had the reins, and his pace got faster and faster. By the time Naomi took control again, we were both laughing merrily at the furious pace.

Finding a friend in a place where I least expected it was enough of a gift. But as we trotted along, twilight turned to nightfall and the sounds of spring added sweetness to the serene quality of the evening. Absent were all the noises I'd become accustomed to all my life: car wheels on pavement, the honk of a horn, televisions talking, radios playing. In this place, the night sounds were peeper frogs and spring insects, the distant lowing of cattle in the darkening fields, and the clip-clop of Naomi's sturdy little horse as he trotted along home.

"Would you like me to write to you as you ride across the country?" Naomi asked as we pulled up to the farmhouse.

I liked that she didn't question whether Rainy, Gypsy, and I would keep going.

"Yes, please do!" I answered warmly...thankfully.

Night settled in completely. I reminded Melvin Stoltzfus and his wife that I could spend the night in the barn with Rainy. I'd observed that although there were animals all over, including kittens and dogs, none of them were allowed inside the house. Gypsy and I had not yet spent a night apart. But there didn't seem to be any right way to refuse the Stoltzfuses' offer, once again, to come into their home and sleep inside.

Gypsy pressed herself up against the screen door when she was shut outside, staring in at me. I noticed Mrs. Stoltzfus looking at the pup once or twice.

"She always stays with you, doesn't she?" Mrs. Stoltzfus asked as she dried her hands on a dishtowel. I nodded my head. She walked to the door and opened it, allowing Gypsy to bound across the kitchen and wrap herself, wagging, around my legs.

"All the animals have a job," Mrs. Stoltzfus explained, "and *her* job is to stay with you."

As if she knew she was in only by special invitation, Gypsy lowered herself down to the floor and stayed very still and quiet until we said goodnight. Then she followed me up the stairs, lying down beside the feathery stuffed bed. I blew out the little lantern they'd given me, and I pondered where I was and the feelings I hadn't expected now coming alive inside me.

I got up from the bed to look out the window at the farmyard below. I could see the road where Naomi and I had taken our buggy ride, now a silver ribbon in the moonlight. No artificial light blocked the stars, no sound marred the silence of the fields around us. I fell asleep with the sense of peace and serenity that these things bring.

## JUST PEOPLE

By the time my animals and I left the farm in the morning, the word of my new friendship with the Stoltzfus family had spread. (Don't underestimate the power of horse-drawn news!) Melvin Stoltzfus recommended I stop at the Fischer Brothers Harness Shop in Madisonburg to get a small split on the seam of my packs repaired. While Amos Fischer worked on my packs, he instructed me to ride to his home where his young wife, Lydia, had lunch waiting for me. Then, the proprietors of the bakery across from the harness shop,

Eli and Katie, packed a bag with cheeses, bread, and brownies for me to take on the road.

As I fastened the newly repaired packs to Rainy's saddle, to my surprise and delight, Melvin Stoltzfus drove up in a fine black carriage, drawing the horse to a stop near us.

"I wanted to be sure you got all the help you needed," he said in greeting. I assured him I had been helped beyond measure, just as a young woman drove her buggy up to the front of Fischer Brothers and handed me a small box of cookies.

I thanked her, and after Melvin drove off, we chatted a bit, she asked bluntly, but not unkindly, "Were you afraid to come and stay with us?"

I paused, then admitted, yes, I had been, but shook my head sheepishly at how silly it all seemed now.

She smiled and declared in her singsong accent, "We're all just people, aren't we, then?"

I smiled back at her.

## FUNHOUSE FACES

We'd been traveling for two weeks, but still, I was having trouble letting go of the need to have a plan, to be secure. My animals and I were in a little downtown called Centre Hall, small, but busy compared to the Amish communities we'd just visited. We rested under the shade of an oak tree as I accepted the fact that it appeared my arrangements had fallen through, and I didn't know what to do.

As I stood there, flustered, a pickup truck pulled up. Chris and Barb Cole, Tennessee Walking Horse enthusiasts, introduced themselves, saying they'd heard that a fellow horseperson might need a hand and had come to get us settled in the horse barn at the local fairgrounds. They had feed for Rainy and dinner for me. It occurred to me that every time we needed help, a kind stranger showed up.

The horse barn at the fairgrounds had old midway rides stored in it, including large cartoonish clown figures from the funhouse. After the Coles had said goodnight and gone on their way, I made my spot in the barn near Rainy, settling into my sleeping bag. I wrote a few short letters by lantern, my light casting shadows and making the dismantled funhouse faces around us seem surreal.

With nightfall, a breeze picked up and blew in through the barn. A ride with long arms and crazy painted faces rattled and bobbed. I dozed fitfully, waking every hour or so to garish clowns with big red-and-white grins staring across the aisle. They clanked and leered at us through the night.

## PENN STATE

As we neared the town of State College, home of Penn State University, a tall, nice-looking guy strode out into the road to meet us. When he informed me that the barn where he worked was full of Tennessee Walkers, exclusively, I knew this connection was thanks to Chris and Barb Cole from the prior town. They had told me they had "Walker contacts" all over the state and were going to help me while we rode through Pennsylvania. Bless them—it appeared they were following through.

Jay, the busy barn manager said her boss, RB Powell, had plans for me, and extended an invitation to stay an extra day. It was intriguing, and it was late anyway, so I accepted.

In the morning I rose early to get to the barn. I worried about Rainy and preferred to feed him myself. He'd so far maintained his weight and his good attitude, despite his constantly changing surroundings, and I wanted to keep it that way.

Within minutes of meeting RB Powell, I was on one of his Tennessee Walkers. I rode around his barnyard on a tall black gelding, getting used to the unfamiliar but comfortable running walk. RB

was convinced that if I rode a Tennesee Walker, I'd want one of my own. The Walker people I'd met were all very enthusiastic promoters of their breed.

RB took me for breakfast at a diner where he knew everyone and then on a tour of the Penn State campus. He looked at me seriously as we walked by a large stone sculpture of a mountain lion on the prowl.

"You know the legend of the Nittany Lion Shrine, don't you?" he asked.

I shook my head no, which was all the encouragement he needed.

"There's an old saying that it will roar when a virgin walks by."

I stood there sheepishly; the statue remained conspicuously silent.

RB escorted me to a campus horse show, where he introduced me to the riding instructor from Grier School, a girls' boarding school about 30 miles down the road. We made arrangements for Rainy to spend our next night at the school barn.

That evening, RB, Gypsy, and I drove down a logging road to a clearing in the woods where a low campfire was ablaze, surrounded by students and staff. RB was an English professor, so the jovial conversation drifted from poetry and Shakespeare to trying to determine what the initials "RB" stood for. His college students were relentless, but RB wouldn't give it up. Jay even confessed to looking around the horse barn office for paperwork with her boss's full name on it. We all had a laugh, as the professor refused to give even a hint.

Someone pulled out a guitar and began playing familiar songs as sparks flew up from the fire. Gypsy enjoyed scratches and food scraps before settling contentedly in the center of everyone and drifting off to sleep.

In the morning, as I got ready to start out, several employees from the barn and friends of Jay's gathered to see us off. RB was the last to say goodbye. He walked with me and Rainy as we moved away from the group.

I put a foot in the stirrup and swung my leg over the saddle while RB held Gypsy for me. When I reached down to take my dog from him, the man leaned forward with a twinkle in his eye and whispered two words in my ear. It took me a moment as he walked away to realize that he just told me what his initials stood for. I laughed out loud, waving an affectionate goodbye to the lovely character who brightened the past two days of my trip.

What?

You don't think I'm going to tell, do you?

## GRIER SCHOOL

Everything was newly washed by rain on the road that wound through the tall oak trees lining the entrance to Grier School's campus. As we rounded a curve imposing stone buildings came into view. Rainy's iron shoes on the wet pavement echoed loudly in the quiet of the stately campus.

As we approached, the sound of sweet voices singing in harmony floated in the air. I brought Rainy to a halt to listen. My horse and dog waited silently, as if they, too, could hear the beauty in the faint sound. A door at the top of stone steps flew open and two teenage girls pounded down the stairs—all over the place and graceful at the same time.

Sophie and Ann Marie, having heard I was coming, had been watching from the window while in choir practice.

"Are you going to get in trouble for being out here?" I asked them with a smile. They laughed and shrugged. Sure enough, soon, we were surrounded by a group of chattering girls. Sophie and Ann Marie, the older "horse girls," took up the role of our guardians. This included special proprietary rights, having been the first to find us.

Jill, the riding instructor RB had introduced me to the day before, was waiting for us at the school barn. Two local reporters were there as well, asking me about my trip, but I was distracted and more interested in making sure Rainy was taken care of. Luckily, the Grier girls were more than happy to give the reporters their attention.

I'd read in one of the articles later that Rainy, Gypsy, and I were treated like "visiting royalty" by the students at Grier School. It was true—some girls went off to find me dry clothes to borrow, others ministered to Rainy's every possible need, while another group gushed over Gypsy, who charmed them with all her puppy ways.

The school barn housed equitation horses, and hunters and jumpers of distinction, but that night it was Rainy who received all the attention of a Kentucky Derby winner. He was bathed, rubbed down, legs wrapped, and mane and tail combed. I thought he actually looked embarrassed when they covered him with a blanket a size or two too large for him.

Jill had made arrangements for me to have a bed and shower at the school infirmary, and my gaggle of girls escorted me there.

"You've created chaos," the infirmary nurse, Adelaide, said good-naturedly when we arrived. "We'll have to address the situation," she warned. "But you'll eat a sandwich and some soup first."

Like one of the Grier School girls, I didn't question her authority.

The infirmary was a quiet, comfortable place to sleep, and Gypsy was given the distinction of being the first canine ever allowed to bed down there. I was, as always, grateful for the latitude allowed me and my animal companions.

I woke, startled to find it was already half past nine in the morning. The blinds were down and there was complete silence. Adelaide had decided that I needed my sleep. It was too late in the day to start out on a long ride... so I got another day to be a schoolgirl again.

I helped Jill and the students set up a hunt course for an upcoming competition, and with the help of a half-dozen girls, gave Rainy all the "day-off" attention he could handle. Gypsy gamboled on the manicured lawns and was generally spoiled. Dogs weren't normally allowed on campus, and the girls couldn't seem to get enough of her.

During the day, Jill was told the school's headmaster received a call from the local television station, asking permission to do a story about my journey and stop at Grier School. Word that the news crew was on its way set off a flurry of excitement among the girls.

The reporter who showed up, however, seemed more concerned with how he looked than hearing about our journey. He kept pulling a comb out of his pocket and checking his reflection in his van window. When he could manage to turn his attention back to our story, the guy appeared almost skeptical that Rainy, Gypsy, and I had come as far as I said we had, and this was not lost on my gaggle of girls. I could hear their muttered remarks and snickering as the interview proceeded under the shade of a tree. The reporter wanted Gypsy on my lap during the filming, but she soon grew bored and began to tug and chew on his microphone wire. I held onto her haunches as I tried to answer his questions, and my pup rolled around, making goofy noises. Muffled giggles could then be heard from the students gathered round, and I felt like the bad kid in school—no matter how old you are, trying to hold in a laugh only makes it want to come out more.

The reporter then asked to borrow a school horse so we could be filmed riding alongside each other.

"Have you ridden before?" one of the girls asked him.

"No," he responded briskly, adjusting his carefully pressed pants. "Will that be a problem?"

I felt a current of joy ripple through the group of students as they set off to get the horse that would be "best" for him.

They returned from the barn minutes later leading an incredibly tall chestnut gelding (called Silo) in an English saddle, a choice that would make the man's mounting and staying in the saddle a little trickier. I looked away to hide my smile at their schoolgirl pranks. *How* would this fellow get on board?

The reporter wanted us to ride side by side for the piece, just two riders on our horses, walking along talking, but Silo kept veering off the walkway, putting his head down, and eating grass. The reporter pulled uselessly on the reins as Silo totally ignored him until one or two smirking girls came to his rescue and led the horse back to start the shot over again.

Undeterred, the reporter brushed back his blow-dried hair, adjusted his microphone, and started once more: "If you think the days of traveling by horse are gone…" he'd start, leaning awkwardly in the saddle—and there went Silo again, back to the grass, while the reporter pulled and tried not to tumble off what was probably the tallest horse in the Grier School stable. The girls kept calling out suggestions as to how to handle the wandering animal, and I wasn't at all sure what I was hearing was the best advice…. There was just no way this guy was going to look cool—even his camera crew was stifling laughter. The interview was over too soon, and with all the laughter and shenanigans, it was the most fun I'd had on the trip so far.

Late in the afternoon, there was much debate and negotiation over whose table I would sit at during dinner. Then the girls remembered that they had to "dress" for dinner—no exceptions. The clothes I had clearly did not meet the dress code. In no time I found myself in sandals and a skirt and blouse. Less than a month on the road and already I felt like a wild child brought in and cleaned up to be presented to civilized society.

After dinner, I walked back to the barns in the warm and lovely May evening so I could check on Rainy. Two girls accompanied me, Tracy and Alex, and we threw the horses an extra leaf of hay for the night.

"I think I need a swim," said Tracy with a laugh, brushing the hay from her blouse. I watched as the girls' eyes met and could see an idea being hatched.

It wasn't long before I was in a borrowed bathing suit and we'd picked up other girls, the idea of an illicit nighttime swim in the school pool catching on.

"But the pool's not officially opened yet!" someone whispered.

Someone else worried, "We're not supposed to go in without a grownup…"

"*She's* a grownup," Tracy said, referring to me.

I didn't feel like a grownup.

The night was balmy, and soon I was floating on my back, enjoying the first swim of the year, listening to the sounds of the Grier girls talking and giggling in subdued tones while the moon rose round and white through the branches of the oak trees.

The headmaster had given the students special permission to stay up and watch the eleven o'clock news in a lounge called "The Smoker." With damp hair and suits hidden beneath clothes, we vied for good seats in the small room. While the story ran, the laughter flowed, because we all knew what was going on during the shoot. Despite the shenanigans, it was agreed that the story of my trip and my stay at Grier School came across pretty well.

I had what seemed like a hundred helpers, getting Rainy ready the next morning. We chatted comfortably and exchanged addresses, our sneakers turning damp in the morning dew. When Rainy stood, packed and ready, and Gypsy waited at his feet, one of my new friends started crying. Then we were all hugging, sniffling, and wiping away tears.

I can't explain it. It's a girl thing.

## LOUIE'S LOUNGE

We followed a trail the Grier girls showed us, and I was instantly reminded of the pleasures of a grassy green path under four hooves. I listened to birdsong and the mild buzz of insects. For me, the smell of spring grass and wildflowers were all the more precious when taken in from the back of a horse.

Rainy, Gypsy, and I enjoyed the quiet trail much of the day, but it came to an abrupt end, feeding out onto a busy road just as it clouded up and started to rain with gusto. All three of us stood at the edge of the pavement, shocked by the soaking downpour, when I heard someone shouting.

"Over here! Right here!" A barely visible figure on the other side of the street was waving and jumping up and down. I looked for a break in the traffic and urged Rainy across the road.

The man continued shouting, even though I stopped right in front of him.

"Hey! Are you the girl who's riding the horse around the world?"

I laughed and nodded as he gestured for me to follow him down a driveway and through a garage door. I leaned over and put Gypsy on the ground, then pulled off my hood and jumped down from the saddle. I was surprised to find myself surrounded by people in white aprons, beaming at us. Everyone was talking at once, and I heard several comments of disbelief that "Louie" was actually backing his Cadillac out into the rain for us.

We'd stumbled upon Louie's Coral Lounge, a tavern and restaurant tucked in the hills of western Pennsylvania. It was Louie himself who pulled me, with Gypsy at my heels, into the kitchen of the restaurant, assuring me his workers would take good care of Rainy while I had something to eat. He handed me a bunch of white tablecloths to use to dry myself off.

"We got a horse in the garage!" Louie proudly informed the staff as he led me through a set of swinging doors into the dining area.

The room had gleaming hardwood floors and tables set with the same white tablecloths I'd just used as towels. Half a dozen men ate sandwiches and drank mugs of cold beer in the bar area; they nodded hello as Louie deposited me at a table with my journal and pen, and orders to choose whatever I wanted from the menu. Before going back to the kitchen, Louie dumped a handful of quarters in front of me.

"Here," he cheerfully insisted. "Put some songs on the jukebox to listen to while you eat."

I walked a little self-consciously into the bar area and flipped through the jukebox, punching in the numbers until Louie's quarters were gone. The strains of the first song filled the restaurant: Ricky Skaggs' "Crying my Heart Out Over You." One of the men at the bar murmured, "Good choice," and I smiled over my shoulder at him before peeking out the window at Rainy, still peaceful in the garage. I knew Gypsy was where I'd left her, resting contentedly on the pile of tablecloths in the kitchen. I returned to my table and wrote notes in my journal while the rain drummed a steady beat on the tavern window, as if part of the song in the background.

The men who'd been sitting at the bar made their way over to talk to me—all of them truck drivers, stopping for lunch. We shared our traveling stories, as outside the rain slowed, then stopped. One by one, the truckers took their leave, having schedules to keep. The first tried to pay for my lunch, but Louie wouldn't hear of it. So in passing, the man placed a five-dollar bill on my table, telling me, "For lunch down the road." I promised I'd remember him with my next cheeseburger.

The other drivers tried to give me money, too. "I'm okay, really!" I protested, but they left it anyway, shaking my hand, kissing my cheek, and wishing me luck and safety on my journey.

The last truck driver paid his bill at the bar and walked over to my table.

"Your parents must be worried about you," he observed. I nodded in agreement.

"I have a daughter of my own," he went on, "and if she wanted to do something like this...." He closed his eyes and shook his head. "But y'know," he said after the pause, "I think I'd give her my blessings."

The man reached out and tucked a tightly folded five-dollar bill into my hand. I objected, offering it back, but he again shook his head.

"Just take it, please," he insisted. "It'll make me feel good and make me think that someday, someone will do something nice for my daughter, too, when she's out there in the world."

We smiled at each other in understanding. I asked him if he wanted me to send him a postcard from California.

"Naw," he replied. "Just remember Ed the truck driver from Jamestown, New York."

The man turned to leave, stopping to wave again from the doorway, the sun now out and shining brightly behind him.

I watched his truck pull out of the parking lot, then unfolded the five-dollar bill, still clutched in my fist.

It wasn't a five-dollar bill. It was a fifty. A fifty-dollar bill that had been folded up so I could not insist it was too much. A fifty-dollar bill from Ed the truck driver, with a daughter of his own, back in Jamestown, New York.

## STORM ON THE MOUNTAIN

A need for fresh batteries meant I had to ride into Duncansville, and after being featured on the news for several nights, arriving in town slowed our progress to a crawl. People approached and called us by name. They took pictures and offered us meals. Twice, I was asked to sign my autograph.

While I made polite conversation with the group around us, a policeman approached.

"Can I make a suggestion?" he asked, pointing toward the railroad tracks that led out of town. "If you're going to get out of here before dark, that's the way you want to go. There's some bad weather headed this way."

I said a hastened goodbye to the kind Duncansville folks, and in minutes, we were riding along empty tracks through a patch of dense forest. The air was so heavy with moisture it felt like we were walking through cobwebs of mist. Then the rain started, cloaking the already shadowy woods in a heavy veil of gray. Ahead, I could just make out a break in the trees and headed toward it.

When we came out of the woods, I knew we were riding into trouble. I could just barely see the wet, darkened road and the little strip of gravel shoulder beside it, where Rainy carefully trod. The road disappeared in front of us, around a curve, heading up the mountain. Cars splashed past, their headlights reflecting off the damp pavement.

The road cut into Cresson Mountain, part of the Allegheny Mountain Range. Steep, almost vertical outcroppings rose on either side, clothed in thick swathes of pine trees that clung to the rocks, adding to the darkness the storm had brought. It was a bad place for us to be, but I had little choice but to keep going forward. Turning back would put us on the equally narrow downhill side of the road, and there was more traffic going that way. I watched in vain for a side road or turnoff, cringing every time a vehicle swooshed within inches of us.

Feeling unsure and nervous in the saddle, I dismounted as quickly as I could, given the shivering puppy in my arms. Passing vehicles showered us with water, coming so close that my rain poncho swirled around. As a bitter reminder that things could always get worse, thunder rolled and a flash of lightning momentarily brightened the road before us. I could see there was so little room between where the cars passed and the steep incline on our right, it couldn't even be called a shoulder. Yet this was where I guided Rainy, keeping myself between him and the traffic. Being on foot made us a wider target, but I figured if we were going to get hit by a car, it was better if it was me that took the impact. I knew that someone would call an ambulance and try to save me. If Rainy got hit, no one would know what to do.

So I plodded on, a death grip on the reins in my right hand, struggling to hold Gypsy at the same time. My back and arms ached, but there was no way I could put the dog down in the situation.

It hardly seemed possible, but it got darker and steeper. The thunder got louder. I could barely see, and I knew drivers, rushing up the road through the rain, could barely see us. I thought of my parents and said prayers.

Through the sound of the wind whipping my poncho, I sensed something close behind us. I turned and tugged at my hood to find a pickup truck hovering a dozen feet back. Weary and scared, I thought, *What now?* The truck stopped and a guy got out, standing behind his open door and cupping his hands to his mouth.

"Stay in front of my truck!" he shouted. "I'll be behind you and keep cars from coming up on you—I've got a friend who is going to box you in up front!"

I watched as another vehicle carefully eased by us and slowed, waiting with its hazard lights throwing strange red flashes into the night.

"Come on!" the guy behind me yelled. "Let's get going! Keep between us to the top of the hill—let's get you off this road!"

The man climbed back in his truck as the car in front started forward, and we began to move slowly up the hill. I could move more freely now with our escorts and the room they made for us, so I thankfully let Gypsy down on a short leash and unclamped my cramping arm. The two vehicles crawled along at the walking pace of a tired horse, girl, and dog, struggling up the steep roadway.

Gradually the incline leveled out and soon the shoulder widened enough to ride, though I stayed on the ground for Rainy's sake—he'd worked so hard and been so brave. I figured my jeans were too heavy with water and the saddle too soaked for me to manage to get on anyway.

As the rain let up and the sky brightened, I could see the side road ahead that would lead us to the Egers' house—our resting place for the night. My intense relief sent a tremble through my body. I felt weak and helpless in the face of how scary the situation we'd just come through had been. I felt a rush of need to thank my rescuers, but the front car had already increased its pace, and soon was gone, out of sight. I turned as the pickup pulled up beside us, and through the window, opened slightly, my hero asked if we were all right. I could now see he had really red hair.

I nodded, then called out, "What's your name?" He just smiled and waved, accelerating away.

"Thank you!" I shouted after the truck. "Thank you." I said again, quietly this time, knowing he couldn't hear me. "Thank you, thank you," I whispered as his taillights disappeared.

I pressed my forehead against Rainy's steaming, wet neck. "Thank you," I whispered to him, too.


## TUNNEL

The tunnel ahead of us looked cartoon-like, the arched entryway filled with darkness. I gently brought Rainy to a stop. Peering in, the blackness robbed me of perspective—I couldn't see how long it might be. Every now and then, a car rushed out, headlights on.

Rainy stood patiently with Gypsy sprawled across the saddle as I looked around for an alternative route. A cursory glance revealed roughhewn steps winding up and around, but they were narrow and crumbling, and it was impossible to tell where they led. Forward it had to be, then. Through the tunnel was the only way.

I urged Rainy on, then halted him again before entering the passage. I could see there wasn't a sidewalk or breakdown lane, just two lanes for traffic. It was quiet, though, with no cars coming, so I gripped Gypsy a little tighter and gave Rainy his cue to start through the cave-like arch.

Our senses on edge, we all three tensed for the sound that would signal an oncoming car in the dark space, but there was only the echo of Rainy's hoof beats. Our trip through the tunnel felt endless. I'd freeze up for a second, thinking I heard the sound of an approaching vehicle; then I'd realize it was only a little wind. I nervously looked back over my shoulder every few minutes to make sure no one came up behind us unexpectedly. Gypsy gave a little whine, looking up at me, and I realized I must be holding her collar too tight. I rarely asked Rainy for any gait but a walk when he was packed, but I squeezed my legs, asking him to trot. At last I saw light up ahead. As we approached the tunnel's exit, I blew out a big sigh of relief, thankful for the good fortune that was on our side once again.

Stepping out of the shadows and into the bright sun, for some reason, made me laugh out loud. Gypsy looked up at me again and thumped her tail, sensing the lightening of the tension we'd all felt as we hurried our way through the dark, damp tunnel. I clapped Rainy on the neck in celebration.

"You're a trooper, buddy!" I exclaimed, my heart surging with appreciation for my brave four-legged partner. "You're such a good boy!"

Rainy's ears twitched back and forth and he extended his pace as we continued on into the sunlight.

# RAINY'S TWIN...AND THE NEWS

On the outskirts of Johnstown we stayed with the Harties, a horse family connection I'd made through the Egers. Charlie Harties asked if I'd come to the local saddle club meeting and say a few words to the members about my trip. I was happy to—who would better appreciate hearing about Rainy and the remarkable strength he'd shown so far than a group of horse people?

The riding club was a friendly group, full of questions. They were especially intrigued by the way people connected to the horse world along our route had begun passing us along, from one to another, ensuring we had places to stay as our journey continued. By the time the meeting was over, I'd collected dozens of new names and addresses, many in Ohio, of families and individuals who were willing to help. Everyone in the saddle club just assumed Rainy, Gypsy, and I would make it past Pennsylvania...and beyond. It strengthened my faith knowing others believed in us.

The Harties and I looked over maps and city directories to find a way my animals and I could go on without going through Johnstown, but there didn't seem to be a way around that made sense. So right through the city it would be. Rainy had handled traffic and people, but this would be a first. Charlie Harties thought if we got going really early, it should still be quiet on the streets, and it being Sunday, most of the businesses would be closed.

With the sun just rising, we said goodbye to the Harties family, and Rainy, Gypsy, and I set out in the morning sunshine. Before long, we were in the city, winding our way up one empty street and down another, past row houses and apartments and storefronts. In an area of commerce, with businesses on one side of the avenue and apartment houses backed into the hillside on the other, we came to a building with a huge plate-glass window-front. The glass reflected the street, the buildings, and the blue sky back at us like a mirror.

It reflected our images, too.

Rainy, perhaps tired of being the only equine around, pricked his ears and raised his head in excitement at seeing "another horse" looking back at him. His muscles tensed, and his head rose to the fullest height he could manage as he bugled out great, loud whinnies, over and over again. The concrete and glass echoed his calls back, making them seem louder and longer as they broke the easy silence of the early morning.

Doors and windows popped open. People stepped outside their doors and gestured for their kids and spouses to come out and see, too. My face turned red, now that we were suddenly on display, and so out of place on the urban street—my dog and horse and I, who had been trying to sneak through the city undetected.

I turned Rainy away from the "other horse" in the window. He called out once or twice more, and even tried to turn back for another glimpse as I urged him on down the block.

We weren't much farther along when a reporter showed up and asked if I'd stop and talk a bit, which I did. We were often stopped by reporters now, and I thought back to the first reporter who'd asked me for an interview. At first, I didn't want to be in the news for fear that someone unsavory would see the story and realize I was a female traveling alone. In the end, I had agreed to that first interview, and that decision had led to something interesting. It turned out that being in the news actually *helped* rather than hurt me and my animals. It gave us credibility. It meant that I often didn't have to introduce and explain myself—many people knew all about us and our story before we even met. They began to watch for us. Folks who'd seen or read the story would come looking for us to see if we needed anything, like the army veteran who had given me his army rain poncho. It was much sturdier than the one I had and big enough to cover me, the packs, and Gypsy, when she was riding with me.

I rarely got to see the news stories, though I did, of course, see the one with the Grier School girls, and another when I stayed with Dale and Nina Siedell, trainers at a Tennessee Walking Horse facility. A cameraman had filmed us on the road during different parts of the day, and the piece ran the scenes while "California Dreamin'" by The Mamas and the Papas played in the background. Dale and Nina watched it wistfully.

"I wish we could go with you," both of them said, more than once.

It made me realize how lucky I was, on the road with my animals. We moseyed along each day, part of the world around us yet in our own world, too.

Between my chain of helpful horse people passing the word along and the different news stories on television and radio, and in print, people were looking out for us, watching for when we would come through their town, chasing a dream.

## ▓▓ DEAD HEAD

We rode in the shade of tall oak trees that lined the streets of a quiet neighborhood, then turned toward a local corner market where I could see a cluster of young folks were hanging out, drinking sodas and soaking up the sun. I halted near the group, and Rainy stood politely while several approached to pet him as I went inside to buy a few provisions.

As I came back out, a heavyset fellow in an oversized tie-dye shirt pushed himself off the store wall he was leaning against and ambled over, his happy, vacant grin reflecting the distinctive smoky smell that lingered around him. He stared at Rainy as I added items to my saddlebags, and after picking up bits of the conversation I was having with the others, he turned his gaze to me.

"Whoa...whoa...." he said, dragging out the words while slowly shaking his head from side to side. "Dude. You rode this big boy here all the way from New York?"

"Dude," I replied, grinning at his mannerisms. "I did."

Tie-dye guy rocked on his feet a little, still shaking his head. "Where're you goin'?"

"California," I told him.

"No way! California!" He paused, thinking. "Dude, you must be going out there to see the Dead. They're playing in Bakersfield on the nineteenth!"

"No, I don't think I'm going to make it to see the Dead," I said with a laugh. "I'm going to be on the road for a long time still before I'm anywhere near California."

But the idea had obviously taken hold.

I put my foot in the stirrup, about to mount up again, and my new friend clumsily patted me on the back, shaking his head and staring at me with admiration in his eyes.

"Dude," he said again. "You're riding a horse from New York to California to see the Grateful Dead. It's like the ultimate pilgrimage, man. The. Ultimate. Pilgrimage."

## ANIMAL RIGHTS

*HOOOOONK!*

A horn broke the quiet of our morning on the road, coming up behind Rainy, going around us, making me grimace. I thought again how lucky I was that Rainy had very steady nerves.

A well-dressed woman emerged from the driver's side of the new Jeep, which she'd pulled over just ahead, and her high heels clacked on the pavement as she approached us, a clipboard in one hand. Her off-white skirt and muted pastel blouse looked perfect…for a business meeting or a lunch date. She gave me, Rainy, and Gypsy a visual going over—one that made me realize that I now knew what the expression "looking down your nose" at someone meant.

The woman introduced herself as a representative of an animal welfare agency. "There are some things I need to find out from you," she stated sternly. I waited in silence for her to continue. Rainy cocked one hind foot, taking advantage of our unplanned stop to relax a bit. Gypsy looked expectantly at the woman—she was used to people fussing over her—but no attention came her way.

"We've seen you in the newspaper." The woman looked down at the clipboard. "You're having this horse carry you all the way to California—is that right?"

I nodded.

"Don't you think that's cruel?"

*That's* what this was about? I was used to addressing questions about Rainy and his welfare, but I had to think carefully about how I wanted to answer her. The woman was probably well meaning, although obviously not well informed. Anyone who knew anything about horses would not pull up behind one and lean on her car horn.

"Walking all day is what horses do naturally in the wild," I began politely. "Studies show wild Mustangs walk over fifteen miles a day, just foraging and grazing."

The woman looked at her clipboard. I could tell she was not listening, but I plowed on with my speech: Rainy was in good shape; we'd conditioned for the trip; he had custom-made shoes; I had veterinarians regularly check him.

Without acknowledging a thing I said, the woman finally looked up and proclaimed, "We think you're making him work too hard."

There she stood, off to the side, away from Rainy. She hadn't reached a hand out to stroke his neck, or cast an eye down the clean, unblemished lines of his legs, or considered his trimmed and shod hooves. She didn't see the sleek healthy shine to his coat, his excellent muscle tone. His behavior and condition spoke volumes about his training and care.

"I think it's cruel what you're doing to him," she said accusingly.

"Look, lady," I snapped. Gypsy looked up at me in surprise at my sharp tone. "There are horses all over that really need someone to watch out for them. Do you have any idea how many people buy horses and then lose interest? I bet you can find a horse within a few miles of here, not 'working too hard' in a tiny stall full of manure. But look at *my* horse!" I took a deep breath, aiming a glare at her heavily made-up face. "You're not qualified to talk to me about this. If your group or whatever has any *real* questions about horse welfare, I'll talk to someone who knows something about the subject. Now excuse me. You're in my way."

I woke Rainy with a nudge of my heels, urging him past her. She blinked, but didn't move, and seemingly unfazed by my rant, turned her attention to Gypsy, sprawled on the saddle in front of me.

"What's wrong with your dog?" she demanded. "Why is it panting like that?"

I wanted to shout, "Because she's hot! That's what dogs do when they're hot!"

But what good would it do? I shook my head in disgust as we rode on, walking into the road to get around the shiny Jeep. I didn't look back.

All the rest of the day, I kept thinking of things I wish I'd said to the woman, the better ways I could have handled her. In the weeks that followed, I prepared myself for another confrontation, but we never did see her or anyone else from her animal welfare agency—if there really was one—again.

## COUNTRY CLUB

A luxury car stopped just ahead, and I cued Rainy to a halt, watching warily. I was braced for anything, the encounter with the animal welfare lady fresh in my mind. A distinguished-looking older woman stepped out and walked to Rainy's head, which he lowered obligingly for her, and she stroked him gently. She then came to my side, reached up, and offered me a firm handshake.

"My name is Ted," she said, meeting my eyes. "I'd like you to be my guest for lunch at the Ligonier Country Club."

My hesitation clearly showed, because the woman smiled reassuringly and patted my leg.

"My lady friends and I would love to hear your stories. I saw you on the news, and it's funny, I just knew I'd meet you when you came through town."

There was something about Ted that I liked, and lunch sure did sound tempting, but a country club? I gestured toward my dusty clothing, stating, "This is all I have to wear."

"Don't worry." Ted waved off my concern. "I'll meet you there. Just tell them you're with Ted Beebe. Up ahead, you'll see a driveway to the left. There's no sign. Follow it. We'll watch for you." She smiled, returned to her big car, and drove off.

Would Rainy and Gypsy and I really be welcome on the grounds of a fancy-schmancy country club? Ted Beebe's car had faded into the distance, and she was now expecting me. She did seem like a cool lady. And there was that free lunch.

The driveway was easy to locate, and having turned down it, we found ourselves in a world of manicured green. I carefully kept Rainy off the grass as we made our way to the clubhouse. There was a reasonable place where I could tie Rainy in the shade of a tree outside the main building, and I did so hesitantly, ready at any moment for someone in one of the golf carts that buzzed around to come and tell me to get my scruffy self out of there. With misgivings, I left Rainy behind and opened the door to the clubhouse, stepping inside. Gypsy was pressed tightly against my leg.

We entered a large room, one I could imagine had been the site of many a wedding reception and gala event. Today it was filled with country clubbers who did lunch. Glasses and silverware clinked delicately, and a conversational murmur ebbed and flowed. Not everyone was dressed up, but they were all well dressed. I stood there like the stable help who'd taken a wrong turn, ready to bolt as I scanned the tables for Ted. Finally, a braceleted wrist rose from the tables, beckoning me toward a group of four women. As I self-consciously headed their way, they all turned toward me and smiled warmly.

Ted Beebe introduced me as I apologized for my attire. The women laughed, and one of them announced that she loved it as she motioned toward an empty chair.

"What are you supposed to be wearing when you're riding a horse across the country?" she asked, putting me at ease. The others immediately peppered me with questions, and I warmed to the subjects: Rainy, Gypsy, our travels. A waiter in a white jacket took my lunch order.

Suddenly Ted noticed Gypsy, sitting quietly by my feet. "Oh dear, we forgot to get something for your dog!" She called the waiter back to our table to order something for the pup, but I was concerned that someone would insist Gypsy go outside to eat. My companions laughed at my worries. "No one will bother us, dear," Ted assured me, and no one did.

I wasn't sure who these ladies were but they *counted*. They wanted to hear all the details of my cross-country trip; they didn't want to talk about golf or gossip with the other members who stopped by our table. In fact, they seemed to delight in *not* introducing me or explaining the dog under the table or the horse tied outside. I was amused that no one questioned these four ladies, the obvious queens of the country club, and began to relax, enjoying their banter and their interest. And we all had a really good laugh when the waiter came bearing Gypsy's hamburger… on a silver tray covered in glass!

Much later I learned that the area I rode through that day and its country club was home to some of the richest families in America. Gypsy and I had lunched with a "who's who" in banking and steel. None of it mattered then, though—they were just kind women getting together to eat and talk and make a stranger feel like a friend.

## A SIGN

The morning sky was heavy with rain and it never really got all-the-way light. We traveled along a grassy strip between the road and the woods, where the leaves on the trees were shiny green, fluttering and waving in the moist, blowing air. Branches hung low, forcing me to duck down over Rainy's neck at times under the heavy canopy. It was an unexpected place to come upon a sign, its words partially obscured by limbs and leaves.

*Welcome to West Virginia.*

I gasped, and Rainy stood quietly while I savored the colored words, flowers, and birds on a faded white background. We had ridden from New York all the way to West Virginia! My jubilation spread to the animals: Gypsy looked at me, wagging her tail, and Rainy took the opportunity to steal a celebratory bite of grass. We lingered in the rain, getting double soaked as the branches above dripped water onto us, too—but I didn't care. We'd ridden to West Virginia!

In West Virginia, it rained and rained. In the drab army poncho that covered us, we were not a color. We were drier than we would have been in the old, bright, plastic raincoat I'd used early in the trip, but now we didn't stand out at all amongst the green of the trees and the gray of the pavement beside us. It felt fitting, symbolic of what we were becoming, how we were more a part of what was around us, blending in with the woods and the grass and the rain-drops dancing on the road.

I saw a sudden flash of color—a deep violet blue against the canopy of trees. It was a delicate bird; a flying jewel whose color had not found a perfect name yet.

At my host's house that evening, I described the bird we saw.

"Ah," she said with a smile. "That must've been an Indigo Bunting."

In bed, with Gypsy curled beside me, my eyes closed as images from the day drifted through my mind. I again saw the sign welcoming us to West Virginia. I saw green leaves and everything dark and wet...and the Indigo Bunting fluttering by like something enchanted in the rain.

# PART THREE

---

# ON THE ROAD

# LOCUSTS

It took a long time for us to ride to West Virginia, which made it seem almost funny how soon we crossed the narrow northern panhandle and out of the state. We traveled into Ohio and followed "Old 40" up and down hilly streets in St. Clairsville.

I called Mike from one of the first places we stayed in Ohio. Right from the beginning our conversation had an awkward quality to it: I talked about traveling and weather and a few of the people we had met. He described the furniture he'd picked out for his house. How many male egos would not be aware of how different our relationship had already become?

I noticed a strange hum or clacking sound as we made our way through the state. When a young couple approached and said hello, inquiring if they could pat Rainy, I asked them about it.

"It's the seventeen-year locusts," the woman answered nonchalantly.

Maybe people in Ohio were used to it, but the noise had me on edge.

We rode along old strip-mine roads that wound around mild hills. I got off and walked often. I could hear the locusts grow louder as we passed under the trees where they gathered. Occasionally, one bumped into my face, or into Rainy, causing him to shake his head and stomp his feet in frustration. I heard *crunch crunch* as Rainy's hooves landed on the shells that littered the road.

We picked up the pace a little, all three of us seeming to want to get through the area as quickly as possible. Seventeen years, and the locusts had to hatch the year we were passing through.

It was seventeen years too soon, if you asked me.

## BRAD

The town of Hendrysburg, Ohio, was just a smattering of houses all lined up; a closed store, a church, and a bait shop sat where the old road became Main Street in the little village.

As we neared the town center, I could see a figure in the middle of the road up ahead. Rainy saw it too—the unfamiliar shape and the way the shadow formed on the street had my horse on alert. He raised his head, ears forward and nostrils flaring. I took up the usual slack in the reins as a whirring noise became audible.

Coming toward us, moving slowly, was a huddled figure in a motorized wheelchair. We approached each other like duelists in an old Western town.

I brought Rainy to a halt, and we watched the guy maneuver the chair around until he was alongside us and we were all facing the same direction. After a few snorts, the always unflappable Rainy settled, and Gypsy wagged her tail as soon as the fellow in the chair started to speak.

"My name is Brad," he announced.

Brad had come to escort us through Hendrysburg as we made our way to the barn a few miles west of town where Rainy, Gypsy, and I were staying the night. He admitted he'd been watching for us all afternoon, slowly going up and down the quiet Main Street.

"This is what I do every day," he said with a shrug. "Today you were something different to watch for."

Brad and I discovered we were the same age, and he told me he used to ride horses, too, before he was paralyzed in a car accident when he was seventeen. This hit me hard; I simply couldn't imagine what he'd been through. I wanted to ask him about it, but he changed the subject quickly.

Brad's head was tilted toward one shoulder, but I could see him give Rainy a once over with his eyes.

"Quarter Horse?" he asked.

"Yup," I answered.

"That's our breed, too," he told me. "Everyone used to get together and rodeo a little on the weekends around here." I didn't know what to say; I thought about how he must miss that.

Rainy, having accepted the wheelchair, slowed his pace to keep Brad abreast of us. We made a strange procession as we walked through Hendrysburg: me, my steady horse, Gypsy, and Brad in his motorized wheelchair. Like a small parade, we passed by a woman in gardening gloves who looked up from her planting and waved hello. A few children yelled, "Hi, Brad!" and one small kid ran up with a hopeful look, but Brad shook his head. "No rides today, buddy," he said. I could tell by the exchanges that Brad had made his Main Street routine a bright spot in his day. I could see the smile reach his eyes when he talked.

Soon we were at the western edge of town where I would keep going and where Brad would not. I thought about how all the next days, and the days after that, as I rode westward, Brad would be riding up and down the empty Main Street, waving hello to whomever was out, and then stopping at the edge of town and doing it all over again.

We stopped, and sat quietly for a minute, facing west. Then Brad and I said goodbye. Rainy, Gypsy, and I headed off slowly. I turned in the saddle to wave, but Brad had already started back on his route. I could still hear the whirring noise, growing faint. He did not watch us ride away.

# DANGER ON THE ROAD

In this southern part of Ohio, the sun was always shining, the grass was green, and corn was growing everywhere. I enjoyed the sun on my shoulders and feeling the roll of Rainy's gait in sync with the way the land rolled on in front of us. Gypsy was slung across the front of the saddle—although Route 22 was pleasant, it's a busy thoroughfare. I sang as we walked along, lulled into a hazy, day-dreaming frame of mind.

Out of nowhere, a massive eighteen-wheel semi suddenly topped a rise in the road behind us, frighteningly close. The driver, no doubt surprised to find himself bearing down on a horse on the shoulder of the road, laid on the truck's air horn and hit the brakes with a deafening hiss.

The surprise and the noise was more than even solid Rainy could handle. He leaped forward in fear and bolted into the road, panicking as the truck bore down on us. He galloped wildly, the packs flapping against his sides, and his feet pounding the hard surface of the pavement. Gypsy started to slide off the side of the saddle as everything went off balance. I desperately hung on to my dog with one hand while struggling with the reins, and trying not to think about the massive truck right behind us.

Rainy suddenly turned on his haunches, jumping the roadside ditch. How Gypsy and I stayed on I don't know. My mind felt frozen—*This could be the end of us*. I could only focus on keeping a grip on Gypsy and staying in the saddle as Rainy continued his fear-filled race into the grassy roadside field. Precariously tipping, the stirrups lost, I summoned all the strength I could muster and somehow pulled my runaway horse into a circle, where he dropped to a trot, and finally a walk and shaky halt. Still tightly holding poor Gypsy with one arm, I slid down out of the saddle, limp from fear and adrenaline, and leaned against my trembling horse's neck.

My legs were weak—I didn't know if they would hold me. Rainy's sides were heaving and rivulets of sweat ran down his barrel and haunches from beneath my gear.

I could see the big truck stopped on the road, pulled over to the shoulder, along with several other cars, near the place Rainy had made his wild run and leap to safety. Seeing I now had my horse under control, the truck driver who had started it all got back in his rig and pulled away. But a woman from one of the other cars walked toward us.

"You okay?" she asked with concern as she drew near. I nodded. I didn't trust my voice just yet. "Take deep breaths," the woman said soothingly, taking Gypsy's leash from my hand and gently rubbing my back. Still not speaking, I turned and began to check Rainy all over. His breathing had slowed—a good sign.

"My name is Jesse Walker," the kind woman said as I finished running my hands down the buckskin's legs, thankful he seemed to have come through the ordeal unscathed. "Wait here a minute."

Gypsy trotted along beside Jesse as the woman went back to her car and leaned against the hood for a minute, drawing something. She returned with a sketch of a map of side roads that would get us off Route 22, and then she pointed to an intersection she'd circled. "Here's where we can meet at the end of the day," she told me matter-of-factly. "I'll bring this sweet dog and your packs to you there."

I didn't question the arrangement Jesse proposed. I just let myself trust her, watching as most of my stuff and Gypsy rode away in her car. I stood with Rainy for a bit longer, again leaning my head against his neck. He was calm enough now to nibble at the grass.

I thought about the saying: *There are no strangers, only friends I haven't met yet.* Jesse Walker set aside her life for a moment in order to help me. It was this kindness of a stranger that got me back up in the saddle.

## GOODMANS

Once in a while, you meet someone, and there's an instant connection. I was lucky to experience that when I stayed with Butch and Nancy Goodman. After they showed me where Rainy could be settled for the night in their spacious barn, Butch and Nancy had pizza delivered. Nancy, Gypsy, and I sat on the floor, pizza boxes open beside us, long after Butch got tired and went to bed. Nancy shared stories about the first time she traveled alone and asked to see the pictures I carried of Mike and my family. She and I talked so late into the night that I spent an extra day with them...just to rest!

When I woke up late the next morning, I hurried to get to Rainy. I wasn't used to sleeping in these days, and I was supposed to meet a local reporter at the Goodmans' barn. Rainy's nicker greeted us when we walked in. There was something about that sound that made me happy.

That evening, I accompanied the Goodmans to a local horse show. Trucks and trailers filled the parking lot of the show grounds; wooden bleachers filled with people. Butch, along with his sons, Greg and Jeff, competed in barrel racing and other timed events. Butch was in his element in the friendly show atmosphere—he knew everyone at the event, and everyone knew him. He kept stopping and introducing me to people, bragging about how I'd ridden my horse from New York all by myself. Gypsy stood patiently beside me as I shook hands with dozens of people.

Then I heard my name over the loudspeaker.

"We have a special guest with us tonight, folks," echoed the deep voice across the big arena. "Her name is Missy Priblo, and she's ridden her horse here all the way from New York!"

I heard some scattered claps and a few whistles. Then the announcer continued: "Let's give Missy a big loud welcome because tonight is going to be her first speed event ever!"

I looked at Nancy helplessly as Butch dragged me out to the middle of the ring and grasped my hand in his, raising it high, while his other hand pumped the air like he was Rocky or something. I knew my face was red as a tomato—but I was laughing, too, kind of enjoying Butch's act.

And then, suddenly, it hit me… *What did that announcer say about me riding in a speed event?*

There was no turning back, it would seem, because Butch was dragging me over to a leggy sorrel gelding that his son Jeff was holding by the entry gate. The horse danced around in excitement. The whites of his eyes showed as he pawed the ground. I'd been traveling literally at a walk on the back of a steady-paced, calm-headed horse, for weeks and weeks. The difference between my kind of riding and this amped-up running machine was like the difference between your granny driving you to church and going shotgun in an Indy car. I pulled back, telling Butch rather frantically, "I don't know what I'm doing!"

"Yes, you do," he calmly reassured me. "It's just a flag race, no big deal. Just reach over and pull the little stick out of each barrel when you ride by it, and let the horse do the rest. On the stretch home, just let him go. You're gonna love it, I guarantee."

Even as I protested I knew I was going to do it. I could hear the crowd yelling, urging me into the saddle. Butch gave me a leg up, and suddenly I was holding the reins. My big sorrel horse pawed and jigged in place in anticipation of what was to come. I swallowed and tried to sit deeper on his back, taking a real feel of the great force of energy I was holding back with just my fingers and a set of thin leather reins.

"You rode that horse of yours out here for an adventure, didn't you?" Butch asked with a grin, slapping my leg.

I barely had time to nod at the timers, and then we were flying through the gate, headed for the first barrel with a bucket on top, the little flag sticking up, waiting for me to grab it.

The sorrel horse knew his job. His hooves pounded, dirt flew, and with one hand clenched tightly round the saddle horn, I leaned in…but missed the flag. Tears streamed straight back from the corners of my eyes as the sorrel leaned in low to the ground—awfully low—around the next barrel, but…I got the flag! I held it tightly in my hand as we ran for the last barrel and then the straightaway home, galloping full out.

I reined the horse to a stop, laughing. "That was a blast!" I admitted as I jumped off. Butch beamed and the crowd applauded as the announcer read my time. I reached out to pat the neck of the gelding, breathing hard beside me. We left the ring together, Butch clapping me on the back as I acknowledged that he was right: *this* was an adventure.

Butch stood by, watching thoughtfully as several people came over to us to say hello and have a chuckle about my run on the fast sorrel.

"You tell everyone how good the people you've met have been to you and your animals," Butch said to me later as we drove back to the Goodmans' home. "Well, maybe you're doing something good for them, too." He paused as he guided the truck along the night-dark road. "I think your trip brings people together, and it makes *them* feel good to help *you*. It gives people a little piece of your dream."

I liked to believe what Butch said was true. It gave me a sense of purpose and happiness to think of my trip that way.

It was dark when we reached town, but to Butch Goodman, the night was still young. He proudly informed me that Lancaster, Ohio, was home to The Charlie Horse, the third largest country dance bar in the nation (second only to Gillie's and Billie Bob's in Texas).

"We feel it's our duty to take you there," said Nancy.

There was a big crowd at The Charlie Horse, and we parked far from the door. Country-singing legend Kitty Wells was performing. The place was so big, and there was so much going on, I didn't know where to look. Unfortunately, on one of his trips to the bar, Butch spotted something for me that he just could not resist.

"There's something over here you have to try," he said, motioning for me to follow him. I caught him winking at Nancy as I got up from the table.

The "something" was a mechanical bull, complete with a crowd gathered round to watch those crazy or drunk enough to give it a try.

"Oh...no, no, no," I said, shaking my head at him as I watched would-be cowboys get tossed to the mat.

"No, c'mon, it's easy," Butch insisted. "People who ride horses can stay on these things. It's just like when your horse feels good in the spring and gives a couple of crow hops."

I gave that mechanical bull a long, hard look. I bet I could stay on the dumb thing. "All right," I said to Butch, and in a blink he was paying my entry fee and pushing a form at me to sign.

"Don't turn it up to the highest level or anything," I insisted.

"Of course not," Butch replied, grinning as I climbed on. The last thing I saw before the bucking got going was my host, making a turning motion with his hand, telling the guy operating the mechanical bull to *crank it up*.

You know what? I think Butch was right. Riding horses did help. I didn't get tossed for a few really long seconds. And I won a Charlie Horse t-shirt out of the deal.

I sat at our table afterward, catching my breath. Kitty Wells' band started in with the opening chords of her signature hit, "It Wasn't God Who Made Honky Tonk Angels," signaling the near-end of her show. And there was Butch, waiting up by the stage, getting her autograph for me.

It was the middle of the night when we finally headed home. My sides hurt from laughing so much. Nancy started to explain why I should plan on staying another day, to rest and recharge.

"Besides," said Butch. "You haven't tried water skiing yet."

## JUMP ABOARD

Gypsy had grown quite a bit since we'd left home, and it had gotten harder to mount up while holding her. We had developed an awkward system where Gypsy stood on her hind legs and put her front paws along Rainy's flanks; then, from the saddle, I leaned over and grabbed her paws. She pushed, I pulled, Rainy stood patiently, and Gypsy eventually scrambled into the saddle.

After traveling all morning with Gypsy on foot, meandering and sniffing and doing what dogs do, we stopped in the shade of some trees to cool off. I could tell Gypsy was weary of walking and wanted a ride by the way she positioned herself alongside Rainy. I leaned over to do our usual "grab thing," but this time, my pup sprang forward and shot herself up and across the saddle, all on her own. I was so surprised I barely had time to grab her so she wouldn't go right over the other side.

"Gypsy! You smart, smart girl!" I exclaimed, holding her face in my hands. The pup beat her tail against Rainy's shoulder, looking pleased. I ran my hands over her body the way she liked and praised her again.

From that moment on, all I had to do was pat the saddle when I wanted Gypsy to ride with me, and she would jump up from the ground. When reporters asked me how I trained my dog to get on a horse, I told them the truth.

She taught herself.

## ICE CREAM SHOP

Sometimes our "chain of people" introduced me to someone who rode with us for a while. But one sunny June day in Ohio, we had a support team driving a car with us along our route. Sherry, Jean, and Grace from the Orihood and Stinson families, checked on us, brought us cool drinks, and let me know what was up ahead. I agreed to meet them at an ice cream shop in a nearby town and then look at saddles at the local tack shop.

Rainy clip-clopped through town until I spotted the ice cream place up ahead, with Sherry, Grace, and Jean at an outdoor table, leaning out and waving so I could see them. A few other scattered groups of people were eating ice cream, too. When Rainy, Gypsy, and I rode into view, everyone burst out laughing.

We approached and Rainy stopped with his nose practically on one of the tables, and everyone laughed even more raucously. I felt uncomfortable but then quickly noticed the laughter was directed toward a lean, middle-aged man near the takeout window of the shop. The customers around me were urging him in our direction.

"Go on!" I heard them encourage him, laughing some more. "You *have* to do it!"

I soon learned that, apparently, when my friends kept getting up from their seats and looking down the sidewalk for our arrival, they had explained to the shop owner they were watching for a horse and rider who had come all the way from New York. The owner's reaction, not altogether wisely, was: "Yeah, right. If a horse rides down my sidewalk—and it's walked here all the way from New York—*I'll kiss its ass!*"

A man of his word, the man did what he said he'd do. He made a show of it, too, to the delight of his audience.

We all got free ice cream cones after that, and buckets of cold water were brought out for Rainy and Gypsy.

I also got a "Coney Isle Ice Cream" tee shirt to join what was beginning to be a collection.

## ON SADDLES

Rainy had been strong and steady, but I couldn't shake a concern I had about his back. Being around so many different horse people as we traveled had only muddied the waters, since opinions on saddle fit and symptoms of a sore back varied greatly. Even veterinarians I met didn't agree. It bothered me to even *think* I might be doing something wrong with my hardworking horse, and I was soon consumed with worry that my Western saddle might not be the best option for Rainy on our long walk.

In the simplest of terms, most saddles are referred to as "Western" or "English," but the subject is deeper than that. The saddle, whatever the style, has to fit the horse correctly, or the horse will get saddle sores (raw, painful wounds from chafing or pressure) or become sore-backed. To make matters more complex, the saddle needs to fit the rider also, for a good seat, stability, and comfort.

It was with reservations that I considered any changes to our rig. I didn't know for sure that anything was wrong with Rainy's back. He hadn't had saddle sores, usually the bane of long-distance riders. My saddle had gotten us from New York to western Ohio; I worried that if I traded it in, I might end up with one that was worse. I decided I needed another expert to weigh in.

The helpful Orihood and Stinson families directed me to a well-known saddle shop outside Sabina, Ohio. The owner was available and I had the advantage of tying my horse right outside so we could discuss multiple fittings. It wasn't long before I was convinced a better saddle existed for Rainy.

"Don't look at fashion or style," urged the shop owner. "Just think about fit, how your horse is built, and how he moves."

Trying the saddles on Rainy told a surprising story. The one saddle that seemed perfect was neither Western nor English. It was a "plantation saddle"—so named as the style was once used by plantation overseers, country doctors, and others who spent long hours on horseback and needed a saddle that was comfortable for themselves and their mounts. It was light and sat on my horse correctly. He walked freely and easily in it, the saddle covering all it should yet leaving his withers and shoulders free. It was comfortable for me, too, with an easy sloping seat and generous padding.

Each saddle is unique, but the truth was, I simply *liked* my saddle. It had been my saddle through almost all my riding career, as well as the memorable miles I'd ridden to reach the saddle shop. It was with a twinge of sadness that I handed it over in trade, hoping I was doing the right thing.

## COWBOYS FOR CHRIST

We'd ridden for hundreds of miles and more than six weeks, and Rainy's shoes needed to be reset. Horses' feet grow and need to be trimmed periodically, like our fingernails. With a "reset," a farrier (a hoof care professional) removes the horse's metal shoes, trims the hooves, and places the shoes back on—as long as they're not worn out. Back home, we had a standing appointment with our farrier every six weeks. Now I was at the mercy of the reputations and schedules of the farriers used by the horse owners I met on the road. The boarders at Decker Road/Springwood Stables, where we were spending the night, assured me that their farrier, Doug, was well respected and specialized in corrective and unusual shoeing jobs. This was an important detail because the shoes Rainy wore our trip were custom-made by our farrier at home to keep Rainy sound and comfortable.

Late in the day a pickup truck, showing the wear of many miles on country roads and a sticker on the tailgate that said "Cowboys for Christ," pulled in by the barn.

Doug had a quiet shyness that for some reason made me trust him. I held Rainy as the man got to work on my horse's feet. A few boarders from the barn stood around, chatting and watching, interested in the special shoes that Rainy wore: borium (extra metal added to shoes that increases the friction against the surfaces a horse is working on) so he wouldn't slip; toe clips to help secure the shoes to the horse's hooves and prevent them twisting and moving rearward; pads to protect the soft part of Rainy's feet from stones; and liquid silicone injected between the pads and hooves to add extra cushion and protection from concussion with the ground.

As he finished, Doug praised my farrier's work and Rainy's solid, healthy hooves. He handed me a folded sheet of paper. "Here are names of other Cowboys for Christ who you can find as you get farther west," he said. "These are people who will help you out." He paused, then asked, "Do you have a Bible with you?"

I shook my head.

"If you don't mind, I'd like to give you this one," he offered, taking a small leather-bound Bible from his pocket. "Would you keep it with you?"

I nodded yes as he passed it to me.

It was clear that Doug's faith was such that he felt better knowing I was carrying a Bible on our journey. As I reached out to take the small book, I noticed it did not appear to be a free "handout" Bible like I expected. Instead, its leather cover was worn soft, and the whole thing curved gently into the shape of things carried in a back pocket over time. Certain passages on certain pages were marked by dog-eared corners.

It was clear that this was Doug's own Bible, well used and read, that he had handed to me.


## SHADOWS

Because of the hours I was spending outdoors with my animals, day after day, walking at a calm and steady pace, I had started to notice things I'd never paid attention to before.

Like our shadows.

Shadows are often used as the literary representation of darkness and evil, but they didn't seem this way to me. Instead our shadows seemed like something cheery—always companionably, silently near. I'd come to notice how their size and the shape changed as the day wore on and the sun made its way across our sky. How giant and misshapen, yet always benevolent, our shadows looked, stretching out across the cornfields beside us. They were the best of fair-weather friends.

The shadows showed our shapes—a horse and rider and a dog—with our feet on the ground, but not exactly earthbound.

They made me aware, always, of the passage of time, and the vague feeling that even if I had no maps and no compass, we could find our way west by just following the path of the setting sun. I liked riding best when the sun was in our eyes and the shadows were long behind us.

## WELCOME TO INDIANA

The land rolled out before us in little rises, making the road we were on look like a strand of old-fashioned ribbon candy.

On the north side of the two-lane road, with nothing but hayfields beyond it, stood the sign that welcomed us to Indiana. As we neared it, I felt the excitement, again, as I had when we crossed into all the states before. I pulled out my camera and took a picture: just rolling fields, an empty road, and a sign.

Tucking my camera back into my saddlebag, I smiled at the accomplishment: *We'd made it to another state!* And this time, we'd crossed into a different time zone. I patted both my partners, congratulating them for another milestone, a source of quiet happiness for travelers like us.

Our first night in Indiana brought us to the barn of horse-woman Marge Jones, a connection through several Ohio farm families, including the Nelsons and the Caplingers, who in turn were connections all the way back to Butch and Nancy Goodman. While getting settled in Marge's horse trailer, where I was going to sleep, I suddenly remembered that it was the day of my younger brother Vince's high school graduation. I hesitated, then walked through the damp grass to knock on Marge's door. She answered, assuring me it was all right to call home. I spoke to everyone in my family, listening to the distant sounds of celebrations in the background. When I hung up, I had to press my hands against my eyes for a minute. I tried Mike, but his phone just rang and rang.

In the morning, Marge fed us breakfast and handed me a list of people she'd contacted and who were happy to host us as we made our way through Indiana.

We rode almost 30 miles the next day, and though the terrain was easy, the heat had all of us worn down. We arrived at the riding club grounds off Route 44 near Rushville, where Marge had said someone would meet us and let us in...but no one had shown up yet.

I let Rainy graze while I sat in the grass and rubbed my eyes. Gypsy sprawled panting beside me. No one appeared. We waited.

I still got just a little bit thrown off when plans fell through. It wasn't panic. I didn't cry like I had in the early days of the trip. It was more of a let-down feeling, like we'd been forgotten somehow. Pushing my disappointment and weariness aside, I tried to think up a Plan B. I didn't mind camping and there was grass and water, so it wasn't like we didn't have a place to stay. It occurred to me that it might not be the accommodations that I needed at that moment; maybe it was the human connection. Spending so much time on the road alone made even small amounts of contact meaningful, and the kindness we had received from people always recharged me.

I pushed myself up from the ground and tied Rainy to the club's corral fence. Gypsy and I set off down the road to see if we could find a place to buy a little hay or feed, and we lucked out with the Needenthals at the very first farm we came to. By the time I returned to Rainy at the corral, Bill Moster from the riding club had arrived, ready to assist us with anything we might need. The Needenthals pulled in with hay for Rainy on their truck. And the Johnsons, whose house was just down the road, came by to visit, too.

Isn't it funny how once you decide you can be self-sufficient, help seems to come around?

As we continued our way through southern Indiana, loosely following Route 44, I kept a close watch on Rainy. The new saddle seemed to be good for him. And his re-set shoes seemed to be working out, as well. I felt thankful as we headed toward Shelbyville, adding a detour to Kopp's Tack Shop, where I had mail waiting. The extra miles were more than worth it: My mail was the first thing Dale Kopp handed me. The farther we traveled, the more envelopes I received at my pre-arranged stops—it was a comforting sign of how many new friends we were making.

Dale refused to accept money for the tack I needed—a better-fitting breast collar, a good, new saddle pad to further protect Rainy's back, and a new headstall to replace the broken one I'd repaired in Ohio. I thanked him warmly as I called Gypsy up onto the front of the saddle, and off we set once more.

Mid-afternoon, we found a shady spot to take a break. I removed the saddle and checked my horse's back to make sure all was going well with the new saddle-and-pad combination, then scratched his back for a minute. He wiggled his lips in pleasure before dropping his head to graze. I sat in the shade near him and took out the letters we'd retrieved from Kopp's Tack Shop.

Though it was the one I had been most looking forward to, it didn't take long to read the few short, impersonal lines of Mike's letter. With his disappointing note in my hand, I looked up at my dog and my horse, and the packs on the ground that held everything we needed. The leaves of the tree above us traced a lacy pattern of shadows where we sat. The cars on the road hummed off in the distance. The world at home, the world with Mike in it, felt like a million miles away.

As I put away the remaining letters and began to tack up, adjusting the new breast collar on Rainy, it occurred to me that here we were, a couple months on the road, and I did not have one single piece of Rainy's tack that we had started the journey with. Everything I'd had at home and thought was a sure thing was different now.

We rode onward, surrounded by Indiana cornfields, with our new and necessary things, leaving much of what we'd started out with behind.

## GOLDEN BOY

Rainy was a "buckskin," a word used to describe a horse with a light-colored body with black legs, mane, tail, muzzle, and ears, a striking combination. His summer coat now shone as golden as the sunshine. He glowed with health and vitality. Life on the road seemed to suit him.

I loved how Rainy looked and was especially partial to his muzzle. It was a dusky charcoal and soft, soft, soft. He possessed a curious nature and was always making use of his muzzle, reaching forward to test new things with his lips—picking up objects and then dropping them to the ground.

My buckskin's affectionate moments touched me the most. That muzzle, part of such a powerful animal, would come to rest in the spot between my shoulder and ear. There he would pause, waiting for me to scratch his neck. I could feel his breath and the velvet of his lips grazing my ear. Having a moment like that every now and then, where he showed affection in his horsey way—to me, that was heaven.

## CONSTRUCTION SITE

After the animals and I had spent a pleasant night at Ben and Mercy Phillips' farm in Martinsville, Mercy was able to join us on her well-behaved Appaloosa for part of the day as we traveled west on Route 44. Mercy was good company, and the morning passed quickly.

After a few hours together, Mercy reined her horse to a stop. "I wish I could go on with you," she said, "but this is where I have to turn around."

I halted Rainy, our two horses lined up, side by side. I think he enjoyed the company, too.

"You're going to come to a huge construction site on 44," Mercy warned me. "I'm not sure you'll be able to go on without a detour. And remember, you can call us if you need anything, anywhere in Indiana!"

We waved to each other, and I watched her ride back the way we'd come for a long moment before turning Rainy and continuing west.

After a mile or so, I heard the sound of heavy machinery. The noise got louder as we rode around a bend and came upon a "ROAD CLOSED" sign, blocking the way in front of us. The ground was all torn up and it appeared a new bridge was being built. I sat on my horse, one hand on Gypsy's back, trying to discern through the dust and noise if there was a way we could get through and stay on Route 44. I really didn't like the idea of going miles out of our way.

A construction worker marking something out on the ground looked up and noticed us. I pointed to where Route 44 was supposed to be and tried to indicate that was where I wanted to go. He lifted a walkie-talkie to his mouth.

A minute later a grader slowed down and ground to a halt. One by one the other giant vehicles, lurking beyond the sign, shut down. The worker walked over to me.

"You need to get over there?" he asked, looking in the direction I'd pointed.

"Can I?" I responded, feeling doubtful by the look of things.

"We can get you through," he said with a nod. He eyed our packs and gear. "Where are you from? Are you traveling far?"

"New York," I answered, "and we're on our way to California."

The worker's eyes widened in surprise. He got on his handheld radio again.

Soon a group of guys in safety goggles and steel-toed boots were all around, the dust of their work settling on us as we talked. I couldn't help but enjoy their responses as I told them about our trip. They seemed like such a fun, friendly bunch.

"Thank you so much for this," I said as one of the men reached out to pat Rainy's neck. "I feel guilty having you shut down the whole construction site for us."

The whole group looked at the worker with the walkie-talkie for a second, and then one guy asked with a grin, "Did *he* tell you that he shut it down for you?" He and the others laughed as I nodded. "It's lunchtime! We always stop work about this time!" I had to laugh, too.

"When are you going to have *your* lunch?" one of the men asked. I shrugged, having made no plans beyond getting past the construction site, and he teased, "Come on, time for a break! Give that poor horse a rest."

So I dismounted, loosened Rainy's girth, and led him to a patch of grass in the shade. The men sat on the ground, so I did, too. Gypsy was happy to flop in a cool spot next to me. We chatted companionably as the workers pulled items from their metal lunch boxes, offering me choices from their own midday meals. I felt bad, taking their food on what was surely a long work day, but they all insisted, so I agreed to half a ham-and-cheese sandwich and an apple.

When it was time to go, a few guys showed me the way Rainy could get down a bank, up the opposite side, then along the tracks made by the construction machinery. This would lead me back to Route 44 on the other side of the site. I was saying my goodbyes and getting ready to head out when one of the men said, "Wait! Let's get a picture."

The workers joked and laughed as they jostled into position for the photograph. Someone located the work camera in the trailer they used as a construction site office. Someone else picked up Gypsy and handed her to me. We posed, me sitting tall on Rainy with Gypsy in my lap, smiling down at the group of hard-hatted men, also smiling, all around us.

## ▨▨ SUNDAYS

I rarely knew what day of the week it was anymore. Somehow, though, I usually knew when it was Sunday. Our route through rural areas and small towns had taught me that Sundays had a certain feel to them—they were still a day of rest and respect in much of the countryside. As we rode along quiet country roads, I was aware of this subtle shift in the lives around us.

On Sunday mornings, when cars passed us, it was not like the usual weekday stream of vehicles that carried one or two people, doing errands and going to work. On Sundays, families were together in their automobiles, old and young, dressed up in good clothes. They slowed and stared as they went around us—an unexpected stranger on a horse on their road where they knew everyone. Most often they waved. On country roads, people usually wave when they pass each other.

On Sunday afternoons, the folks in the cars would often stop, curious about us. "Where are you going?" "Where are you from?" "What do you call your horse?"

There was a familiar sameness on Sundays: a friendly ritual in stopping and talking to people.

When we passed people at home, sitting on their porches, I raised an arm, waving hello. The little ice cream stands, a staple in small towns, always seemed to have more cars parked out front on Sundays. Sometimes, Rainy, Gypsy, and I stopped and visited there, too.

On Sundays, we got invited to dinner, we received offers of cold drinks, and we were welcomed onto shady lawns to rest. When we kept on our way, we were given best wishes and safe travels. These were the ways I always knew when it was a Sunday.

Rainy, Gypsy, and I had rituals of our own: the people who had shown us kindness, the sun shining on us and on the great fields of corn, the way the road curved ahead beckoning us, and our steady quiet walk together. This was our church.

## REVIVAL

It was a long day's ride to the road to the Bo-San-Bo Arena. We turned in and maneuvered through a parking area crowded with campers and RVs. Children ran around in herds, and our arrival caused a bit of a stir. Before long kids were lined up with treats to give Rainy: He crunched the apple right up, accepted a piece of a cookie, then, to the delight of all his little fans, shook his head and tossed a banana from his lips.

A few adults came over to say hello, and one asked if I was there for the show. Many in the crowd were wearing cowboy hats and Western shirts, but I was confused—Bo-San-Bo was a horse event venue, yet Rainy was the only equine in sight.

Bob Brown, part of the family that owned the place, made his way over and led us to the barns where Rainy would be stabled for the night. Finally, I saw other horses.

Teenaged Bob Junior helped me get Rainy settled, explaining the story behind Bo-San-Bo Arena. Bob ("Bo") and Sandy ("San"), and their son Bob Junior ("Bo") had built the business on their property in order to host barrel racing and horse shows. On nights that horses weren't the focus on the grounds, the venue was often rented out for other events. A gospel concert and revival meeting was filling the place that night.

I called to Gypsy, and we wandered out to explore the grounds, following the smell of barbecue. Lights strung around tents glowed in the evening dusk. The sound of a band tuning their instruments and the sounds of many conversations drifted in the air. Children approached, asking where Rainy was, then settled for petting Gypsy instead.

One gentleman inquired whether I was the person who'd ridden on a horse all the way from New York. I said yes, and he insisted on buying me dinner from a concession tent. I sat at a picnic table with him and his friends and family. No one asked if I'd been saved or anything like that. They just smiled a lot and invited me to join them for the gospel music show.

It grew dark. I thanked the family for the meal and began walking back to the barn when I heard the announcement that the concert was starting. People who had been milling about now hurried toward the big tent. It sounded pretty lively inside.

*What the heck*, I thought, turning back to the tent with Gypsy right beside me. I entered a little nervously and stood at the back of the crowd.

Everyone around us seemed caught up in the loud music, and after a few minutes, I saw why. It was hard to sit still. The music swept you along into it—if you liked harmony and a foot-tapping beat! Someone spotted me trying to remain unnoticed in the back and motioned to an empty chair. I ventured forward and sat, Gypsy right beside me. The crowd got rowdier, and I couldn't help but clap along. After every song the claps and hollers and yee-haws rang out—this was not like any church music I'd ever heard. This was rockin'!

By the time the band, called The Pathways, started a rousing version of "I Would Crawl All the Way to the River," any feelings of self-consciousness or not belonging were forgotten. I jumped up, stood on my seat, and stomped and clapped and swayed along with everyone else. Gypsy gave a few excited barks, not sure what all the wild movement was about but ready to join in the game nonetheless. Soon my t-shirt was stuck to my back with a joyful kind of sweat, and I was hoarse from shouting and singing.

The band stopped playing and a tall gentleman joined them on stage and introduced himself as Brother Redmond. In a black cowboy hat and an abundance of heavy turquoise jewelry, he looked down upon the crowd, raising one hand high above his head as he took the microphone with the other.

"BROTHERS AND SISTERS!" he bellowed, whipping the crowd into further frenzy. "There are people in this world who have not yet accepted Jesus Christ as their personal savior!" The crowd murmured and mumbled in response. "What are we going to do about that?" he demanded. After another pause, "WHAT ARE WE SUPPOSED TO DO?" he shouted.

"PRAISE THE LORD!" the shouts rang back, and "SPREAD THE WORD!" someone screamed near me. The band broke out playing again, and Brother Redmond pointed at people, who raised their hands and called to him when they saw him look in their direction. Men paraded into the audience with baskets to collect money. "For our missions!" Brother Redmond reminded all of us. "For our mission work!"

As people closed their eyes in prayer, Gypsy and I slipped out the back flap of the tent. The evening air cooled my damp skin, and the clamor from the gathering was slightly muffled now that I was on the outside. I hummed to myself as Gypsy and I walked back to the camper we'd been given for the night. Even with the aluminum door closed, I could still hear music and shouts of "Praise the Lord!" floating through the summer night.

## LAND OF LINCOLN

The whole state of Indiana had a small town feel, at least on the back roads where we traveled, and I became accustomed to people stopping us and knowing about our journey. The days in this state felt safe and friendly. We rode on in an easy way through the low hills that rolled gently before us, and arrived at the town of Vincennes, on the Wabash River in the southwest corner of Indiana. There, we crossed the bridge and passed the sign welcoming us to Illinois.

The Land of Lincoln! Another milestone on our trek. My animals and I would get to know its back roads, one step at a time.

We began in southeast Illinois on Route 50, an early and well-known coast-to-coast road, starting in Ocean City, Maryland, and terminating in Sacramento, California. Route 50 crossed the United States through farmland and small towns, just like Rainy, and Gypsy, and me.

We spent our first Illinois night in the town of Olney with a gracious young woman named Julie Hurn. Julie was helping me get Rainy ready in the morning when we turned to find Gypsy standing near the barn with Julie's kitten hanging from her jaws. We both held our breath for a second, but Gypsy set the kitten down gently, and they began to play together. After a romp, the kitten sat between Gypsy's outstretched front legs, leaning against the pup's chest. We had to gently persuade the new friends to part when it came time to set out.

West of town, a woman stopped us, curious about our travels. When I told her we had just left Olney, she said, "I suppose someone told you about the white squirrels? They're kind of famous. They've even been written up in *National Geographic*."

"No," I admitted. "I didn't hear about them. What's the story?"

The woman shrugged. "Olney isn't even the only town that has 'em anyway," she said with a sniff. "There's some other town in Missouri or Tennessee or something, and people there say they had the white squirrels first."

It struck me as mighty funny that squirrels could stir up such human competitiveness. They spent their time leaping from tree limbs to fence rails and across power lines. They didn't care where they came from or who saw them first.

It was pleasant riding along Route 50, and we made good progress. We spent one night in an old barn, where I placed my sleeping bag on the floor by Rainy's stall at first...but hearing mice (and quite possibly other critters) in the barn, I moved to an old picnic table stored inside. Adaptable Gypsy climbed up and curled on the table alongside me.

Near Sandoval, we met a friendly newspaper reporter who bought me lunch on a swelteringly hot afternoon. The paper was so small, the printing presses were right next to his office—and he was the only one working there! Of all the things Virgil Downen and I talked about over our sandwiches, the deep connection between Rainy, Gypsy, and me was what he most wanted his readers to understand. I found that discussing it all with him and then reading his words about our trip helped with my own clarity of thought.

I used to tell people, "I want to ride a horse across the country, from New York to California!" like getting from one place to the other was the reason. It was different to me now. It was not a goal so much as it was a way of life.

If we made it to California, great. But it took a small town reporter to word things in a way that made me realize the heart of the story was the adventure. It was about back roads and small towns and good people—and about Rainy, Gypsy, and me, and all that we shared together.

As I traveled, I'd come to believe that roads had their own personalities. As we rode along Route 50, I grew fond of its two lanes; it was a "friendly" road. A wide strip of green grass kept us from being too close to the pavement and the traffic, and often, a line of trees shaded us from the hot afternoon sun. We were on Route 50 for days, and we began to see the same people pass by, heading to and coming home from work. Some began to stop and check on us. They offered cold drinks, advice, and friendly greetings. In this way, Rainy, Gypsy, and I became part of the road for a time.

Marty and Ray, two soft-spoken men who worked in the oil fields, professed worry for us. The last day I saw them, they tried to give me money. We stopped by the Owens family home, and their small children were so excited to have Rainy in their yard, they hauled bucket after bucket of water to him, spilling most of it on each trip. If the folks along Route 50 were a fair sampling, then I definitely liked the people of southern Illinois.

## CARLYLE

A veterinarian who checked Rainy over as we neared the midline of the state of Illinois arranged for us to stay at the barn of Bob Lewis in the Route 50 town of Salem. Bob, in turn, was a well-known horseman in the area, and sent us onward saying he'd organized horse people he knew to look out for us in several other towns we'd pass through.

It was a particularly long day after leaving Salem, and Rainy wasn't himself. My usually good boy with the willing attitude was cranky and lethargic. I needed to "listen" to what he was communicating by this change in personality. First thing was to give him time off.

I took it slow, stopping plenty of times for Rainy to rest, and it was evening by the time we rode into the town of Carlyle. I realized

I should've asked for more details, as my directions from Bob Lewis consisted of simply, "Ride into Carlyle and go to the Court House. Someone will find you there."

The Court House was a stately building right in the middle of town. I let Rainy graze on the lawn and sat beside him. It was quiet. The evening light was soft as streetlamps began to flicker on. I wondered whether it was legal for us to camp right there on the Court House lawn.

In the distance, I heard hoof beats. Three horses and riders came into view from a side street. My escorts had arrived.

Mike Kohlbrecher and his two boys, Chris and Steve, greeted me warmly. There was a flurry of friendly handshaking and a lot of questions, then: "It's getting dark," Mike said. "We'd better head out to the barn."

We mounted back up, Rainy stepping lively now, invigorated by the company of other horses. We rode abreast down the main street under the light from the street lamps, as if we and our horses owned the road.

As we headed toward the Kohlbrechers' barn outside town, the darkness became complete. It lowered the temperature enough to feel cool and wonderful after the heat and worry of the day. A big gorgeous moon rose in the sky, and it lit our way as we clip-clopped on in the lovely evening. The moonlight made soft shadows and our new friends felt like old and dear ones. We stayed out at the barn longer than we needed to, drinking Old Style beer, talking, and swiping at mosquitoes that landed on the necks of our horses, standing near.

As we ate a late dinner, Mike and his wife Sue invited us to stay with them longer than one night. It was like a small miracle: With my belief that Rainy needed a rest, I couldn't have been more relieved.

"I'll stay out at the barn with him," I offered, not wanting to impose.

"The barn is for horses," Mike answered. "You'll stay right here."

Mike also had no doubts about what we'd do the next day.

"Your trip across the country won't be complete unless you meet Cletus Hulling," he insisted. When I admitted I'd never heard of Cletus, Mike exclaimed in surprise. "He's the 'World's Largest Horse Dealer!'"

In the morning, Sue looked skeptical as we prepared to head out.

"We're just taking a ride out to Cletus's place so Missy can see the countryside and the Hulling operation," Mike said innocently.

Sue looked at her husband and shook her head. "No new horses," she insisted.

"It's just a quick visit," Mike assured her.

We then promptly stopped at the barn, and he and the boys hooked up his stock trailer.

We headed west, joking around in the cab of the pickup as the empty trailer bounced along behind us. Mike told tall tales of the incredible "horse-dealing empire" run by Cletus Hulling.

Cletus was a big man in a cowboy hat, and as soon as he learned I'd ridden all the way from New York, he asked if I wanted to trade my horse in for another.

"Not for anything in the world," I promptly replied.

Cletus laughed and invited us to have a look around.

We moved leisurely from one long barn to another, viewing every size, color, and breed of horse imaginable. I noticed Cletus and Mike deep in conversation in one aisle, and watched curiously as they shook hands.

Next thing I knew we were loading a stocky, sturdy-looking strawberry roan gelding up the ramp of the Kohlbrechers' trailer.

Cletus handed me one of his "World's Largest Horse Dealer" souvenir pens. "Good luck on your trip, young lady," he said, "and come back when it's time for a new horse."

During our extra time with the Kohlbrechers, Rainy relaxed out in the barn and paddocks, grazing peacefully with Mike's horses. The break proved to be just what he needed. He stepped out smartly when it came time to say goodbye and set out once again.

## ▨ BIG RIVER

I rode with no concerns since Mike Kohlbrecher had made arrangements for us to stay with Bucket and Ethel Peters, about twenty miles or so away from his place, in the town of Trenton. "They are two of the nicest people you're ever going to meet," he assured me, and he was right: After spending the night at Bucket and Ethel's place, the couple gave me a two-dollar bill, faded and pressed flat from spending years tucked in their Bible.

"It's been our good-luck charm since the day we got married," they informed me warmly, "and now we want you to have it."

I tucked the token carefully into the little Bible I'd been given by the farrier in Ohio, which I knew they'd appreciate. We all hugged, then the animals and I turned back onto Route 50, heading toward the Mississippi River.

Ever since we'd ridden into Illinois, people had been asking how I planned to cross the Mississippi or warning me about the problems we would encounter when we neared it. I hadn't seen the "Big River" yet, but as we rode closer, I felt a growing sense of its presence, an awareness of something massive looming ahead.

Staying on Route 50 would take us right into East St. Louis, some of the roughest inner city in the country. It joined several other roads that all merged with the interstate there, crossing the Big River on a curve, with the muddy water churning hundreds of feet below and highway traffic all around.

We'd experienced crossing other bridges in traffic, but I could tell that this one was very different. I felt riding into a dangerous situation would be unforgivable—Rainy's and Gypsy's safety was paramount. The Kohlbrechers, the Peters, and several other Illinois horse families had impressed upon me that I couldn't just "ride across" near St. Louis; they had been kind enough to arrange a trailer ride to get us over the Mississippi.

I was glad to arrive in the town of Mascoutah, where I had mail waiting at the post office. My last phone call with Mike had been strained, and he was on my mind. I thought about calling him from town but decided I'd wait and read his letter first.

I'd been told that the driver with the trailer who was to ferry us across the river would find us on the road just west of Mascoutah. It wasn't long before a red pickup truck hauling a red stock trailer pulled over, the driver leaning out the window and calling, "Needin' a ride across the river?"

We loaded Rainy right in, tack and all, and Gypsy and I climbed in the cab.

"I'm Tim," said our driver with a nod and a smile. "You've never seen the Mississippi?" He looked at me, and I shook my head. "Just wait. You'll see why you had to accept a trailer ride!"

Tim went on and on about all the places he'd been, talking almost nonstop. Gypsy sat quietly at my feet. I turned to look out the back window and could see the top of Rainy's head with his ears pricked forward. The Big River came into view, along with tall buildings and the famous arch on the St. Louis side. Traffic increased greatly, merging in from all directions as we began the crossing. Below were river boats and big paddle-wheel boats, and then the river curved away, into the distance. It was so wide it took several minutes to cross, even traveling at 65 miles an hour. The horsemen of Illinois who'd warned me were right: There was no way Rainy, Gypsy, and I could have crossed this long high bridge or somehow forged our way across this great body of water.

"Welcome to St. Louis, Missouri," read a big sign on the far side of the bridge, "Gateway to the West!"

The West! I looked back again. Rainy's head was still up; he was still looking forward.

Rainy and Gypsy and I had made it from New York to the Mississippi River! I could almost sense the terrain, spreading out in front of us. We were ready for whatever was on the other side.

## A MYSTERY

Tim dropped us a little north of the city. Before the dust from the truck and trailer had settled, I opened the pack of mail I'd had sitting beside me in the cab of the truck. It only took a minute to see there wasn't a letter from Mike back home. I stared at the small pile of envelopes for a moment, seeing only what wasn't there.

I pushed the mail back in the big envelope; reading it was something to look forward to later. I expected we'd make good time to our night's stop—another friend of the Kohlbrechers, a man Mike Kohbrecher referred to as "Diamond Jim." I'd promised to call the Kohlbrechers and let them know that we'd safely gotten across the river, so before we headed out, I stopped at a convenience store to use the payphone.

"Hi, Mike!" I said when he answered. "It's Missy!"

"Where are you? Are you okay?" he interrupted before I could tell him we were in Missouri. "We've all been on the phone, looking for you! Everyone's worried about you!"

"Worried about me?" I asked, frowning in confusion. "Why? I got on the trailer you guys sent and—"

"No," Mike interrupted again. "We've been calling around, seeing if anyone saw you trying to cross the bridge or if you went a different way or what. Our friend with the trailer called here, confused. He looked around where he was supposed to pick you up, but he couldn't find you. He waited, he backtracked toward Trenton, but no sign of you."

"He did find me," I replied. "His name is Tim, right? With a red truck, red trailer…"

Mike was silent for a second on the other end of the line, then said, "Nope. The man we made arrangements with is not named Tim. And his rig is not red."

It was my turn to be silent. I had gotten into a truck with the wrong man; I'd loaded Rainy right into his trailer. My mind replayed how Tim had pulled over as soon as he saw me and my horse and dog on Route 50. It never occurred to me to think that he was *not* the person who'd been sent to drive us across the Big River. I also thought about the moment on the ride when he'd asked if I wanted to get out and go for a walk in a cornfield. I'd said no thanks, and nothing more had happened, but the odd moment looked different now, and shook me a little.

I hung up after apologizing for making my new friends worry, and I promised again to keep in touch. As we rode on, I wondered about Tim in the red rig. It was a mystery.

## DIAMOND JIM

Rainy, Gypsy, and I arrived at Diamond Jim Ribbings' and found no one home. The place had a fenced paddock and a neat barn in a nice area. Unsure of what to do, I tied Rainy to the fence rail and took off his saddle and packs so he could graze in comfort. A horse whinnied from inside the barn, aware of our presence.

Next to the house was a garage with the door open. A phone was visible on the wall. Knowing I probably wouldn't have privacy for much longer, I stepped inside the garage and dialed Mike in New York, collect.

I heard him accept the charges.

"Mike?" I ventured.

"Hi," he responded. Then silence.

It made me nervous, so I rushed on. "I got my mail today, and there wasn't a letter from you, so I got worried."

"I know. I've been busy."

His flat statement just sort of hung there. My stomach started to feel a little weird.

Afraid to ask him what "too busy" meant, I changed the subject, as if somehow that could change what was happening between us. I told him about the Mississippi and seeing the arch, trying to sound upbeat and excited, trying not to show how his coldness was affecting me. I told him how I'd found out I'd jumped in the wrong truck for the bridge crossing, childishly hoping he would show concern, admonishing me about the dangers of such a thing. But he didn't. In fact, he didn't say much at all.

After a few more awkward minutes, we hung up. It was the first time ever a phone call had ended without Mike saying, "I love you." I started to cry even before he disconnected and I heard the buzz of the long-distance dial tone in my ear—the buzz of many, many miles.

I held the phone to my ear, absorbing the words that had been said—and not said—for a minute. Then, as I slowly put it back in the receiver, a man—"Diamond Jim" Ribbings, I assumed—appeared in front of me in the doorway. I was a stranger in his garage, with his phone in my hand. But before I could explain who I was and that it had been a collect call, he saw the tears running down my cheeks. He simply opened his arms and pulled me into a great, comforting hug.

"Tell me about it," he said.

And I did.

Jim, still in his work shirt and tie, sat in his garage, talking with me, for a long time. His family came home; he introduced me to his wife and daughter. I thought about how someday, when some guy caused her heartache, Jim's daughter would be glad she had the dad she had.

Later, after my trip, when I tried to think of one act that symbolized the way people in every state we passed through reached out to me and made me feel *not* like a stranger, I thought of Diamond Jim Ribbings—how he walked onto his own property, found me there, crying, and just opened his arms, no questions asked.

## SOOTHING SUNSETS

Heading south from the outskirts of St. Louis, I swore to myself that I would not think about Mike. But I did. It made me sad, and a little mad, too, that he hadn't had enough character to at least say something—make his statement, so to speak—rather than silently waiting for me to just figure out that he was finished with the relationship.

The Missouri terrain rose into rolling hills, and the cornfields shrank to a more modest size than those we'd seen in Indiana and Illinois. I couldn't shake my melancholy, especially when I realized I'd left my extra fleece girth cover, the bandanna that kept my neck from sunburn, and the denim jacket I folded and used for a pillow, behind. But then the sky put on a show for us at sundown. No one told me the sun set so beautifully in Missouri. Rainy and Gypsy and I faced west with a clear view of the fingers of color, spreading across the clouds, dusting the land with soft light and streaking the whole sky in front of us with shades of peach and plum. The light bathed us, allowing contentment to ease back into my soul.

## LUXENHAUS FARM

Riding onto the grounds of Luxenhaus Farm outside Marthasville, Missouri, we passed a windmill, a covered bridge, and several more charming outbuildings. From the paddocks next to the horse barn a palomino and a bay whinnied out a welcome to Rainy. A screen door slammed, and a man and a young girl emerged from the tidy log farmhouse.

Bob Hostkoetter and his daughter Jill reached out to clasp my hand in greeting, then led us to the barn where Jill unsaddled Rainy and Bob made room for my things in their tack room. Rainy had developed a small chip in his hoof, causing me some concern. When I'd called the Hostkoetters the day before, I'd asked if they knew a farrier who could take a look at it.

"Our farrier can come out while you're here," Bob reassured me. "But he can't make it until tomorrow. Can you stay an extra night?"

I thought Jill looked just a few years younger than me, and I smiled at her, thinking it might be fun to spend a little more time with them. Gypsy was already running around, reveling in being one in their pack of dogs, and Rainy looked quite comfortable in his roomy stall with hay and water.

When someone's heart and soul is in a place, you can feel it. The Hostkoetters had made Luxenhaus Farm their life's work. All the structures were original or mostly original buildings built in the 1800s. Bob brought them from their original sites around Missouri and reassembled them on his plot of land, remaining faithful to their original design. He explained that he had done it to preserve the heritage of the German-American homesteaders who'd settled this part of the country.

That evening I sat around in easy conversation with the Hostkoetters and mentioned that I'd lost some of my things, topping off a pretty rotten day.

"When things go bad, it comes in streaks," Jill's mom Lois mused.

"Let me tell you about my dream and my bad day," Bob interjected as he cleaned his pipe. "I've always been interested in

American history, especially the settlers who first came to these Missouri hills. I knew of an original settler's log cabin in Perryville that was built around 1820—it was slated to be destroyed. I decided to buy the building and have it moved here." Bob imagined the house would be carefully taken apart and marked for him so he could start reassembling it when it was delivered to his land. "When I got to my property," he said, closing his eyes for a moment with the memory, "I found a huge pile of logs, dropped in a jumble."

Reality turning out differently than the idea…I could identify with that!

The weather had been terrible, Bob had sustained a minor injury, and other factors had interfered with his ability to see his dream through. "I felt like giving up more than once," Bob admitted.

It really hit home with me that evening how sometimes the bumps in the road on the way to achieving a goal can seem insurmountable. When you've gone out on a limb to follow your dream, the highs are really high, but that makes the lows seem even lower. But if things were always pleasant and always easy, there would be no grand and unusual accomplishments. By keeping on when the going gets tough, the challenges just become part of the story.

In the morning, the whole family joined me in the barn as the farrier filled in the little chip in Rainy's front hoof and rasped it down a little. "His feet and legs look really good," he assured me, "especially with all the miles he's got on him!"

As he said this, I happened to look over at Jill. I could see in her face that something was bothering her.

"You're not going to leave now, are you?" she asked. "I mean, now that your horse's hoof is okay?"

It was early enough in the day for me to get some miles in, but I wanted to spend an extra day as much as Jill wanted me to. "We're here for the day to hang out with you!" I promised.

The Hostkoetters all noted my plantation saddle, and Bob asked why I chose it over a Western one. "It's comfortable, and it seems to be good for Rainy," I explained, sharing a bit of my saddle-fitting adventure in Ohio. "But I miss my saddle horn. I'd hang things there, and Gypsy leaned on it and used it to brace herself."

Bob frowned in concentration as he walked around the saddle, sitting on its stand, staring at it.

"Do you mind if I try something?" he asked. I shrugged, indicating he was more than welcome to take a look.

Jill and Lois had planned for us to enjoy some "girl stuff" in town, which of course meant we ended up in a tack shop before long. Then I joined them at their 4-H meeting, and we even fit in roller-skating before calling it a day.

When we got back to Luxenhaus Farm, Bob emerged from his workshop with my saddle over his arm. In the spot where a horn would be on a Western saddle, he'd bolted a metal bracket about five inches high and five inches across. It was padded and wrapped with sturdy fabric. Gypsy could lean into it, and I'd once again be able to hang items I needed, like my canteen, within easy reach.

Lois helped me, too: As a 4-H leader and "horse show mom," she knew horse families throughout the state of Missouri. She worked all evening at the kitchen table with a map and a phone, setting up places for us to stay.

That second night at Luxenhaus Farm, strong winds swirled through the leaves in the treetops outside. Gypsy and I woke to the sound of a storm battering the roof of the sturdy log home. There was a knock on my door.

"We want you to be ready, just in case," Lois warned me in a quiet voice. "There are tornado warnings in effect for our whole area."

The word tornado made me shiver. I sat with my arm around Gypsy, listening to the wind. Sometime in the late hours, Jill rapped gently on my door, bringing me a candle, and the two of us, with

Gypsy squeezed between us, sat on the edge of the bed, talking about nothing just to avoid thinking about the battering wind. The electricity was down, and although dawn was only a few hours away, the darkness was thick and heavy.

With the gray light of sunrise, the worst of the storm had passed. Jill and I went to let the horses out. Downed branches were scattered everywhere, and rivulets of water and small stones ran down the driveway. But by early afternoon, the weather had brightened again; it was time to get on the road.

I knew I would keep in touch with the Hostkoetters, but it was hard to say goodbye, especially when Jill handed me her jade horse necklace and a note.

"Don't forget your Missouri family, now," Lois said as we hugged. "Call us if you need anything."

With Gypsy comfortably snuggled against the modified saddle horn, we headed west once again.

## GOOD DOG, BAD DOG

We left Luxenhaus Farm with a wealth of contacts, but sometimes that simply meant a safe place for my horse and a spot where I could camp. I set up my tent for the night next to a small pen where I could corral Rainy. I didn't have much to eat in my packs, so I decided to walk the few miles into a nearby town. Gypsy started out eagerly, bouncing and running ahead, but soon the heat had her walking behind me, her tongue hanging out. I focused on all the ways I'd treat myself when I got to town.

My spirits plunged when we arrived to find few businesses, all closed. It was Sunday. I should have known. My imagined splurge on all manner of tasty items ended up nothing more than crackers and chips from a vending machine at a gas station. Disheartened, Gypsy and I retraced our steps to Rainy and our tent.

I filled my canteen from the hose alongside the catch pen and sat on the grass with my disappointing picnic. Gypsy placed her paw on my arm.

"What's up, Gyps?" I asked absentmindedly.

Suddenly, the pup grabbed the brim of the hat I was wearing in her teeth and pulled it off my head. She posed with her front legs outstretched, the hat in her mouth, her tail and hind end up in the air. She wanted to play.

"Naw, it's too hot," I said as she darted back and forth in front of me. But finally I made a grab for the hat. That was just what she wanted. Her "fierce" growls were muffled and goofy because of the hat in her mouth. I had to laugh and finally jumped up and chased her, which was her favorite game of all. We played tug of war, another thing she loved, until I flopped back on the grass, sweaty and smiling. Gypsy plopped down next to me, dropped the hat, and rolled over for a belly scratch.

"What a good dog you are," I murmured with affection. I knew she had sensed my mood and had tried to cheer me up, in her own way.

Before we went to bed, a small black dog wandered into our campsite. I watched, amused as he and Gypsy played and ran around Rainy's pen. When Gypsy had enough of the fun, she crawled into our tent by me, panting. Her new friend sat outside, waiting for her to come out and play again.

Soon the dog began to whine. He paced outside, going from one end of the tent to the other, looking in the screened openings at us and scratching to be let in.

"Get!" I said, and, "Shoo!" My tent was designed for moun-tain climbers—lightweight, freestanding, and compact, with finely woven mesh screens to keep insects out. Now, this one small dog was going to destroy it. I heard the first rip as his scratching became more urgent. I yelled and shook the tent, but it was too late. My wonderful insect-free tent soon had gaping holes on both ends. Within minutes I heard the whine of mosquitoes in my ear.

All night Gypsy snapped and I swatted as bites accumulated on my arms, ears, and scalp. In the morning, I felt downright miserable as I packed up to leave. As summer had progressed and we'd ridden south in Missouri, biting critters were everywhere. I climbed on Rainy and headed out into the day, distressed and scratching.

## SERENDIPITY

Rolling back roads took us to Bland, Missouri, where we spent the night with the Krause family. They had five children and many horses, and the way the farm was built into the wooded hillside created the impression that kids and ponies were popping out from behind trees everywhere I looked.

"Bland is tiny," Mr. Krause said at dinner. "There's only one place for jobs around here—the little factory in town."

"What kind of factory is it?" I asked out of curiosity. I liked to know about the places we rode through.

Mr. Krause chewed his food, taking a minute to answer. "It's not a very big factory," he said. "They just make screens for tents."

I stopped eating and set my fork down. "What did you say?" I wanted to make sure I'd heard him right.

"I said there's a small factory back in town where they make tent screens. Maybe tents, too, I'm not sure."

I shook my head in disbelief. "How far away is it?" I pressed.

"'Bout two miles, kind of back in the direction you came from," he replied, taking another bite of his dinner.

"Do you think they would fix my tent for me?" And I quickly told them about my run-in with the bad black dog the night before.

Mr. and Mrs. Krause look at each other and shrugged. Then, they began to run through all the people they knew who worked at the factory before deciding on someone to tap for help. Mr. Krause made the call for us.

It was just incredible to me that my tent needed repairs in the rural back roads of the Ozarks, and there we were, within reach of the one small industry nearby that just happened to make tent screens.

Mrs. Krause said it meant someone was watching out for us.

Early in the morning we headed back east for the first time since we'd left New York, following the Krauses' directions to Kellco, the tent screen factory. Riding toward the rising sun felt strange after months of starting the day with the morning light at our backs.

Gypsy and I waited in the factory's little lobby. In the time it took Rainy to graze a close-cropped circle around the flagpole where he was tied, a girl returned with my tent, the holes sewn up perfectly with fine nylon.

"Thank you so much!" I exclaimed.

By mid-afternoon, we were not much farther than we'd been at the same time the day before, but the delay, in this case, was more than worth it.

## COPPERHEAD

Due to the heat, Gypsy had been riding with me a lot, leaning against the new backrest Bob Hostkoetter had added to the saddle. I was glad she wasn't insisting on being on the ground because I'd seen snakes along the road, slithering quietly into the grass as we rode by. When we stopped at a ramshackle convenience store that was really little more than a shed in someone's yard, the young woman there told me they were copperheads and I'd better watch out for them.

By midmorning the humidity was oppressive. Gypsy trotted along, stopping every once in a while to dig or stick her nose in a hole. After several miles, she asked to climb up in the saddle. Up close, I saw she had mud caked on her snout, making it look fat and puffy. As I brushed the dirt off I realized it was not just mud. Her nose was swollen.

"Gyps?" I said out loud. She looked up at me and wagged her tail. The more I looked, the odder her nose appeared. I thought about the copperhead snakes and how Gypsy liked to dig and explore and felt a flip of fear in my belly.

I desperately hoped the town we were riding toward was big enough to have a veterinarian. I urged Rainy into a faster walk. For the first time in all our months on the road, I wished that Rainy wasn't my only form of transportation. Worry was a lump in my throat by the time we rode into Vienna.

I asked the first person I saw where we could find a vet, and he pointed up the street. I tied Rainy to a street sign outside the small office and hurried inside with Gypsy. Her nose was now very puffy and sort of raw looking. I tried to comfort her, telling her to hang in there. She wagged her tail as I murmured in her ear.

A young woman was seated on the office floor, playing with a baby. She looked up when we entered, inquiring, "Can I help you?"

"My dog needs a vet!" I said urgently.

"The doctor's out on farm calls right now," she responded in a matter-of-fact way, turning back to the baby.

My heart sunk. "Is there any way you can get ahold of him? My dog needs to see a vet really badly."

The woman looked at Gypsy, who was happily sniffing around the open room, then looked back at me. "You *could* go out to where he is," she suggested doubtfully.

I shook my head, indicating Rainy where he stood patiently outside the window. "I can't get anywhere far away fast enough."

She glanced out the window at my buckskin. "Oh, you're *that* girl. I heard something about you."

"Yes, that's me," I agreed impatiently, "and that's Rainy, my horse, and this is Gypsy, my dog. I think she got bit by a copperhead!"

The woman looked at Gypsy again, who was eyeing a ball near the baby and wagging her tail.

"Are you sure?" she asked.

"Well, no, I'm not *sure*," I admitted, "but she was digging and then her nose got all puffy."

"Well, I can call out to where he is and see if he can stop back between appointments," she said. "I'm Irene, Dr. Henderson's wife."

I realized I didn't really have a choice but to wait patiently.

Over an hour later, Loyal Henderson, veterinarian, walked in the door. He had on coveralls and smelled pleasantly farm-like. Overwhelmed with worry, I immediately explained why I was there. Dr. Henderson knelt on the floor, setting his travel bag beside him, and called to Gypsy. She wagged up to him; he stroked her head and then brushed the gunk off her nose with his thumb. Under the layer of dry dirt I could see it was pink and scaly in one puffy spot.

Calmly, he pronounced, "She's not snake-bit." Digging through his bag, he said, "She's got ringworm."

I felt a surge of relief. "So she's going to be okay?"

"Oh, yeah, she's okay right now. It's contagious, though," Dr. Henderson warned. "Here's ointment for it. Be careful or you'll get it, too." He handed me a few small tubes, which I took, a little sheepishly.

"I'm sorry I dragged you back to town," I apologized. "All I could think was she got bit by a snake and then I couldn't think of anything else."

"It's okay, you have to treat ringworm anyway." The busy man was already washing his hands, kissing his child, and saying good-bye to his wife. On his way out the door he called, "Good luck to you. And don't let the snakes around here get you spooked."

**1.** In preparation for our cross-country journey, Rainy and I conditioned on trails and back roads as often as possible, building up to riding for about six hours a day, six days a week.

*Photo by Colin Moriarty Photography*

**2.** My older horse Bo (left) stayed at home in New York State with friends when Rainy and I set out on our adventure.

*Photo by Colin Moriarty Photography*

3. Getting ready to leave on our very first day. None of us had any idea what we were getting into.

4. Gypsy was just a puppy at the beginning of our journey. She adapted very quickly to the tent and the traveling life.

5. After staying at her family's farm in Springville, Pennsylvania, Julie Heitsman rode with us to Meshoppen.

6. At our campsite along the creek in Meshoppen. Gypsy was obviously a very tired pup!

7. Rainy and Gypsy "discussing things" during a roadside break in the Endless Mountain Region of Pennsylvania.

**8.** This picture in the Sunday paper in Williamsport, Pennsylvania, is the one that first resulted in people recognizing us on the road.

*Photo from* The Williamsport Sun-Gazette

**9.** On a lunch break in Dushore, Pennsylvania, a policeman came along and told us to put money in the parking meter!

Tyrone Daily Herald 5/19/82

BOUND FOR CALIFORNIA — Melissa Priblo, in the 18th day of a cross-country trip on horseback, stops to rest in the Warriors Mark area and to pose for the Daily Herald photographer. The horse is Arizona Raindance. The pup draped across the saddle is their inseparable companion, Gypsy.

**Missy, Raindance And Gypsy:**

# Traveling Trio Pauses On Trek To California

By Mary Michaels and Peg Hurd

All her life it has been Melissa Priblo's dream to travel.

It's not an unusual dream; we all have it. But, for most of us, the dream doesn't become reality while crossing the country on the back of a quarterhorse named Arizona Raindance with a puppy named Gypsy either sleeping across the saddle or running alongside.

Last night 22-year-old "Missy" who left her home in Binghamton, N.Y. on May 1

bound for the San Bernardino Valley in Southern California, found an ideal place to spend the night.

At Grier School, Arizona Raindance was tenderly cared for by the school's riding director, Jill Walter-Robinson, and two riding students, Sophie Sharp and Ann Marie Strand, while Missy spent the night snuggly bedded down in the Grier infirmary.

Except for five or six nights, sh (Cont'd on Page 2)

**10.** One of the many articles collected by my parents. This one appeared in the *Tyrone Daily Herald*.
*Photo and article by Mary Michaels and Peg Hurd*

**11.** I really bonded with the girls from the Grier School, where we stayed for a long weekend.

**12.** At a campsite in western Pennsylvania.

13. At Louie's Coral Lounge, where we found shelter from a storm. The restaurant owner and his family posed with us after the rain stopped as we were getting back on the road.

14. Almost to West Virginia! We quite frequently dealt with rain on the first part of the trip.

*Photo by Kate Fagan of the* Tribune-Review

**Missy Priblo And Rain Dance: The Ride Has Been Encouraging**

15. A good view of the packs Rainy carried and how Gypsy rode across the front of the saddle much of the way. An estimate of the weight Rainy carried at this stage of the trip, including me, Gypsy, my saddle, and our packs is about 190 pounds.

16. We spent several days riding strip mine roads in Ohio.

17. With Butch and Nancy Goodman at a horse show in Lancaster, Ohio.

18, 19, 20. These photos were taken by a woman in Ohio who wrote for a gaited horse publication. She was nice enough to send prints and the article to my parents—although I was a little miffed to find she had written disparaging comments about doing a long-distance ride on what she called a "walk, trot, canter" horse like Rainy instead of a gaited horse!

## INSIDE HORSE

After days of heat the afternoon brought a slight breeze and a few gray clouds skittering across the blue sky. More clouds darkened the day, and before long, a pelting rain beat down on me and my companions.

I usually tried to find an open barn or garage where we could wait out this kind of heavy downpour. I hunkered down, shielding Gypsy as best I could, and kept watch for shelter as Rainy gamely plowed onward. Finally, I spotted a carport jutting out from a home in a little cluster of several houses along the road. I turned Rainy in at the driveway and jumped off. With my poncho hood and the heavy rainy limiting my vision, I led him through the entrance to the carport with Gypsy right behind. I thought it was an unusually low and narrow doorway for such a structure.

When I pulled my hood back, I saw why. We'd walked into an enclosed patio. There was a bench, a nice rocking chair, and some wicker furniture covered in chintz cushions. A glass-topped table with a candle and a potted plant sat in one corner. It was homey and pleasant—a sort of indoor/outdoor room. And it was definitely *not* a place a horse should be. I looked out at the rain pouring down and decided to take our chances where we were for just a few more minutes until the storm passed.

"Hello?" I called toward the door to the house. No response. I led Rainy carefully around the table across the flagstone floor and knocked at the door. No one answered, and no sounds came from inside.

I sat down gingerly on the wicker chair, holding Rainy's reins in my hand. I hoped if the people who lived there came upon us, they would see we were doing no harm. It would only be a few minutes until the rain stopped.

I leaned back in the chair, which was surprisingly comfortable. The air was warm and heavy, and the rain tap-tapped on the roof.

Rainy lowered his head and his bottom lip drooped. Gypsy curled up by my feet with a sigh. I felt my head bob a little as I listened to the pattern of the raindrops and the sound of Rainy and Gypsy's slow breathing.

My head jerked up, my heart jump-started from sleep by a loud ripping noise.

I looked around, confused for a minute in the unfamiliar sur-roundings. A strange cloud of white filled the air. Rainy was shak-ing his head and snorting from across the room.

I tried to shake off sleep and get my wits about me. The white powdery stuff was everywhere. It covered the glass table, the plants and pillows, and gathered in white spots on Rainy's coat so he looked like an Appaloosa. A brown bag stood ripped open, spilling the powder across the stone floor.

I figured that when I'd dozed off, the reins fell from my hands, and my Rainy, always curious and a bit mouthy, had spied the large brown bag that looked remarkably the same as the bags that usu-ally contained his sweet feed. He must've walked across the room to the bag and ripped it open—something he'd done before back home with feed bags if I didn't get them into the tack room fast enough. Only this time, he'd torn open a fifty-pound bag of lime.

I looked his buckskin coat over carefully. He seemed all right, other than the white speckles I had to brush off his nose as he snorted. Keeping the reins in one hand so he couldn't get into more mischief, I looked around for a broom or something—anything—I could use to clean up the mess. I tried brushing with my bare hands, but it was futile. A lame attempt at sort of sweeping with my sneak-ered foot only ground the lime into the floor. There was no rag in sight, no old newspapers, nothing I could do to make the mess better.

The afternoon sunlight was breaking through. Feeling guilty but having little choice, I called to Gypsy and led Rainy across the patio and on out the screen door.

When I turned back to view the chaos again, I knew what would mystify the homeowners even more than the torn bag and coating of white powder were the large, perfect hoof prints that led from their home's back door, across the patio floor, and out.

## MY RAINY

The last veterinarian who had seen Rainy had declared him fit and healthy, his feet and legs holding up well to all the miles he walked every day. As we rode on, I thought about how I could rely on moments every day that reminded me to be thankful for this horse of mine. Rainy was so good-natured and willing that riding him was, quite simply, a pleasure.

In this part of Missouri, the roadside was wooded and green, intersected with streams and muddy runoffs. Moisture and humidity was a constant presence, and dewy grass wet our feet as we started out each morning. When we cut through the forest, the air hummed and chirped and tweeted with bugs and birds. I felt exposed and out in the open...in a good way.

Rainy had curiosity—not something you often hear about in horses. He didn't find the world to be fraught with danger as some horses do, and that made him a wonderful partner for a journey like ours.

Many fingers of water and dirt roads twisted and turned around Lake of the Ozarks, and it felt like a place where it would be easy to get lost. We turned down a shady road of soft dirt—a good road for riding...until we found ourselves faced with a bridge. Rainy had crossed plenty of bridges in our time together, but none like this one. It was wooden and rickety and suspended in a way that caused it to sway when he placed a hoof on it.

Tracks across the bridge showed that cars used it, so I focused straight ahead at where we wanted to go. Rainy stepped forward and the whole bridge moved a bit from side to side. Slow-moving, muddy water below was visible between the wooden slats. But my good boy walked with his steady pace until we stepped on solid ground on the other side. I patted his withers, grateful for how sensible and willing this horse of mine was.

After days of traveling unnamed back roads, we rode out onto Route 54 and its paved two lanes. Just as I'd come to expect in Missouri, the setting sun had brushed dramatic streaks of darkening orange across the dark navy of the coming night sky. The air was so warm and the sky so pretty, the evening felt almost dreamlike.

That night Rainy whinnied a soft greeting when I checked on him before bed. I stroked his cheek, and he pressed his muzzle against my leg. This small moment made me realize how perfect life was sometimes.

Some people want a horse for status or to win ribbons. But true horsemen seek this: a connection with an animal that wants to please you and be with you. This was what Rainy gave me, and it filled my heart.

## NANNIE AND ANTHIS

Nannie Jenkins stood by the side of the road watching as Rainy, Gypsy, and I approached. Her white hair was pulled back in a bun, and a faded pastel cotton dress covered her sturdy shape. Chickens pecked the ground around her.

I asked Rainy to halt and jumped down. From the nearby farmhouse, another white-haired woman came to join us—this one small and diminutive. I shook hands with Anthis Wright, Nannie's sister.

Nannie laid her hand on Rainy's neck. "Let's get this good horse taken care of," she said, "and then you'll have supper with us."

It seemed awfully early to be thinking about supper. Besides, these women seemed so, well, *old*, that I didn't want to make any work for them. "Don't go to any trouble for me," I said. "I'll just stay out in the barn with Rainy."

Both women looked at me with stern expressions.

"Of course you won't stay in the barn," Nannie insisted. "You have to eat. We've been getting ready for you since we heard you were coming."

"Oh, of course, then," I replied, giving in. "Thank you."

Because of the white hair and the old-fashioned clothes, Nannie and Anthis's age was what first made an impression on me. Years had worn lines on their faces. But these were not frail women. They had strong hands and clear, intelligent eyes.

In the barn stood an old black-and-white dairy cow, and next to her a few boards had been nailed up to partition off a square stall. Straw bedding covered the floor, and a water bucket sat in the corner. Everything looked freshly done, and I wondered if the sisters did it all for us.

I hosed down Rainy with Nannie and Anthis watching, then led him into the makeshift stall. He stuck his nose over the boards to meet the cow. She looked over her shoulder at him with her big dark eyes, then went back to her food. This established, Rainy went to work on his own pile of hay. Chickens mingled around his feet. It was peaceful watching the scene play out, and I was again thankful for Rainy, how nice he was and the way he could fit in anywhere.

The sisters offered a tour of their farm, which I accepted. I admired their garden—a perfect square of beans, tomatoes, squash, and corn, growing in neat rows. They talked as we walked, and though they never said their exact ages, they mentioned they were both members of the "Over Eighty Club."

I offered to help with dinner, but Anthis waved me over to sit with Nannie, who was pulling out photo albums. We sat, our heads close together, as she opened up a big black book.

The pictures were black and white: old friends, farm homes being framed up, horses. Once in a while Nannie pointed out certain friends and family. "This is Ada," she said. "She's ninety-two here." Or, "This is Nel. We lost her last year." She showed me a picture of the "Johnson Girls," as she called them—the "girls" being eighty-nine and ninety-four at the time of the photo.

Nannie told me that she regularly contributed to the local paper and had helped write several books about the local history and Missouri pioneers. I was totally engrossed in her tales of how settlers claimed the land where panthers and wolves ranged, and the details she knew of the hardships of life back then—when Missouri and Arkansas were still the "Wild West." Though my trip was a far cry from what early cross-country travelers endured, learning about the pioneers somehow connected me to the people who made hoof prints heading west, long before Rainy, Gypsy, and I did. Nannie had actually known some of those early settlers when she was young, and hearing her stories and sharing her old photographs made me feel like the journey my animals and I were on was a part of something bigger.

I looked at Nannie and Anthis, there on their farm, still doing the work it took to keep it going. How wonderful to grow old that well, with the strength they had and the interest they had in the world around them. I was grateful the paths of our lives had crossed.

## ▓ DEERFIELD

Near the western border of Missouri, having crossed the state from the affluent suburbs of St. Louis to the worn shacks in the Ozarks, I thought about what stood out about the state, and I called up a kaleidoscope of images. I thought of dark woodsy nights, farmland, and snakes and ticks. And the way people all seemed to know each other, even in towns twenty and forty miles apart. And of course the sunsets—how in the evenings we rode west into pink sky, the very air seemingly rose-colored around us.

Riding along 54 and drooping in the heat, I spotted a sign welcoming us to Deerfield, and with it, a notice for a general store. Perking up at the prospect, I followed the path until we came to the store. I tied Rainy to the porch railing, loosened his girth, and took the few steps up to the door. Little bells tinkled as I pushed my way inside, and I had to squint, stepping in from the bright sun to the shadows within.

"Hello there," said a voice.

Amongst the shelves of canned goods and cereal, along the scuffed and worn wooden floor, several men sat on overturned boxes and a folding chair or two, playing checkers.

One of them touched his hand to the brim of his dusty and worn hat.

I let the door creak shut behind me, and Gypsy, always right on my heels, walked over to the men, looked at one of them the right way, and started getting her ears scratched.

"Hello there," the same man said again, and they all nodded or smiled at me, and another one said, "Ridin' across the country, are ya?"

I smiled back at them. For just a moment I remained still, holding the picture in my mind: old men playing checkers in a general store, the swayed wooden shelves, the dust motes in the sunlight from the door and the windows.

That was how I would remember Missouri.

## DELAYS

The sun burned high and hot when I stopped Rainy in the shadow cast by a large billboard along the side of the two lanes of Route 54. Rainy snatched at the green grass growing thick there, the reins lying loose on his neck. Gypsy's tongue hung out as she stretched in front of me on the saddle.

Me, I just stared, in wonder you could say, up at the great sunflower welcoming us to Kansas.

Halfway.

We were halfway across the country.

Rainy got a complete checkup at the veterinary clinic in Fort Scott, the first town we came to in our new state. One of the vets, Dr. Durling, offered us a place to stay the night.

In the morning, the family bustled about, getting ready to leave on vacation. Despite all she had to do, Mrs. Durling was kind enough to make a big breakfast before I hit the road. I appreciated it, but for some reason, I could hardly eat.

I felt weak when I tried to tighten the girth of my saddle, but I swung up and waved goodbye as the Durlings packed up their car.

Two miles. That's about how far I got before my vision started to turn black around the edges. I slid off Rainy and stood there, leaning on him. It felt like I was going to faint. My legs trembled. My horse stood motionless, not pulling to eat like he usually did whenever we stopped. Gypsy sat quietly, staring up at me. I felt a sharp pain in my side and wooziness in my head. The dizziness came again as I rested my head on Rainy's side.

I walked a few steps on wobbly legs and threw up in the tall grass, holding the reins behind my back. Gypsy whined nervously. I was sweating like crazy and could barely pull myself back up in the saddle.

Rainy began to walk slowly along. I struggled to stay upright. I didn't hear a car pull up beside us, my head was buzzing so. Then, distantly, I heard my name.

"Missy? We came to say goodbye. We're—hey, Missy...are you okay?" It was the Durlings, heading out on their trip. Mrs. Durling's face was full of concern as she said, "You're bright red."

I looked at them with watery eyes. "I think I'm sick."

"Go back," Mrs. Durling said without hesitation. "Go back to our house. You can stay until you feel better."

She told me where to find a key, and I thanked her feebly before turning around and backtracking to the Durlings' place. It was all I could do to untack Rainy and turn him out in their pasture. I fumbled my way into their house and immediately crashed on a sofa in their basement.

The whole day passed as I drifted in and out of sleep. I got sick again. I managed to get up once to check Rainy. Gypsy stayed right beside me, wherever I was.

When I woke once again, it was almost evening. I checked on Rainy again and didn't feel as bad—just weak. I even managed to drink a little water. I stood outside on the deck for a few minutes, looking down at my horse, when I heard a sound from inside the empty house. I turned to see someone walking toward me and yelped in surprise.

"Sorry! Sorry! I didn't mean to scare you! But John asked me to come check on you, see if you're all right. I'm Dr. Reid Scifers, Dr. Durling's partner."

I stuttered, trying to find a response, unsettled because I'd been in my own strange world all day, sick, and I knew I must look a fright. And maybe a little bit because Dr. Reid Scifers was really, really cute.

"I think I'm feeling better," I offered with a weak smile. I was so glad this guy hadn't shown up while I was heaving in the toilet or lying in oblivion on the basement sofa.

"So, they tell me at the clinic that you rode here? From New York?" Reid motioned toward one of the deck chairs, and I thankfully sat down, acknowledging I was pretty shaky.

"I did." I was relieved to have something to talk about other than being sick. "With him." I indicated Rainy, out in the pasture.

"And Gypsy, too." I nodded toward my dog, who it occurred to me should've barked when this young vet had come into the house, what with me in my weakened state and all. But she hadn't. In fact, there she was, scooched up to him, practically sitting on his feet, gazing up at him adoringly.

"Why are you riding your horse across the country?" Reid asked. "And how's he holding up?"

About an hour later, Reid and I were still talking on the deck; we were both surprised when we realized how much time had passed.

"I better get going," he said. "I have to stop back at the clinic."

He rose and walked toward the door, then turned back toward me.

"Are you feeling well enough to go to the rodeo at the fair tonight, maybe get something to eat?"

"Sure," I answered, trying not to seem too eager or show how glad I was that he'd asked. And I was definitely feeling better.

The Little Britches Rodeo was pretty funny—the equivalent of Little League to baseball, basically giving little guys a chance at a sport for big guys. Reid and I laughed and talked and walked around the fair. My stomach reminded me I was not ready for any midway offerings yet.

It felt like everyone at the fair knew Reid and stopped him to say hello or ask him about a calf or pony. He spoke kindly to everyone. It's easy to tell when someone is just putting on an act and when someone is for real.

Back at the Durlings', Reid came out to meet Rainy as I did night check.

"Will you be here tomorrow?" he asked.

I still felt a little weak, and fun with Reid aside, I'd already decided I was going to stay and rest one more day.

"Because if you're here," he went on, "I could come back over and give Rainy a really good check up. If you want me to," he added.

I could have mentioned that his partner, Dr. Durling, had just checked Rainy. But I didn't. Truth was, it made my heart light to think of seeing him again the next day. Besides, it wouldn't hurt for Rainy to have as many vet checks as possible.

"Yes, I will be here tomorrow," I answered.

For Rainy. Of course.

## VET CALL

In the morning, feeling far better and well rested, I called home and had long conversations with my brothers, Vince and Jack, and my sister Jan. I enjoyed catching up after so many weeks and appreciated their enthusiastic response to the news that we had made it to Kansas. I gave Rainy a bath and turned him out to graze again. I got my packs in order and made sure everything was neat in the Durlings' house.

Reid showed up about noon, and we chatted casually as we walked out to Rainy together. Reid spent a great deal of time checking my horse over—the exam he gave could not have been more thorough. And he offered to come by again when his workday was done.

For a short while, the time spent with Reid made all the miles and the times I'd felt alone over the past months just fall away. But after he drove away at the end of the evening, I went and stood with Rainy. I was beginning to feel worn down by all the goodbyes. Over and over on this trip, I would get attached or feel connected to someone, and then we had to say goodbye. I told myself it was part of the journey. I'd always been sentimental, always felt connections deeply, and always hated goodbyes. I never could have known how many people would touch this dream of mine.

Of course, Reid and I said the usual things about writing, keeping in touch, but really, I thought, how likely was that? Moving on was the very nature of what I did. Most of the time it was a great way to be, but sometimes, it just made me feel lonesome.

After packing up and grooming Rainy carefully the next morning, I left a note for the Durlings, thanking them for their kindness both while they were with me and while they were not. I walked slowly down the driveway, holding Rainy's reins as he ambled beside me, head and ears up and interested. Gypsy trotted ahead and loped back again over and over to make sure we were coming. She seemed happy we were starting back out again, and her enthusiasm was contagious. I started to feel good to be getting back on the road, too.

At the end of the driveway, we turned west on Route 54 once again. Along the shoulder of the road, little kangaroo rats popped in and out of view. They were so comical in their jumpy movements and always traveled in gangs or families—I never saw just one.

After a few miles, Gypsy stopped and gazed back behind us. A minute later, a familiar white pickup slowly passed and pulled to the shoulder a short distance ahead. Reid got out and walked toward us, a can of Dr. Pepper in his hand. Gypsy danced around trying to get his attention, but he was looking up, smiling at me.

"I wanted to see how you were feeling and say goodbye again," he said.

I jumped down and let Rainy graze. Reid and I sat on the tailgate of his truck as I drank the soda he'd brought me. Gypsy jumped into the bed of the truck and happily squeezed between us, her tongue hanging out. We just let time go slow and the sun shine down on all of us.

But Reid had to get back to work, and I had some riding to do. I watched as he climbed back in his pickup and pulled away, his arm waving out the window.

I felt something on my hand and looked down to see a ladybug had landed near the reins. Remembering a childhood game called,

"Ladybug, ladybug, fly away home," I made a wish and blew a soft breath toward her. Her miniature wings lifted and she flew off as I made my wish to somehow see Reid again.

Not once, ever, on that blissful sunny morning, did it occur to me to think of that old adage: *Be careful what you wish for.*

## OH NO

Maybe my "sick days" were a needed respite from the road, or the brief but pleasant time with Reid was a nice way to finally put the hurt from Mike behind me. Maybe the humidity wasn't quite as bad as it had been in prior weeks. Maybe it was that Kansas was roughly the halfway point between New York and California. Whatever the reason, I enjoyed myself in the simplest little ways as we made our way deeper into the state.

I liked Kansas. There was an airiness and openness that pleased my senses. Green grass was abundant any time I wanted to let Rainy graze, and water was easy to find. I rode along watching birds fly by and the swirls of road dust, and waving at the friendly folks who passed us. I felt like Rainy, Gypsy, and I fit in well, moving slowly under the wide blue sky.

In the first weeks of our trek, if I caught the weather report on someone's television, I'd look away. I couldn't bear to see a map of the whole United States. The amount of land we had to cross was so vast it was intimidating to think about. So I focused on small steps. I'd always known that any one thing could end our trip. The slightest injury to my horse or myself, for example, and the journey would be over. But now we were in Kansas. We'd ridden halfway across the country! I could actually picture us making it the whole way.

We left a little town called Gas City early in the morning and headed west, still on the long straight 54. The land was level but it was quite hot, so we made frequent rest stops during the day. I removed the saddle and checked Rainy all over each time.

In the tiny crossroads town called Piqua (pronounced *Pic-way*) we turned down a lane toward a diner just off the main road. I tied Rainy out back, and when I pulled the saddle off, my breath caught sharply. To my horror, a big ugly swelling had started to grow near Rainy's withers.

I reached to touch it, but Rainy skittered away. The area was round and as big as a golf ball. I could feel heat all around it.

Rainy was hurt.

My horse had never taken a lame step. The whole morning that hurtful thing must have been growing. *And he just kept on walking.*

Desperate to do anything to help Rainy, I pulled everything off him, carelessly scattering my belongings over the ground. I stroked his neck, and whispered to him that I'd make it right. Then I hurried into the diner, using my tee shirt to smear at the tears that streaked my face.

Inside, a waitress let me use the phone, and I pulled out the scrap of paper with the name and phone number of Tom and Barb Kee. They were our contact that night in Yates Center, a little farther west. My plan, or I should say my hope, was to ask if they could help me get a truck and trailer to get Rainy to a vet. I was so upset and worried that I didn't care that it was presumptuous thinking that someone I'd never met would go to the trouble of stopping whatever they were doing in the middle of their day, hitching up their trailer, and hauling some stranger to a vet. It was the only hope I had. I dialed over and over, but no one answered the phone at the Kees' farm.

Yates Center was about twelve miles away, not much of a ride for us under normal circumstances, but Rainy was done working— done carrying me, done carrying our packs, done with all of it, for now.

I gathered up a pile of gear that I would have hated to lose—my packs, my camera, things from home—and with my arms wrapped around it, I went back into the diner and asked if I could leave it somewhere safe. I had no idea if I would make it back, or if someone would steal it, or if the staff would throw it out. But the waitress seemed nice. I left everything.

I hoped walking was okay for Rainy as long as there was no pressure near the sore and no weight on his back. I took hold of his neck rope, and we started off, side by side. Some instinct told me to try and make it to the Kees'—I didn't know them, but I simply had nowhere else to go.

Rainy kept his head close to me; I stopped often to pet his neck and rub his head. "I'm sorry, buddy," I kept telling him. "I am so sorry."

## THE WORRIED WALK

Each time I checked the swelling on Rainy it made my stomach queasy. Gypsy, aware of the somberness of this trek, stayed close. All I could think of was helping my brave, kind horse. And the fact that the steps we were taking along Route 54 could well be the last of our journey.

I wasn't sure how many miles we'd traveled when I saw a figure in the distance. The shimmer of heat off the pavement made everything a little distorted. When at last we reached the woman on the roadside, she looked me in the eyes and said simply, "Missy. I've been looking for you."

Amid tears, it all spilled out at once: "Rainy's hurt. I need to have a vet look at him. I think maybe the trip is over."

Barb Kee somehow absorbed it all: how far we'd come, what the trip meant to me, how I felt about my horse. Worry furrowed her brow and showed in her warm, open face. She unselfconsciously laid her arm across my shoulders and said, "Let's get you all to our place. We'll find my husband. He'll know what to do."

Then Barb Kee, Rainy, Gypsy, and I finished the walk together to the farm on Prairie Road.

## TWISTS AND TURNS

Tom Kee was a lifelong rancher and farmer. I watched his face while he examined the lump on Rainy's back. I could tell he didn't like the look of it, although he didn't say a word. He just quietly filled up a trough with cold water from a hose, and we both stood there wordlessly while Rainy drank.

"Do you have a vet that would come out and see him?" I asked, guessing the state of things.

"Usually, around here, you haul animals to the vet clinic instead of the vet coming to you," Tom explained. He looked at Barb, and then they both looked at me. "But why don't you stay here tomorrow? I'll come in early from the fields, and we'll hitch up the stock trailer and haul Rainy out to see the vet in Eureka."

"That's a very kind offer," I mumbled, struggling to control my emotions. "Thank you so much." It was all I could think of to say.

I checked on Rainy frequently throughout the evening. Barb asked if I wanted to call home, but I didn't want to call anyone. I was unable to say out loud what I feared: that maybe I'd permanently injured Rainy...and maybe our journey was finished.

I tried to recall any little sign of discomfort or injury from my horse that I might have missed. *I should have known.* Rainy and Gypsy and I, we had this bond. Why didn't I sense something was happening to Rainy? Why didn't I catch it in time?

I rose very early in the morning. Tom was already at the kitchen table, feeding scraps of food to Gypsy. After breakfast, he hitched up his stock trailer, and we headed to Eureka.

Rainy stood quietly for Dr. Drogey's exam. "I'm not really sure what this is," the veterinarian admitted—a frustrating thing to hear. "A hematoma, an unusual bursitis of the withers, or an abscess? In many cases it's worse to biopsy it because it can increase your chances of infection." The doc paused, then: "Let's get him on antibiotics right away. I want him on bute to make him comfortable, and also let's start him on an anti-inflammatory. Can you hose the area with cold water, twice a day for fifteen minutes, then put some DMSO on it?"

I nodded my head yes.

"I'd like to see him after a few days on the meds," Dr. Drogey said. "How 'bout you bring him back on Saturday? I'll be able to tell you a little more then."

Tom nodded in agreement, as if the plan sounded fine to him. He even made an appointment for Saturday before we loaded Rainy back in the trailer.

I turned to the man. "I can't ask you to put us up for the rest of the week."

He brushed off my concern. "Sure you can. Let's see what the next few days do for your horse."

But Saturday didn't yield good news.

"I don't think this is going to heal up right away," Dr. Drogey said after re-examining Rainy.

I felt heat rising within me as I struggled to hold back my emotions.

"It's better...but not better enough to have much weight and pressure on him yet." The vet looked at me and my watering eyes. "He's not in any pain now. Keep up with the hosing and the meds. It just needs time to heal." He smiled and tried to look reassuring. But I was devastated.

I turned away, stroking Rainy and silently crying. I heard Tom ask, "How long would we need to treat him and let him rest until he's right again?" It didn't escape my notice that Tom said "we." He was just being nice, I was sure, not wanting to let the vet know that I was kind of homeless. Homeless with a horse and a dog.

Dr. Drogey considered the question. "Well, if you keep hosing the area, keep him on the meds for the whole course, I'd say three, four weeks?"

I wanted to wail. The doctor had no idea how far we were from home and how we couldn't just stay there waiting, *hoping* Rainy would heal. Tom had told him we were on a long-distance trip, and I'd summarized a few details: our saddle and our gear and the daily miles. But Dr. Drogey didn't ask more than that, and I was so emotional, I couldn't bring myself to explain more.

Tom and Dr. Drogey walked to the vet's office, giving me time alone with Rainy and my sadness.

Could I find a job here? Get an apartment? Or could I find a field or a patch of woods for the tent and make it our home for a month, like a squatter? Anything was better than thinking about giving up on the trip, when we'd come so far. But I also knew those were pretty unrealistic scenarios.

I tried to bury my emotions as I went to pay our bill, only to find that Tom had already paid it. He waved aside my tearful thanks.

I sat in silent despair in the truck cab while Tom slowly backed the rig around and pulled back out onto the road. I had my head turned to the window and the passing prairie when Tom spoke in his slow and easy drawl. "We want you to stay with us."

"I can't ask you to do that," I protested.

"You didn't ask." He smiled. "I asked you."

I looked at him. Who offered to put up a stranger for one night, then happily welcomed her into his home for a month, animals and all? "What about Barb?" I asked.

Tom shook his head, that little smile still there. "I called her from Dr. Drogey's office when we got the news that Rainy'd be laid up for a while. She said to bring you on home."

A glimmer of hope began to grow. "I'll stay out in the barn," I said. "You won't even know I'm there."

Tom laughed. "Oh, Mama wouldn't hear of that."

"I'll help you guys. On the farm, in the house, anything. Anything that needs doing around your place, I'll do." I wiped away tears again.

He just shook his head. "When we get back, call your folks and tell 'em you've got a new home for a while. We're gonna make a Kansas girl out of you."

## TOM AND BARB

When we pulled into the horseshoe driveway, Barb came out of the house, and as soon as I was out of the cab, she threw her arms around me, exclaiming, "I'm so glad you're staying!"

Barb led me inside and down the hall to the room Gypsy and I had been sleeping in for the past few days. "Let's get this room fixed up like you're staying a while." She started pulling things from drawers and pushing aside boxes in the closet.

I realized what a good feeling it was to know there was a place for me. They were simple things—a drawer to put my clothes in and my own bottle of shampoo on the edge of the tub—but they were things that were missing when you lived on the road. I'd adjusted to the traveling life. But the feeling of having a home of sorts, however temporary, was a comfort.

Barb reminded me it was time to tell my folks about Rainy and the change in our travel plans, so I got on the phone. My mom, ever-organized and practical, made a list of what she'd pack and send to me for a few more weeks in Kansas. Both my parents, originally so opposed to my trip, said, "Do what you have to do. We'll do whatever we can from this end."

During a rambling conversation that evening, I told Barb about meeting Reid.

"Well, honey, you should call him," she urged. "He might like to know you're here for a while. Fort Scott might seem far to you, but by car it's only an hour or so."

The next night, Reid's white pickup turned into the Kees' yard, and Barb and I bumped into each other in our hurry to run away from the window, so we wouldn't be caught watching for him. I gave him a minute to walk to the house before stepping outside. Gypsy squeezed out the screen door behind me and trotted past, hurrying toward her favorite vet. I couldn't help the big smile on my face; Reid had a happy grin, too. He strode right over and gave me a big hug, and for a second I enjoyed his clean, fresh-air smell.

We walked together to the corral so he could look at Rainy, and I poured out all my worries on the way. Like the rest of us, Reid was confused by the exact nature of the swelling.

"Gosh, that's an odd-looking thing," he said as he touched and probed the swollen area. "But he doesn't act like it's painful right now. And he looks good."

I was glad Reid wasn't overly bleak about my horse's condition, and pretty soon we were joking in an easy manner. I remembered why I was so glad he'd driven out to see me. Reid patted Rainy affectionately, and we turned back to the house so he could meet Tom and Barb, Gypsy jogging in front of us as if she had to show us the way.

Tom and Reid shook hands and started right in, talking about farming and livestock. Barb caught my eye, mouthing, "*He's cute!*" with a silly grin on her face. The sun was setting big and orange on the grasslands outside the kitchen window. For a minute, in this new place, it felt just like a real home and a real family.

## ▨ HAYING

When I overheard Tom talking to Barb about how he'd be working in the hay fields the next day, I thought, *Here's a way I can help repay their kindness*. There's always room for another hand at haying time.

"I'll help!" I interrupted. Tom and Barb stopped their conversation and looked at me.

"Oh, that's okay," Tom said, shaking his head. "My uncle drives the tractor, and we got a couple boys working for us, but thanks anyway."

"Seriously," I persisted. "I've been helping put in hay since I was like fourteen. That's how I earn some of my horse board back home."

Tom and Barb exchanged a glance but didn't argue further.

In the morning I was up extra early to see to my animals, and Tom, who had already been out in the fields, came back to pick me up.

"I really wish you wouldn't try haying with the boys," he tried once more as he drove south on the gravel road toward the hay fields.

"I'll be fine!" I assured him.

Tom pulled the pickup off the road and onto the mown field where a tractor took slow turns as bales of hay shot into the wagon that lumbered behind it. The tractor stopped here and there, allowing one of the four or five young men nearby to jump up in the wagon and throw the bales into a neat formation so more could be loaded on top. When they noticed Tom's truck, they all stopped and stared as we got out and walked toward them.

Tom had his hand on my arm when we reached the crew. "This is Missy," he said. "She's gonna help, if you boys don't mind." Tom turned to me. "I'll be back for you in a while."

There was an awkward silence after Tom left. I climbed up on the hay wagon. The scent of the cut hay and the feel of the warm sun were intoxicating. Standing on the low row of bales, I said cheerfully, "I can stack if you guys want."

The boys exchanged glances. It seemed they didn't know what to think of me. They looked wiry and strong but very young. I could tell I'd changed the dynamic they'd established working together. I felt their discomfort.

The one with a shock of dark hair falling on his forehead finally spoke, stuttering, "Uh, well, we almost got this field picked up. We'll just be taking it to the barn soon."

*Well, I knew that.* I knew it got stored when the wagon was full. Maybe that meant they wanted me to help when we got to the barn. The boys shuffled back to what they were doing. They had a system in place, and they stacked the last of the bales without offering a way for me to join in. I took a seat high on the bales and held on to the wooden slats of the wagon when we took a wobbly turn and headed to the barn.

The guys jumped up in the wagon for the ride back. They ignored me as they picked up what appeared to be an ongoing conversation. The topic had them fired up, and they argued and debated with fierce enthusiasm. Not about girls or sports. About Cars, with a capital C. I had no idea that a topic like Ford versus Chevy could inspire such passion.

The fellow who'd shyly spoken to me was apparently a Ford man. He brushed the hair from his face with the back of his hand while his buddy taunted him, "You know what Ford stands for, don't you?"

"What?"

"Fix Or Repair Daily!" the blonde kid answered gleefully.

Before the one who liked Fords could think of a comeback, one of the other boys spoke up: "No way, man. I heard Ford stands for Found On Road Dead!"

The two Chevy guys had a hearty guffaw.

My Ford guy was flustered, and struggled with a retort of his own. "Oh, yeah?" he tried. "Well, Chevy stands for…" He sputtered, obviously making it up as he went. "Chevy stands for Ching Chong Eck..." and he sort of faded out then, not sure what to do with it.

"'The hell does that mean?" one of the others boy asked.

"It's cuz everything on a Chevy is made in Japan or China or something!" Everyone, me included, laughed a little at his attempted comeback.

The banter lasted all the way to the barn, but up in the loft, everyone got to work. It was hot, hay dust floated in beams of sunlight, and the roof was high overhead, where the bales dropped off the hay elevator. Again, the crew didn't seem to want my help. Again, I insisted I could do it. Finally the blonde one sighed.

"Okay." He gestured to me and stepped away from the bale he'd been about to grasp.

As I went to grab the bale, I noticed for the first time that there were wires, not twine, holding it together, and there were three, not two. It suddenly looked mighty big compared to the bales I was used to. I couldn't get my hands around all three wires, so I grabbed two of them, and attempted to heave it over to the guy waiting to stack them.

I couldn't move the bale. At all. I thought these kids were playing a trick on me. They'd weighed it down with something. I planted my feet and got myself mentally psyched and tried again. The effort lifted my heels from the ground and all I managed was to move it a few meager inches. On my third try, I pushed and pulled and dragged the bale to the guy who was waiting to throw it along the line. He took it without making eye contact and spared me whatever he, and no doubt the others, were thinking.

I continued to slow the previously smooth-running operation as I attempted a few more times to drag the monstrous bales over to the line-thrower. It must have been painful to watch, as they all looked away and stopped the casual joking that had previously lightened the mood. I was sweating like I never had before. My arms and legs were shaking. Finally, one of the guys mercifully asked me to do something else—a job I think he made up, out of pity or frustration. I was directed to stand by the hay elevator and make sure the bales were on straight as they made their way up the rattling machine. Even just standing there, my arms ached.

When Tom arrived, looking for me, I climbed up in the cab with him, still sweaty and trembling. He pulled out silently, waiting for me to speak first.

"I couldn't even lift one bale!" I admitted, baffled. "I really have helped with haying *so many times!*"

"What does one of your bales at home weigh?" Tom asked, turning the wheel as we headed for home.

"Depending on the baler and stuff, like, forty pounds." I measured with my hands in front of me the approximate size of the bales I was used to.

Tom laughed in his friendly way. "Well, there you go. Our three-wire bales are at least twice that long and weigh more than three times what yours do. I've never seen a bale of hay from New York, but I'd say that explains your problem right there." He chuckled again. "I was wondering why you were talking like you were gonna throw those bales around so easy. It's hard work for anyone, even the men we got."

I hadn't accomplished anything that day except to look silly. I reminded myself to listen and look a little more carefully, out here in Kansas.

## DAYS

Reid and I went on dates. Barb and I talked and laughed all the time. Gypsy developed an attachment to Tom and followed him around the farm. Rainy grazed in his private pasture and stretched flat out in the sun when the mood hit him. I ran errands for Barb in town, and the people I saw greeted me and Gypsy by name. There were many connections, large and small, that made up everyday life, and time passed in a pleasant way.

Reid invited me to visit the clinic in Fort Scott where he and Dr. Durling worked and hopefully be of some help on a farm call where he was vaccinating and tagging a whole herd of calves. When we arrived at the farm, a small group of men were waiting, dressed in overalls, and drinking coffee from thermoses.

"This is Missy," Reid introduced me when we got out. "She's the one you may have heard of, riding her horse across the country. She's sticking around these parts a little longer than originally planned."

The men were friendly, and some indicated they knew my story from the news. They joked with Reid while he prepared his veterinary instruments. I was the only female, and I wondered whether they would want my help, but it was a large herd, and Reid had said, the more hands around, the easier and faster it would go.

It was soon clear that everyone had a job. Two of the men wove into the nervous herd and cut one calf away from the others, driving him into the cattle chute. Another hand slammed the gate shut while one big guy wrapped his arms around the protesting calf, keeping him pretty immobile. Reid drew blood, got the syringe with the vaccine into the muscle, and shot a tag, like a pierced earring, into the calf's ear. I stood near Reid and recorded the calf's ear tag number, vaccinations, and the number on the label of his tube of blood. Reid explained this was part of the work required by the government to prevent outbreaks that could harm livestock and the food and dairy products the country depended on.

Although I'd never heard a farmer or a rancher or a cowboy say they disliked their work, I had to think that people who did this kind of labor every day might not describe it as "fun." Me, I was having a great time. The men managed to joke and laugh a lot as we moved through the herd.

At midday, we headed for the farmhouse, where we left our muddy, manure-caked boots out by the back door and took a seat at the kitchen table. I figured they probably took this break at the same time every day, because it got them out of the sun when it was at its highest and hottest point.

As we ate lunch, the guys talked nonstop about something they called "Days." I was confused until I figured out it was their "shorthand" for *Days of Our Lives*, an afternoon soap opera that they discussed fervently. It seemed everyone at the table had an opinion about the show: who belonged with whom and who was up to no good. The biggest, gruffest fellow in the group kept saying, "I like that Kayla. She's my pick."

For some reason that got to me. I wanted to laugh with joy. Joy for the dirt on my boots… and for being reminded that people are forever full of surprises.

## KANSAS TIME

We had another checkup with Dr. Drogey, and he was pleased with Rainy's progress. With my desire to continue our trip in mind, he suggested I consider getting a pack animal to share Rainy's load. I pushed the suggestion to the back of my mind. He also recommended that I begin riding Rainy bareback so that he maintained his fitness in the hopes we would be able to continue on our trek.

It became my habit each evening to take my bridle from the peg in the barn, lead Rainy up to the back steps of the house, and climb onto his back for a ramble. Gypsy would leap around happily as we headed out. It was unusual to see even one vehicle as we wandered the unmarked dirt roads that crisscrossed the prairie. On our first ride, we found ourselves back at the field where I was bested by the giant bales of hay. Another evening, we made our way to Tom's Uncle Poe's farm. West of town was a "hanging tree" where the last man was hung a hundred years before for rustling cattle in Woodson County. But one discovery in particular got me thinking. It was on a road just east of the Kees' place, where we came upon an old-looking stone wall, complete with a heavy door made of thick wood and black iron, built into the ground, as solid as if it grew up from the earth. I guessed it was a tornado shelter, but when I asked Barb about it, she said it was a fort "left over from Indian-fighting days," and that much of it still stood, intact and little-altered since the days of the frontier.

I'd driven Tom's truck and Barb's car around the area, running errands for them, and Reid and I had driven back roads on our adventures together, but it was the ritual of my peaceful evening rides with Rainy and Gypsy that made me feel close to and familiar with the prairie around us. I loved the land in Kansas. I felt like we were part of the place now, much the same as its history, the smell of fresh-cut hay, and the dusky twilight.

## PHONE CALL

Tom, Barb, and I sat in the living room one night, watching *Dallas.* Like *Days of Our Lives,* the show was something of a ritual in the area, although the reception was poor and the picture fuzzy. The phone rang, and Tom answered it, turning his back to me and Barb, purposely saying little tidbits in a louder voice, though he pretended not to notice we were listening.

"Yep, she's here all right. Yep, she's the one," he said. Barb and I looked at each other, wondering which of us was the "she" he was referring to.

"Well, that sounds mighty interesting.... Uh-huh. I don't know.... She might.... Is that right? Well, whaddya know." He chuckled.

Barb and I were like two little kids, dying to know what was up. But Tom said goodbye and settled back down in his chair, slowly picking up his paper and shaking it, then holding it so we couldn't see his face.

Barb didn't last one minute of the game. "Well?" she demanded immediately.

Still behind his newspaper, Tom said innocently, "What?"

"Who was that on the phone?" Barb asked.

"My friend."

"What friend?"

"Arlo."

"Well, what did he want?"

"To talk to me."

"What do you mean? What did he want to talk to you *about*?"

"Stuff."

I could have sworn Barb was about to jump up and rip the paper from his hands, though she was laughing, too. "That man!" she said when Tom finally put his newspaper down, his own eyes crinkling with laughter.

"Arlo called because he heard someone at our place might be looking for a mule," he explained. It took a minute for me to realize he was referring to *me*. Was I looking for a mule? Then I remembered the veterinarian's suggestion about considering a pack animal. The small-town grapevine had done its work.

"Fellow Arlo knows down in Fall River has a little mule for sale," Tom continued. "I told him I'd ask Missy if she'd be interested in going to take a look."

I hadn't taken the suggestion about a pack animal seriously. Rainy, Gypsy, and I were such a well-matched team, I was hesitant to disturb the balance. On the other hand, if it might help Rainy, I knew I should look into it.

I looked at Tom. "How much do they want?" I asked.

"One hundred and twenty-five dollars," he replied. "I figured we could go look at her tomorrow afternoon, after the fields are done, if you want to."

One hundred and twenty-five dollars? Where I came from, no working equine of any kind would be priced that low. Maybe animals were cheaper in the Midwest. Or maybe just mules? I'd never been around a mule, but I was good with horses, and how different could a mule be from a horse?

"Okay," I agreed with a shrug. "Let's go have a look at her then."

## THREE SIMPLE WORDS

Old Yeller, Tom's mustard-colored Ford truck, had stock racks built onto the back—a tall framework that enclosed the bed of the pickup like a small cattle chute. The tailgate was converted to a ramp. Farmers commonly used such a setup to transport livestock without hauling a trailer around.

The stock racks rattled as we rode over dusty back roads on the way to Fall River to look at the mule. Charley Pride played on the radio. You couldn't see above the top of the cornstalks, they were so high, and the narrow roads we drove were like channels cut through the fields. When I looked out the back window, I saw a long dust plume trailing behind us.

The Yohos had the mule for sale, and their home was a pretty little place. A few large shade trees cooled a large fenced lot where I could make out several animals. Mrs. Frank Yoho (she introduced herself in the old-fashioned way, using her husband's name) greeted us.

"I guess you came to see Sweetie," she said, leading us through a gate to the lot.

Sweetie, apparently, was the mule, and Sweetie, apparently, was hard to catch. Mrs. Yoho was armed with a can of 7-Up and a bag of licorice—"The mule's favorite," she explained. Sweetie, apparently, had a sweet tooth.

Mrs. Yoho was soon haltering a dark little beast and leading her up to us, and I got a good look at her.

The mule was about twelve, maybe thirteen hands high—like a decent-size pony. Nothing described her color as well as "dark chocolate." She didn't have a speck of white, just rich, deep dark brown with a hint of dappling on her hindquarters. What you noticed most, of course, were her ears. Magnificent and long, like royalty among equine ears, they stood tall at attention as the little mule focused her gaze on us, and we sized each other up. I reached my hand, palm down, to her. She ignored it.

I was at a loss. What kind of questions did you ask about a prospective pack mule? With my head still in the horse world, all I could think to say was, "Is she broke to ride?"

Mr. Frank Yoho had joined us, and in unison, he and his wife answered, "Sure." Without hesitation, Frank tossed the lead rope around Sweetie's neck and tied it on the other side of the halter, threw a leg over and was on her back. Frank was a large man, and this was a little mule, but the weight didn't appear to bother her at all.

Frank gave a cluck, and using the lead like a direct rein, turned the long-eared animal in a few circles, brought her to a stop, then clucked again until she went off into a perky, cute trot. His feet hung mere inches from the ground.

Frank jumped off. "Fetch me a two-by-four from the barn," he called to his wife. He turned back to me and Tom. "She's a coon-huntin' mule. I got her from Arkansas on a trade."

"Coon-huntin' mule?" I repeated in the form of a question.

"In Arkansas and other places, they raise these mules to go hunt raccoons at night. They can see better in the dark than horses do," he explained. "When they're out huntin' and come to a wire fence, the hunter takes off his coat and drapes it over the top wire to make it more visible. The mules jump right over, easy as pie. I don't know any horse that'll do that, especially in the dark."

Mrs. Yoho returned with the board. "Grab that end there," she said to Tom.

They stood, the two-by-four horizontal held pretty high between them. Frank led Sweetie up to the makeshift fence. She was a pudgy thing, her belly protruding roundly on both sides, and the board was as high as her neck—a height she was unlikely to be able to jump over, in my opinion.

Frank tugged on the lead and clucked yet again, and from practically a standstill right in front of the board, the little mule popped clear over it. My jaw dropped, Tom chuckled, and Frank had Sweetie jump it from the other direction. Mrs. Yoho and Tom raised the board higher and again, up and over, no problem for the mule.

I was amazed. A horse would have to have the strides and the pace just right, but this mule just stood there and popped over the board like a cat would jump up on a dresser.

Everyone turned to look at me as if to say, *Well, what do you think?*

All the practical things I should have considered and asked about, like whether she had experience being packed, if she ponied off other horses, and whether her feet were in good shape, came nowhere near my mind. I didn't ask how she might deal with the road, traffic, or bad weather. When my mouth opened, all that came out were three simple words.

"I want her."

## A MEETING

Tom had somehow guessed the outcome of our visit and had come prepared to pay for the mule. I promise to pay him back. He just chuckled. With little fuss, we loaded what was now *my* mule onto Tom's truck to take her home to Yates Center. She walked right up the ramp, showing no hesitation about going with us. As Tom cranked Old Yeller around, Sweetie turned her dark face once and looked at the home she was leaving. Then she found a comfortable spot up toward the front of the truck bed, just on the other side of the cab window. Her little mule muzzle rode just inches from us, between Tom's shoulder and mine, the whole way home.

This mule was so docile about leaving the Yohos' place that I was totally unprepared for her reaction when we turned into the drive at the Kees'. Suddenly, she transformed into a pacing, pawing dervish, causing the truck to rock. With her face just inches from our ears, she let loose the loudest, most ungodly noise I'd ever heard. It couldn't be called a bray, or a whinny, or anything else I was familiar with. Tom and I both about jumped out of our seats.

I felt a rush of worry. Was this mule doped up with tranquilizers that were now wearing off? Was she actually a crazy, uncontrollable animal?

No. It was just that she had caught her first glimpse of Rainy.

The mule's strange noise got Rainy's attention, and we could see his head over the pasture gate, looking our way. Sweetie was frantic in the back. I was afraid to let the ramp down or try to grab hold of her halter. Why was she acting like this? What if she attacked Rainy?

Tom undid the bolts on the back of the truck, and sure enough, as soon as he started to lower the ramp, the mule charged out, almost knocking both of us down. Tom and I both grabbed for her lead rope, but even with the two of us holding tight, we could barely keep Sweetie under control as she pulled and made her weird noises and pointed those long ears straight at Rainy. She dragged the two of us toward the pen.

Just as I began to fear I'd bought a crazy mule and brought her to the Kees' farm, Sweetie yanked the lead we both had a hold of out of our hands and charged off in a surprising burst of speed. Tom looked down at his brush-burned hands and then up at me.

"Have you considered any other name for her?" he asked slowly in his laidback Midwestern drawl. "I don't think Sweetie suits her, do you?"

The mule made it across the yard in a flash and stood pressed against the pen's gate, nuzzling Rainy through the bars. She was perfectly calm again, the rapid in-and-out of her breathing the only hint of her mighty rampage. After a few minutes of snuffling, muzzle to muzzle, Rainy calmly returned to his grazing.

I was getting my first inkling that dealing with mules might not be exactly like dealing with horses.

## GETTING TO KNOW HER

"What are you going to call her?" Barb wanted to know. A new name for the mule had become a frequent topic of discussion. Barb and I both happened to like the name Amanda, and we just started calling her that. I didn't know it at the time, but it was an old tradition to give mules a human name.

I figured I had my work cut out for me, getting the little mule used to carrying packs and accustomed to dealing with unfamiliar situations on the road. But once she had a few days to absorb how steady and unflappable Rainy was, it all came easily.

The first day I tried ponying her she fell into place a little behind Rainy as he walked. Within a few days, she was venturing out, exploring the roads with us. As Rainy moved forward smart and steady, that's what Amanda did, too. It was like she had decided that being with Rainy was her life's calling. If I was going to throw some packs on her and ask her to walk a thousand miles, so be it. I marveled at my luck in finding a mule who was likely the exception, not the rule.

In learning what I could about mules, I read that they were known for "picking out" who they liked and who they didn't. She loved Rainy. That was clear. Luckily, she seemed to have decided she liked me okay, and Tom, too.

But Amanda was convinced that Reid was up to no good.

Reid was what Barb called "the last of a dying breed." He was a true gentleman. He always came in and visited with Tom and Barb when he came to pick me up for a date. When we went to the movies, he blushed when he had to say *The Best Little Whorehouse in Texas* when purchasing the tickets. But a hundred-and-twenty-five-dollar mule brought out another side of him.

Reid kindly offered to vaccinate Amanda. But Amanda decided she didn't care for needles. Or vets. Or Reid. It took me, Tom, Barb, Reid, and a solid steel livestock chute to get a needle in her, and Reid was rewarded with a hard knock to his arm against the bars of the chute. It was then that we heard the first "Shit!" and "Damn mule!" We'd just discovered that the mannerly vet could swear. Amanda kicked, tossed her head, slammed against the bars, and pinned her ears. And Reid cussed with the best of 'em. Barb and I kept glancing at each other across Amanda's humped brown back, biting our lips, trying our best not to laugh.

## TIME IS OURS

I have always dreamed in equine. And in sky blue and grass green. They say girls imagine Prince Charming or the perfect wedding, but I belonged to a different tribe of women. I never had a fantasy car, a job in mind, or a wish for anything that didn't involve horses, dogs, and wide-open spaces. In the waning days of my time at the

Kees', with Rainy healing and Amanda becoming part of our little family, my time was filled with contentment. I rode Rainy bareback, leading Amanda along as Gypsy ran in the fields. The land seemed to go on forever, and the time and place was ours. I had friends and family who supported me and wished me well. I had the sun on my shoulders and the breeze in my face. When I looked at the view through Rainy's familiar ears in front, and looked back at the smart face and long ears of Amanda behind us, I knew I was in the middle of an abundance of riches.

We'd followed the advice of two vets. Rainy had healed even better than hoped for. Reid was impressed—and told me so.

"You've really done right by him," he said. "A lot of people would have kept him on pain meds and put him back to work. Giving him as much time as you have has worked wonders."

His compliment meant the world to me. I'd done what could be done to assure Rainy was ready to return to our walk across the country. My dream was alive, thank goodness.

That meant the time was coming that I would have to say goodbye.

## GONE DOWN THE ROAD

With Dr. Drogey's approval of Rainy's condition, things went into motion. Drawers were emptied. Saddlebags were packed. Reid and I made plans for one more date—we just drove around the prairie roads we so enjoyed. When it was time for him to go, I acted like it was fine, that it was all part of the deal. From the dark at the Kees' back door, I watched his truck drive away.

Barb stayed home from work the day before we left and helped me pack. We talked companionably, like always, laughing a little, too. Then she pulled off her glasses and wiped at her eyes. I got a lump in my throat and my vision was swimming. She pulled me into a spontaneous hug, knowing we didn't have to say a word.

Leaving Yates Center, Kansas, was almost scarier than starting out from home the first day of the trip. I now had another animal with me, which added a whole new complication to our travels. And I had the nagging worry related to Rainy's injury: What caused it? Would it resurface? But Tom, Barb, and others believed in us. They believed we could ride the rest of the way across the United States. It was time for me to live in the moment again—to put my worries aside and do the best I could.

I said goodbye to Tom and Barb at the Richardsons' farm out along Route 54 in Eureka. It was a ways away from Yates Center, and they had driven out that far with the idea that somehow it would make saying goodbye a little easier. It didn't. I almost couldn't bear watching Tom, a man who spent his words carefully, struggling to keep everything inside. He kept his eyes down while Barb and I hugged, making no attempt to keep the tears at bay. Tom stood apart from us, quietly petting Amanda and then Rainy—the animal he'd helped care for every day for the last four weeks.

Few words were said. We all held each other tight, then Tom took Barb's elbow, and they walked to the truck. Tom came back to us once more and said something quiet in Rainy's ear, then he climbed into the cab beside his wife.

I waved and waved until they were gone, down the road.

## MORNING STAR

The Richardsons gave me a little space after I said goodbye to Tom and Barb. I went into their barn and buried my face in Rainy's mane. I didn't know what else to do to fight the emptiness in me.

I don't know how much time passed before Mrs. Richardson came in and gently asked me if I'd like to see some of their ranch. I pulled myself away from Rainy, grateful for the distraction.

In one pasture, big hairy buffalo grazed, one or two with calves by their sides. The emerald green land rolled out behind them. It made me smile. Buffalo. You had to love Kansas.

I got up in the morning before true light, and Gypsy and I walked to the barn together to get ready for the next step of our journey. Rainy and Amanda turned their bright faces toward me. The sky in the east was beginning its gradual awakening, the edge of the horizon in shades of pink and purple. In the western sky, I saw one bright, shining star—bright enough to be visible even as this part of the world turned slowly toward the sun. It was the brightest morning star I'd ever seen, highlighted by the deep vivid color of the sky. I stared upward, taking it as our sign. I reminded myself to remember to look at the beauty in the land, in the sky, and all around as we moved on. I felt many things inside me, but I also believed this, too: All would be well.

The road west was waiting.

# PART FOUR

# THE ROAD WEST

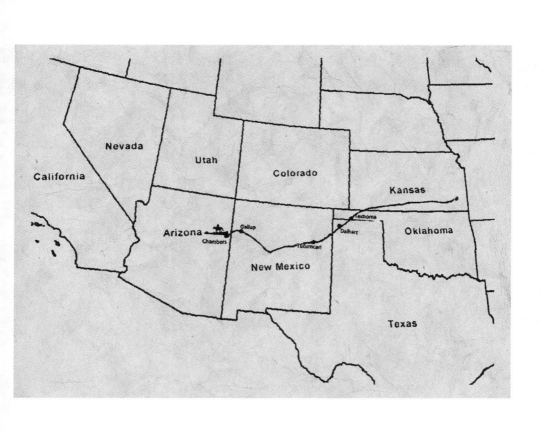

## AMANDA, GYPSY

Tom and I had improvised a pack system for Amanda using an old Western saddle. We fit it with a breast collar and a crupper to keep the saddle in place on the mule's barrel-shaped body, and we covered everything in fleece. We paid close attention to balance and placement of weight. Amanda and Rainy and I even took several trial runs around the fields before we left Yates Center.

Still, practice was not the same thing as being out there, on the road, and the first few days, I stopped often to rearrange things and adjust the packs.

We were almost to our night's destination when a horse and rider came toward us along the road. They passed us at a fast trot, and for some reason, Rainy didn't like that. He fussed and pawed for a minute.

Amanda picked up on this friskiness. She got her head down and started to buck, somehow managing to get her saddle and packs over her head—and off. Everything I owned went flying, ending up in heaps in the grass.

The whole incident was over in a minute. For a second, we all just stood there and looked at all my things on the ground. Then Amanda decided that bucking the packs off had worked out well, so she wandered off to eat grass. Then the sky opened up, and it began to pour.

I had one of those *What I'm doing is crazy* moments before I started grabbing my scattered belongings from where they'd landed and stuffing them in the disheveled packs before the rain soaked everything. I glanced to my left. Gypsy was coming toward me with one small bag in her teeth. She dragged it to where I knelt, sort of repacking, leaving it at my feet. I stared, open-mouthed, as she made a beeline to a plastic bag with some envelopes in it, and pawed at it, trying to grasp it in her teeth. My dog was trying to help me pick up the mess!

Now...now...I wouldn't trade this moment for anything.

## FLINT HILLS

Riding through the Flint Hills was the perfect way to re-acclimate to our traveling lifestyle. The land rolled and swelled in every direction. Red-brown cattle grazed on distant hills, and the great wide sky made me feel like we'd somewhere crossed an invisible line into *The West*.

These were the hills that were home to Indian nations and vast herds of buffalo just over a hundred years before our journey, until the mid-1800s, when the homesteaders came. Much farther back, something like 250 million years ago, shallow seas covered Kansas and Oklahoma. The land we were traveling through was rich in fossils of prehistoric sea creatures.

The hills were mostly treeless and largely uninterrupted by man-made structures. The grassy expanses were the deepest of green, the sky the clearest blue I'd yet seen. It seemed to touch the earth all around us.

Who knows what it is that draws different people to different places? Mountains, seashores, city skylines? I only knew I felt something special surrounded by simple beauty. I felt that if I breathed deeply the sky and the sunlight would fill me up inside.

In this way, I found my peace. It was the same way I'd always found it: being aware of the earth and the sun and the steady rhythm of Rainy's hoof beats on the road.

# LITTLE GUARDIAN

West of Wichita I had a host who was a veterinarian, which gave me the opportunity to have Rainy's back and withers area checked. I was relieved when my horse received the all-clear.

While staying the night, Rainy and Amanda had to be turned out in a pen with an established herd of horses. There's always a tense moment in such situations with equines when you watch the introductions and hold your breath.

As Rainy and Amanda checked out their new surroundings, one horse approached, but my mule immediately flattened her ears, bared her teeth, and charged, running the friendly neighbor off. I watched: If any of my host's horses took even a step toward the newcomers, Amanda pinned those long ears and snaked her head at them. The other horses gave up, letting the little mule make the rules.

I camped right outside the corral, and I woke in the morning to the sight of Amanda, standing between Rainy and the herd, ears up, still on guard.

The animals and I gradually fell into the rhythm of being on the road again. My worries about Rainy's sore back and Amanda's inexperience eased up a little. The number of miles we traveled each day slowly increased.

We were near the town of Pratt when Amanda pulled back on the lead, hesitating to go forward. She'd been such a willing worker up until then, I immediately brought Rainy to a halt, dismounted, and took everything off the mule.

Sure enough, I found the beginning of a small girth sore low down on her belly. Although I'd caught it early, I didn't want to make it worse. I loosened Amanda's girth so it wouldn't rub and transferred the packs from her to my patient buckskin standing near, hoping he'd be okay with the few miles we had left.

The family we were staying with in Pratt—Dennis and Sherry Leighty, along with their two young girls—invited us to stay with them an extra day even before I told them about the girth sore.

"Well then you have to stay!" said Sherry without hesitation. "Tomorrow we can have your mule see a vet."

Rainy and Amanda got a surprise day off, and I soon had an antibiotic salve from the vet, and a new girth and fleece to protect my mule. Our second evening together, we cooked out on the back deck, where we could see Rainy and Amanda, snoozing in the Leightys' backyard pen.

"We were thinking," Dennis started, "that when you ride on tomorrow, you could leave Amanda here with us for a few days. The girls will give her tons of attention. When her sore looks better, we can haul her out to you on the road."

"Besides," Sherry added, "the girls have been begging for a pony, and this will give them a taste of what it will be like caring for one. It'll be a good experience."

So it was just Rainy, Gypsy, and I starting out in the morning. We had a light load and no little mule—I was glad for her opportunity to rest and felt sure she was in kind hands. Amanda didn't fuss as much as I thought she would as I rode away. I decided she was smart enough to understand that she needed to heal and that she would be reunited with her pal soon. I'd spent enough time with Amanda to believe that she usually knew exactly what was going on.

As we slipped around the house, the last view I had before turning west was of the Leighty girls, Heather and Shonda, brushing Amanda in the pen.

## DIAMOND DAY

I loved Amanda, and it sure had been a help to have her along to lighten Rainy's load. But there was something free and easy about riding along the way we had started our journey—no extra packs, no lead rope to hang on to, Gypsy running around the grasslands.

There was an old John Denver song that said, "Some days are diamonds…" For me, this day was a diamond day. The sky was impossibly blue, the land was wide open, and there was so little traffic the road was mostly ours. I even got to canter Rainy for a nice stretch in the morning while the breeze kept the air cool. I had such a feeling of lightness and happiness while we were flying free, like the birds that soared over the prairie above us.

Midday brought us to a feed co-op where I stopped to get water, then led Rainy across the road from the grain elevator to the one big shade tree in sight. I pulled the saddle off his back, and he began contentedly grazing on the rich grass. Gypsy and I sat and shared the over-sized lunch Sherry Leighty had sent along with us.

It was a good spot—the tall tree and cool shade such a contrast to the bright sun and flat land all around. A balmy breeze kept us comfortable. Free from any care or worry, Rainy, Gypsy, and I—all three of us—fell asleep with the rustle of the leaves above and grass around us as our lullaby.

## ROUND HOUSE, ROUND MOON

Being outside all day, I got caught up in the land and the natural world around us. But I still appreciated a unique and special building when I saw one.

My animals and I had been invited to stay in Greensburg with Bob James and his family. Their house was round and built partially into the earth, in a low hillside. This made use of the ground as natural insulation, keeping the house cool in summer and warm in winter. It also offered some protection from tornados.

In the evening, I went out back to see how Rainy was getting along with the Jameses' horses. The pasture was on a gentle rise, and I stepped out in time to see a huge round moon rising. A warm breeze blew just enough to stir the grasses as the small herd made their way across the slope—three horses in a row, perfectly silhouetted against the wondrous moon. Their hooves rose and fell, making the rhythmic steps only horses make.

Never in the East had the moon looked so large and so mesmerizing, or had such a presence, as that wide Kansas moon. Never had I seen horses look more like art or poetry as the three against that giant disc of amber for one quiet moment.

## WIDE OPEN LONESOME

The rolling land had flattened into the long view of West Kansas. We sweltered in the sun and grew accustomed to a hot, constant wind.

We watched for windmills, which meant water, their slowly turning blades working pumps that supplied stock ponds. They taught me the lesson of the flatlands: just because you could see it up ahead didn't mean you were almost there.

My animals and I were staying the night with a woman minister. She lived by herself in a house that stood alone, the only structure on windswept fields. She had one horse in a pasture some ways down from the house—the horse was black, beautiful, and wild. He became aware of Rainy as we made our way up the long drive, and I watched as he pawed the ground and bugled out a shrill whinny, then trotted hard and fast along the fence line.

Rainy was usually so adaptable, but this big horse unnerved him. He didn't relax or graze when I turned him loose in an enclosure. He stayed away from the fence that separated him from his pacing neighbor, keeping his head up and eyes on the black horse.

Reverend Betsy seemed glad to have us; it didn't seem many visitors passed her way.

"That horse needs to be trained," she answered when I asked about the black horse in the pasture. "I can't ride him yet. I spend time with him, though. I brush and feed him and just spend time with him." I could tell she loved her horse, but I thought he would likely be a handful for her.

Reverend Betsy wanted me to stay inside her home for the night so we could visit. I agreed but sat restlessly. I kept looking out the window at the hot-blooded black horse and my quiet Rainy.

Finally, late in the night, I went outside to Rainy. The wind had picked up. The land was as vast and wide as a black ocean, though the moon made enough light to see what was near. I saw the darkened house where the minister slept. I saw the big horse, still pushing against the fence, still anxious and excited. I saw my Rainy, awake and a little nervous all by himself out in all that space, without Amanda or anyone familiar nearby. He turned at the sound of my footsteps.

There are so many different kinds of alone. There on the same homestead, all of us were separate in the faint moonlight. I went to Rainy and stood with him. He turned and lowered his head to my touch.

The wind just kept blowing.

## REUNION ROAD

Rainy, Gypsy, and I came to a crossroads, and my map showed the road going north would lead us to Dodge City. From Dodge City, we could ride straight west into Colorado. Or we could stay on Route 54 as it veered south, passed near the old hideout of the Dalton Gang, then headed into the panhandles of Oklahoma and Texas.

I'd loosely planned on riding through Colorado. After our extended time in Kansas, however, it was weeks later than I'd planned. Even though it was hard to imagine in the heat, summer would be ending soon, and riding toward the Rocky Mountains was maybe not the smartest idea.

Route 54 had been good to us, so the decision came easily. We headed south.

I'd let the Leightys know we were staying on Route 54 from a gas-station payphone, and soon they caught up to us, towing Amanda in a trailer. We all hugged, and I was happy to see familiar faces on the long lonely stretch we were traveling. Amanda squealed and grunted happily as she reunited with Rainy.

Sherry Leighty and the girls had faithfully treated the small girth sore, and I was pleased to see it had scabbed over well. The new and better-fitting girth would prevent any further problems. Amanda belonged with us, and she sure seemed ready to get back to work.

Wary of running low on supplies, I made a stop at the lone store in a very small town. I tied Rainy and Amanda outside, then searched the aisles inside for items that required no preparation and would be light in the saddle packs. I walked to the checkout line with some cans of tuna, a couple cans of fruit salad, and a soda. In front of me were several women, their backs to me, but I could hear them talking.

"Can you imagine calling up and asking to stay with someone you don't even know?" I heard one of them say.

"What is a young girl doing, all alone like that? Asking for trouble, seems like," replied another.

"What kind of mother would let her go off like that, anyway?"

I stood with my little bundle of groceries heavy in my hands. I felt my face burn, realizing it was me they were gossiping about. My instinct, always, was to avoid conflict...but these women had said something about my mother.

"Excuse me," I said as forcefully as I could. "Are you talking about me?"

All three of the women turned, their mouths open in surprise, and immediately looked uncomfortable.

"I have a great mother," I said first. "And everywhere I've been on this trip, people have treated us kindly."

I didn't know what to say next.

The women mumbled a few words I couldn't understand and left quickly. The teenage cashier avoided meeting my eyes as I paid.

My initial anger slipped away, leaving in its place a vague feeling of depression. It really was the first time I'd felt unwelcome in a small town anywhere on our journey. The unpleasantness reminded me that sometimes I was very much alone. I suddenly missed my mom.

I found a payphone on the main street. I was afraid the story would make my mother feel bad, so I called Barb Kee instead. In her wise way, Barb reminded me that some people were not necessarily bad, but they mocked or feared what they didn't understand. What did really bother kind Barb Kee was that the incident had taken place in her Kansas—as if she could make the whole state as nice as she was.

## HEAT AND SWEETNESS

One hundred and five degrees—that's what the static-y voice on my little radio said. The light wind only pushed the hot air around. The insects were worse than any we'd seen, causing crusty scabs inside Rainy and Amanda's ears. I rode with my face scrunched up in a squint to try and keep the flies and gnats and the hard light of the sizzling sun out of my eyes.

We came to a wide spot off the shoulder of the road where a weathered picnic table sat and the remains of an old seesaw rose from the grass near one lone shade tree. I dismounted and stretched my stiff back, scratching Rainy's withers for a moment.

I heard a vehicle on the road, and an old pickup truck chugged up, its paint a faded blue. It raised a small cloud of dust as it slowed to a stop. An old man stepped around from the passenger side, and a younger man did the same from the driver's seat.

"There you are," the old man said, as if we had been playing hide-and-seek. "We seen you on the news and wanted to bring you something."

He was carrying a big oblong watermelon, which he handed to me. It was heavy and hard for me to get my arms around.

"Thanks," I said to both men.

They nodded seriously, then, the older one spoke again: "We grew it, that."

"Wow," I replied, shuffling a little beneath the fruit's weight. "It's a big one…"

They nodded again, then got back in the truck and drove away.

I was grateful for their kindness but unsure what to do with the massive melon. It was too big and heavy to carry or pack, but I didn't want to waste it either.

I shuffled to the oval of shade the tree cast on the ground and set the watermelon down with relief. I pulled my knife from its leather sheath on my belt and plunged it into the green hide, carving out ragged shaped chunks of the deep pink center. I cupped my hands under the dripping treat as I bit in, the sweet juice running down my chin and my wrists and my forearms.

I offered a piece to Gypsy, who licked a little but soon lost interest. Amanda liked her piece, although Rainy seemed unsure. We sat like this for a while, until full of watermelon. I surveyed the scene. There was still a lot left.

I poured a little of the canteen water on my hands to clear the stickiness, then saddled up. Before we left, I stabbed into the melon again, cutting what remained into pieces and spreading them out on the ground.

*This is for the crows and coyotes and kangaroo rats that will come forward onto this dusty patch after we're gone,* I thought, *so they can have a sweet dripping feast in the hot sun, as we did.*

## STATE LINE

The grasslands changed over to low brush and gravelly ground as we made our way to the state line, where the worn sign for a new state had a pinwheel of color on it. I looked back behind us, thinking about our time in Kansas, then turned forward as we passed on into the wide spaces of the narrow panhandle of Oklahoma.

There was something age-old and natural-feeling about camping with a horse. Staying outside and sleeping on the ground was like putting myself in the horse's world for a while. It felt tied to the past and a more natural state for me and all my animals, when our species were somewhat nomadic and slept out in the open with the earth beneath us and the sky above.

I didn't often make a campfire, but on the nights that I did, I admitted it was not for warmth or cooking but because it was cheery. Perhaps it was old Westerns I'd watched that made this seem like a familiar comfort. Maybe it had to do with the debated American "collective memory"—the idea that most of us descended from someone who came from somewhere else, giving us our desire for wandering and finding new places. Westward movement, being part of the outdoors, and the urge to wander... all of these things were far older than me.

I sat with my tin cup and watched the animals settle as my small fire sent sparks spiraling upward to join the blanket of stars spread over us.

## WINNING OVER THE MULE

I've always wanted horses in my world, but I wanted to be a part of their world, too. I wanted to not just be able to ride but to understand and have a connection with them. I was fortunate to have that with Rainy. Our bond showed in the way we communicated, and in the way he wanted to be with me. I was always hugging him, leaning on him, and Rainy followed me, often laying his head on my shoulder.

I hoped Amanda would become attached to me in that way, too, once we had more time together. But when I hugged her neck, the mule swished her tail and stepped away. She was well-behaved and did her new job like a pro...but she wanted no part of the mushy love fest I lavished on Rainy and Gypsy all the time.

Each evening I spent time grooming Rainy and Amanda, going over every inch of them with a brush, cleaning hooves, combing manes and tails. One night, as I used the soft brush for Amanda's ears and face, I noticed she was standing perfectly still. I continued, going over her coat, even where I'd already groomed.

By the time I was combing her tail, the little mule had dropped her head. Her lip drooped and her eyes closed halfway. She got so relaxed that her muzzle actually touched the ground in front of her. It was like she was hypnotized! I wanted to laugh, but I held it in so I didn't disturb her.

I groomed and massaged the mule until my hands were tired. She never moved a muscle—and now I had the key to bonding with Amanda.

## BORDERS

I was pulling a few things from my packs in the guest room of the ranch house on the Oklahoma-Texas border when I heard a car pull up on the gravel outside. Soon there was a soft tap at my door. My host poked her head in; I couldn't quite read the expression on her face.

"There's a policeman here," she said. "He's looking for you."

Does everyone have the same reaction to a policeman? My conscience was clear, but still my heart began to beat nervously. Did I trespass somewhere or leave a spark of a campfire burning? Was there some kind of bad news from home? I followed the woman to the front room.

"I'm Missy Priblo," I said to the officer who was standing just inside the door.

His face was inscrutable. "Can I talk to you outside?" he replied.

I started to feel really nervous as I walked out with him.

"Come with me to my car," he instructed. And then, perhaps seeing my anxiety, went on: "I am the friend of someone you know. That someone is worried about you traveling all alone. That someone made arrangements for me to find you. That's all I'm going to say."

From the back of his patrol car, the officer retrieved a little canvas bag. He unsnapped the flap and pulled out a gun.

"This is a .25 caliber automatic," he explained. "It's small and easy to work with. You should be able to carry it right on your saddle without anyone knowing you have it."

I looked over the gun, then back at the policeman. I didn't know what to say.

"Tonight, you should probably just get used to the feel of it," he went on. "Keep the safety on and practice holding it and carrying it. I'll be back tomorrow morning, and we'll practice shooting when the light is better."

We set a time, and the officer drove away, leaving me with a gun and a lot of questions. Who was the mysterious friend that sent him with this? Should I take it? Why wouldn't he tell me anything else?

Early the next morning, the policeman and I took his patrol car out into the surrounding brushlands. I pulled out the weapon. It felt heavy and unfamiliar in my hand.

"Hold it steady and brace your shooting arm with your other arm," he instructed. Then the officer showed me how to load rounds and hit the clip in the right way. He indicated an area with a low bank and told me to aim and shoot. "Not bad. Try again. Keep your eyes open and be as still as you can. Just get comfortable with it."

It was a strange feeling, hearing the sound and then seeing the spurt of dirt that puffed up from the little hill.

Eventually the officer said, "Okay. We're good."

And that was that. We walked back to his car together, where I thanked him and he nodded acknowledgment. We barely spoke as he returned me to my hosts; he stayed quiet when I asked questions, unless it was specifically related to the gun or shooting. He was apparently perfectly fine with sending me out on the road with an unregistered gun and a box of ammo hanging from my saddle horn.

## TEXAS

Amanda was packed, Rainy was saddled, and Gypsy trotted between the two. After my early-morning shooting lesson, we were back out on the road. A few miles out of town, the road narrowed and traffic died out. We shared the roadside with only a line of telephone poles and cattle in the distance.

The heat that had been our constant companion for months had lifted slightly. It was no longer a heavy, exhausting temperature. Now there was a warm and lazy breeze. It rustled around us all the time.

A granite stone was visible ahead on the side of the roadway, carved into the shape of the state of Texas.

What lay ahead in this land that looked so open and spare? What kind of place had policemen who gave guns to complete strangers? And what about me? Why did I accept it? I had taken a gun when it was offered to me, though I'd never wanted one, or even really thought about one. Now it was hanging on my saddle horn, concealed in its little bag, like it belonged there.

Rainy kept his pace, and we passed the hard rock monument—just like that, Rainy, Gypsy, Amanda, and I crossed the invisible line into the Lone Star State.

The wind whipped bits of grit and dry twigs around Rainy's feet. I noticed the Texas rock had graffiti on it.

When the end-of-day-sun was sitting low in the sky, a car pulled over and the driver rolled down his window. The passenger tilted across the seat so he could see us, too.

"Where you headed?" the driver asked.

"California," I answered.

The two men burst out laughing.

"HA!" the driver barked at me. "You'll never make it!" And they roared off in a cloud of dust.

I wanted to shout, *Hey, do you know how far we've already come?* But I just sat there on the side of the road, smarting from the unaccustomed rudeness.

After a night camping in a rancher's pasture, Rainy came to me in the morning with a cut on his hip and a puffy eye. The other horses must have had a scuffle with him. I cast a look at Amanda. What happened to his Little Guardian? I washed out the cut and put salve on it, and looked over his eye. Neither one looked too serious, but seeing that Rainy had been a little beat up made me feel guilty.

I walked quite a bit that day. With few distractions or changes in the land, I had too much time to think, and a kind of melancholy enveloped me. I questioned decisions and choices I'd made, before and during the trip, and apologized to my animals for having them out on what seemed at the moment like an endless walk.

We finally arrived at the northern Texas town of Stratford only to discover there was a problem with our connections for the night. We walked the streets of the small town, eventually finding our way to the county agent who agreed to let us use the local arena for the night. He looked surprised when I asked if it was okay that I stayed with my animals, but he shrugged and said sure.

I pulled the big heavy doors shut and look around the indoor arena. The ground was covered with soft dirt, and the space was huge. I unrolled my tarp and put it under my sleeping bag, but I figured I'd likely be covered by a fine layer of grime by morning anyway. As darkness arrived fully, I was settled in, and the effect of my small lantern was like a candle in a cave: it made the space around us seem even bigger and darker.

It was hard to sleep. I didn't know how long I stared into blackness before I got up and used my flashlight to scan the arena—I spotted a phone sitting on the announcer's desk. I picked it up and dialed "0." The operator answered immediately with, "What number please?"

"What time is it?" I asked.

"3:10 a.m." she responded in a business-like voice.

I didn't tell her that the time didn't really matter, that I just wanted to hear a voice out there.

Sometime later in the wee dark hours, I heard the unexpected sound of raindrops pinging on the tin roof high above. Rain had been a constant issue in the early months of my journey, but now I couldn't remember the last time I'd heard it. The shower lasted only briefly.

Morning saw us up and out early, the arena locked behind us. There was no sign anywhere that there had been rain in the night. We headed out of town, where everything was still closed up tight. We saw no one.

## NOWHERE

My map showed a small town, Conlen, about twelve or thirteen miles away from Stratford. My plan was to pick up a few supplies there, ride another ten miles, and find a place to camp. The county agent in Stratford had mentioned an abandoned ranch between Stratford and Dalhart, and I kept it in mind in case no other option came our way. The "chain of people" that had been calling ahead, watching out for us, and giving us places to stay was not working in the long desolate stretches of the North Texas Panhandle.

A pickup passed and made a U-turn, pulling over on the opposite side of the two-lane road. A couple of cowboys jumped out.

"Hey, we saw you on the news!" one of them said in greeting. "I'm Darryl, and this is Randy. We're rodeo riders, heading up to Las Vegas."

Randy pulled a bottle from a cooler in their truck bed. "Welcome to Texas!" he said, grinning as he cracked open a Lone Star beer and handed it to me. I smiled gratefully and took a long swig.

Darryl nodded toward my saddle packs where my boots were tied. It had just been too hot to wear them, so I'd been riding in my sneakers. "Is that what New Yorkers do with cowboy boots?" he teased.

Another car pulled up later that day, and the driver called out to me, "Girl, you better put them boots on! And watch for snakes with the horse there."

I started to answer, but he just shook his head at me and drove off. What was it with Texans and cowboy boots anyway?

As we neared what should have been the town of Conlen, according to my map, what came into sight were railroad tracks and a few homes. An old sign for a saloon or restaurant stood broken and peeling and mostly unreadable. The only store looked like it had been closed for some time. I peered in the building's grimy windows, searching for signs of life.

"What do you want?" a woman snapped from behind me, startling me. Gypsy, usually friendly by nature, pressed close to my legs.

"I need to get food and water, and I thought there was a store here," I explained.

"Can't help you," she responded, scowling, hands on hips.

I tried again, explaining who I was and what I was doing. The woman grudgingly allowed us a little water from a hose, then grumbled that she'd see if "someone" could open up and let us inside the pitiful store. She was the only someone I'd seen for miles.

She returned a few minutes later with a set of keys.

We entered the dim store together, with Gypsy at my feet. The woman kept her eye on me as I sized up the few choices. I picked a faded can of corn and one of fruit cocktail, age unknown. She charged too much for the few items, taking my money like she was doing me a favor. I asked if she knew any place I could camp farther along the road, and she bit back, "No. I do not!"

I felt relief when I was back in the saddle, heading out, glad to leave the depressing place behind. We were not much better off than we had been: I had little food and less money, and many of the people we'd encountered lately had not been nice.

We returned to the long empty stretch of two-lane asphalt. No hospitality to be found there, either. Not today.

## ALONG THE TRACKS

Wind blew through the brush. Vultures circled overhead, waiting for us to pass so they could glide down once again toward something dead and unrecognizable on the yellow line in the road.

Railroad tracks ran parallel to us, as they had for miles. I looked over and contemplated the gravel access trail that ran alongside them. It would be nice to get away from the paved road for a while. I turned Rainy and we climbed up a low bank to the path along the tracks, Amanda following behind.

The brush and the rise and fall of the land made the tracks seem far from the road. The world for us was only the sound of hoof beats, the creak of the saddle leather, and Gypsy's steady breathing on the saddle in front of me.

Then, my senses registered a different sound—not loud, but a clear and certain rattling.

Our world exploded.

In the same flash of a second I heard the rattle, Rainy heard it, too. In front of us, the snake was stacked in fat coils, wrapped around itself like a pile of deadly hose. Rainy, contrary to anything I'd ever have imagined him doing, shied hard to the right and then reared straight up in the air. I hung on, but the packs slid, and before I could grab hold of her, Gypsy fell off.

My pup stood looking at the venomous creature before her. The tail of the snake continued to emit its ominous warning. The rattler's head rose, its mouth open enough to see the fangs as it readied itself to strike. Rainy tossed his head and jigged in fear as I struggled to hold on to the reins and Amanda's lead rope.

"*GYPSY!*" I screamed.

My dog turned at the sound just as the rattlesnake, fast as lightning, plunged toward her. The fangs hit air right where Gypsy's face had been a half-second before. The snake's rattle seemed to grow louder as it pulled its head back, ready to strike again, but Gypsy thankfully trotted a few steps toward me and Rainy. With a pounding heart and shaking hands, I managed to pull my pup back up into the saddle, half dragging her by her front legs in my hurry to get her away from the rattler. Rainy moved forward at a fast pace, making a wide berth around the danger.

The packs were askew, the reins were uneven, and I was hanging on to Gypsy in an awkward position. Rainy snorted and tossed his head, on high alert. My hands trembled on the reins. Amanda, bless her, remained steady behind us. I was afraid to let Gypsy down on the ground again. I was afraid to dismount and fix the saddle and the packs. I now saw rattlesnakes hidden in every mound of dirt and behind every rock. Now I knew why Texans told me to put my boots on…why they said Rainy would spook over a snake.

I cut back to the road as soon as I could, where I could see what was around us. I hopped off Rainy and quickly changed from my sneakers to my boots. With a sense of unease, we worked our way onward, looking and listening for that deadly rattle with every step.

The land was tough in the North Texas Panhandle. And so were the few people we'd met. This was not welcoming country.

## ▓ SIGNS

It was hard to feel anything but lonesome and discouraged as we rode on. It didn't help that we were riding to...nowhere—we didn't have a destination...no family farm or cozy campsite. I started to look for houses as the day wore on, but they were few and far between. Sometimes we passed a long drive or dirt road turning off the pavement, but the signs posted near them felt like they went beyond the ordinary "No Trespassing." The signs in this part of Texas had stronger warning messages, like: "STAY OUT! GUARD DOG ON DUTY." One place we passed had at least four signs so that you would make no mistake: "NO TRESPASSING!" "PRO-TECTED BY SMITH AND WESSON!" "PRIVATE PROPERTY STAY OUT!" And just in case you still didn't get it: "ABSOLUTELY DO NOT TURN DOWN THIS PRIVATE ROAD!"

I was getting concerned about being able to find water, but I could also take a hint. Up until very recently, finding water hadn't been a big problem. Normally we came across a feedlot, a grain ele-vator, or a windmill with a stock tank. Today, it just wasn't working out that way.

The sun was burning its way down through the atmosphere when up ahead on the opposite side of the road, I saw a long driveway. A relatively mild "Private Property" notice was posted. I felt this was our chance for water. I also harbored some hope that making contact with someone would bring about good things as it so often had on our trip—an offer of a meal or a place to camp. Hope bloomed as we headed toward the house.

Riding closer, I made out the shadowy shape of someone just inside the screen door, watching us approach.

"Hello?" I called, my hand shading my eyes. No response. "Hello?" I tried again. I heard the sound of a lock sliding shut.

"What do you want!" a woman's voice shrieked from inside the house.

"Um, I …" I was taken aback by the hostility in her voice. "I just wondered if I could possibly get some water for my horse and mule? They haven't had a drink all day and—"

The woman cut me off: "NO! No, you cannot have water!"

I was flabbergasted. Just water? She couldn't be serious.

Optimist that I was, I tried again, thinking that maybe she just didn't really understand. Maybe she was scared, like Barb Kee had explained to me. There was a garden hose lying just a few feet away.

"I can just get it from the hose. You don't even have to come out."

"Get off my property *now*. Get going! *GET OUT NOW!*" she shouted, as if my animals and I were junkyard dogs she'd found tearing up her trash cans. "*GO ON.* I'm sick of people asking me for things!"

I felt emotion inside me, bubbling its way up. I turned Rainy slowly around, passing the green hose lying right by his feet…oh so close. Amanda followed around and we walked back up the dirt drive that somehow felt longer now than it did going in. I could feel the bubble trembling like something about to burst, and when I knew we were clear of the awful house, the tears started pouring out of me in a way I couldn't hold back. Real hard tears spilled out, and I kept snuffling and crying as we walked. On the main road, we turned south again. I cried for several more minutes as we rode onward, until the tears dried up, like everything else in this place.

## THE DARKEST NIGHT

Several times I noticed a gully or a ditch that looked like it should have water, but we'd ride up to find everything dry, dry, dry. We came upon the abandoned homestead I'd heard of, and I turned down its gravel road, praying there would be water there.

The grounds were forlorn and neglected; the windows of the empty home cracked and broken. It had the hollow feel of a long abandonment. The place certainly wasn't ideal, but we needed to get off the road and put the rotten day behind us.

I walked around looking for a spot for the horses and the tent, stomping my feet and making noise in the hope it would scare away any resident reptiles. I jolted to a stop several times, thinking some old stick was a snake. I finally settled on a small gravelly area clear of prickly plants, near an old lean-to and a fallen down wire fence.

I untied our collapsible bucket from the saddle pack and walked to the faucet on the side of the house. As soon as I gave it a turn, a rusty spurt of water rushed out. Then it stopped.

"Oh no!" I gasped. I ran with the little bit of water over to Rainy. He lipped at the bottom of the bucket and sucked it in, drying it in a second.

I sat back on my heels to think for a moment. The water to the house looked like it was shut off, but maybe the pump in the yard connected right to the well. I hurried to the pump and grabbed the handle, using both arms to pump. The water flowed at first and the bucket filled to almost half. Then it stopped. I felt myself crumble a little. I tried again but no more water came out. I got angry and pumped like crazy, as if all the strength I had could change the situation.

I let Amanda have some first this time, then pulled it back and gave the rest to Rainy, amounting to about a quarter of a bucket each. Amanda went right back to nibbling at grass. But Rainy nudged the bucket, nosing it around, looking for more water. It made me want to cry.

I considered packing back up and going onward in search of more water, but if the road behind us was any indication, we'd have little luck riding on. I had to hope and pray that my animals would be okay all night, and in the morning, I would get them water, no matter what. It killed me to think of the way Rainy and Amanda depended on me, the way they went on every mile for me, and now here they were, thirsty and tied to an old fence behind an abandoned house.

I replayed what had happened earlier at the angry woman's house. *I should have jumped off Rainy, grabbed the hose and filled our bucket. What could she have done? Called the police?* I hadn't thought quickly enough; I was so unprepared to be treated in such a way.

With the dusky fading light, the old building loomed like every child's vision of a haunted house. Though the land looked flat, it was deceptive: there were dips and rises, with bunches of grass and weeds, and sitting on the ground, we were hidden from view from any direction, including from the road, about a quarter mile away. It should have made me feel safe, but after a day like we'd had, it just made me feel more alone.

The light was fading fast. I set up the tent, trying to remember anything I'd ever learned about rattlesnakes, knowing most of it probably consisted of old wives' tales. I got up and walked backward, dragging my boot heel in the dirt, making a little furrow circling the campsite. I'd heard that kept away snakes. I hugged Rainy and Amanda, then crawled into the tent, feeling battered from the worries and the miles. Gypsy crawled in beside me, and I zipped us in.

Gypsy and I shared a few sips of water from the canteen, saving a small amount inside. Darkness became complete. I couldn't see a thing if I peeked out the screen window, but hearing Rainy and Amanda stir now and then was a comfort to me.

As I lay still, the emptiness of my belly started to nag at me. I turned the lantern back on. I held the unappetizing cans of cold corn and fruit cocktail near the light, but the labels were so faded they didn't tell me much. My stomach was making noises—I hadn't eaten since the day before. I plunged the can opener on my knife into the can of corn and cranked it around the top. I cupped a handful of dry dog food and placed it on the sleeping bag for Gypsy. She picked at it delicately, and I patted her head affectionately. She showed no interest in my food, which was rare…and probably not a good sign. I used my camp spoon to scoop out kernels of the watery corn, eating about half the can, then pushing it away, hoping maybe the fruit would be better. A minute later I pushed that away, too. I was hungry, but not desperate yet.

I turned off the lantern, listening to mostly silence and the shuffle of hooves, a few insect noises, and the rustle of the brush in the breeze. These sounds lulled me to sleep.

My eyes opened as I felt a feather-like tickle against my calf. I could see Gypsy looking at me in the dark. I felt another movement on my leg—like a pinch this time. I scratched at my head and sat up, grabbing for my flashlight.

The beam illuminated a shadowy column-like shape, like a thick, dark line, out of focus on the tent wall. I scooched backward, unsure of what I was seeing. From the glow of the light, it almost looked like a strange streak of dirt. But was it moving? I rubbed my eyes, still swatting distractedly at the itchy sensation on my arms and legs.

My eyes focused. The dark column moving up the side of the tent was ants.

And they were not on the outside.

I slapped at the spots on my arms and legs even more as I saw the ants crawling down the sides of my tent and over everything in it, including me. They were heading for the open cans of unfinished corn and fruit that I had pushed aside and forgotten.

I scratched and brushed and tried to get all the tiny demons off me, but they fell from the ceiling back into my hair. Desperate, I started to step outside to shake out my sleeping bag when I remembered my new fear of rattlesnakes. What a choice! I grabbed my boots (vigorously shaking them first), pulled them on, then dragged everything out of my tent. *I must be a sight,* I thought, standing there in nothing but a t-shirt and cowboy boots, shaking things wildly like a dog with a rag.

It wasn't working. In the blackness of night, quiet except for my antics, I took the whole tent down and turned it inside out, shaking it until I could shine my light along the seams and the corners and see that the last of the ants were gone. I wearily set it all back up again in the dark. I had no idea what time it was when Gypsy and I crawled in, and at last sleep came again.

For a while.

There's a feeling that comes with being awakened from the depths of sleep by something unknown. It's not the normal stirrings, the ebb and flow of slumber, but a buried knowledge that tangles dreams and sounds together. It was from that primal place that something caused my eyes to open once again, my heart to race, and my sense of recognition to claw its way back to the surface.

My eyes opened to the blackness. I gathered my senses and tried to understand why, in this moment, the one thing I felt was fear.

My mind began to clear and then I knew.

The sound that woke me was the slow turning of tires, crunching on the gravel of the long driveway that led behind the old house, to my tent, to my animals, and to me.

I sat up. Gypsy was up, too, her ears and eyes pointed in the direction of the sound. Why would a vehicle be driving slowly toward this abandoned ranch house in the wee hours of the night?

I crawled onto my hands and knees, instinct making me move as quietly as possible, and peered out the zippered opening of my tent.

Only a little light from the stars filtered through the deep darkness, allowing me to make out a dark-colored truck moving stealthily down the private road. Chillingly, the headlights were turned off. Adrenaline sent my heart rate up.

I tried, for a moment, to calculate the reasons that someone would be coming toward my tent, in the darkest hour, in this darkest spot in the middle of nowhere—and none of them were good. Out the back screen, I saw Rainy and Amanda, two familiar shapes, alert now, too, watching and listening.

There was no one point where I was aware of making a decision. There was just me, and the three animals I would do anything to protect. I did not move impulsively but in a measured, calculated fashion. I unzipped the back of the tent in case I had to run. I did it slowly, but the small clicking of the zipper sounded loud in the darkness.

I reached over to the canvas bag that held the gun and slid the weapon out. With the heel of my palm I shoved the magazine in and turned toward the front of the tent. The truck was almost to me. I used one arm to brace and keep the gun steady, and aimed, flipping the safety off.

I sat in perfect stillness. All thoughts in my brain receded; I focused entirely on keeping my aim steady.

The tires ground to a halt, the sound so close now it made me shiver. I heard the door quietly opening, then the "snick" of it being shut carefully. The sound of boots on gravel, approaching.

I couldn't breathe correctly, as if the right amount of air wouldn't come into my lungs. I heard the person stop right outside the tent. I saw the dark shape of a pair of boots and legs through my screen. Rainy and Amanda stirred and pawed, sensing something in the air. The intruder stood there. I was as still as any human could will herself to be.

"You in there?" came a gruff voice, startlingly near, the sound magnified by the night.

I shrank further into my stillness and didn't answer.

"Hey—you in there?" the man called again.

I weighed whether to warn him I had a loaded gun trained on him, in hopes it would scare him away, or whether I should take advantage of the element of surprise.

"What do you want?" I tried to sound assertive and my voice sounded strange, even to me.

I tensed, waiting for him to take one step closer. My finger on the trigger moved just a hair.

"You awake?" he asked.

Again, I growled, "What do you want?"

His steps had ceased. "Uh, are you the girl that's riding the horse through here?"

"WHAT DO YOU WANT?" I shouted.

"Uh." He paused, his voice sounding almost nervous. "You was lookin' for water earlier? Stopped up the road lookin' for water?"

"Yeah? So?" Who *was* this guy? For a moment, there was only silence between us. The gun began to feel heavy in my hand.

"Well..." Another pause. "Sorry if I scared you. I know it's late, I just..." The boots shuffled and shifted a little. "I been lookin' for you since I got home and my wife told me a gal had ridden up lookin' for water..." He paused, discomfort apparent in his voice.

I kept the gun trained on his torso, but my edge, the high tense edge that kept the gun steady, had eased ever so slightly.

"She, well, I don't know why she'd do that. I tol' her she shoulda helped you," he went on. "Give you some water at least. Anyway. I'm sorry for that. That's not how we was raised. I'm sorry you didn't get no help at our place."

The man sounded old, I realized, and tired. But my nerves were wound way too tight to just shut down my fear. I didn't lower the gun yet, but I relaxed a notch more. I stayed silent.

"So I been lookin for you, to say sorry my wife treated you that way."

After a moment I said, "Okay."

He shuffled again. "And, uh, I got five dollars here for you. In the morning you'll ride up on a diner, this side of Dalhart. I'm leaving this here so you can buy breakfast. On me." Another pause. "And my wife."

"Okay," I repeated. Then, quietly, "Thanks."

"It's right here. I'll put a rock on it so the wind don't blow it away."

I heard him move away, the gravelly sound distinct in the pre-dawn quiet. His black silhouette faded from my tent screen.

There was the sound of the truck door opening, then he called back, "You take care, now, hear?"

I waited for the truck door to slam shut and the engine to come to life and the wheels to crunch on the stones as he turned around. Only then did I lower the gun. Through the screen, I watched the dark shape of the truck crawl up the road and the small red flash of brake lights before he turned east on the two-lane.

I looked down at the weapon in my hand, like I didn't know how it had gotten there. I switched the safety back on and set the gun down beside me, the handle warm from my grip. I pulled my knees up close and wrapped my arms around them, my body shaking all over as if it were cold. Resting my forehead on my knees, I sat for a long time, until the stars grew dim in the endless sky above.

## FULL CIRCLE

At first light we set out toward Dalhart. True to the word of our late-night visitor, after several miles, we came upon a diner on 54 West. I tied Rainy and Amanda, and Gypsy and I walked in with my collapsible bucket.

"I need to get water for my horse and mule," I said to the man at the counter, wasting no time for a greeting or to request permission. Friendly enough, he showed me right away where to fill the bucket.

I watched as at last, Rainy and Amanda had their good long drink. Some of the tension I'd been carrying began to fade with each slurp the two made. In my pocket, I felt the five-dollar bill that had been placed under a rock in the middle of the night. I allowed myself to hope we were working our way back to our usual good fortune.

In Dalhart there was a veterinary clinic with small pens in the back where Rainy and Amanda could stay the night. The vet offered to give both of them wellness exams…and when he charged me twenty dollars, I knew it was a fair price. I silently handed him my last twenty, telling him I'd be back to check on Rainy and Amanda in a bit. I did not mention I had nowhere to go.

I walked into town without one cent on me. I had no plans for food or shelter that night, but along with the pressure to figure it out, there was actually a bit of a thrill, because I didn't know how the day would play out. It was faith and foolishness that provided that strange anticipation and sense of challenge that came from not knowing what would happen next. The way things turned out was up to my wits, and my luck, and *completely* up to me.

Gypsy and I wandered around, trying to get a feel for the town. I half-scouted for spots I could sleep if I had to. I knew I would be able to reach my parents at some point and have them wire me some of my cash, but in the meantime, I was on my own in Dalhart.

By the time I headed back to the vet clinic, I'd pretty much decided to ask the vet if I could sleep on the ground near my animals. But before I had a chance, he handed me a scrap of paper.

"This guy wants to interview you," he mentioned casually. "Said he hoped you'd call before five." The clock on the wall showed five minutes before five o'clock.

I looked at the scrap. *Bob Wilcoxson, Dalhart Times.* I dialed the number from the clinic phone.

"Can I ask you a few questions?" Bob Wilcoxson asked. "I'd also like to show you around and tell you a little about Dalhart."

"Sure," I answer, happy for the company.

Bob turned out to be a kind-eyed older gentleman, and after talking with him a bit, I felt comfortable enough to take a drive and hear about Dalhart and its history. Before long, I'd learned all about the famous XIT Ranch and the big cowboy reunion that the whole town took part in every year. I was entertained with tales of the railroad, Indians, and tornados. Bob stopped to make a phone call and came back with a smile, saying, "My wife Betty would like to meet you. She wants to know if you—and Gypsy, too, of course—can have dinner with us."

"That would be nice," I replied, knowing then that our luck had indeed changed. While eating dinner, the invitation was extended for me to spend the night, and I couldn't help but grin.

As I left the next morning I learned the invitation was a special kindness. In the car Bob explained that Betty was battling a serious illness and hadn't been up to having visitors. He lingered as I packed up Rainy and Amanda, then asked me to write and let them know how we were doing, farther along the road. He handed me a folded-up bill as we said goodbye.

I didn't protest as much as I usually did when people tried to give me money, but I asked, "Are you sure?"

Bob smiled warmly. "Please take it."

I looked down at the twenty dollar bill in my hand and thought of how I'd handed over my last twenty to the vet when we'd arrived in town the day before. What happened was *not* just up to me and my wits and my luck. The kindness of strangers had played much more of a role in our journey. My animals and I had walked pretty much in a straight line, east to west, across the country. But in Dalhart, Texas, I saw it, I really got it, how things went full circle.

**21.** Another photo taken by a reporter in Western Ohio.
*Photo by DM Crawford of* The Herald

**22.** I always asked reporters to send copies of their articles and photos home to my parents.
*Photo by Virginia Peterson of the* Wilmington (Ohio) News Journal

23. Near the Indiana border, waiting for a group from the local boarding barn to join us for half a day's ride. People always requested that Gypsy be in the saddle for pictures, although she grew to spend a lot of time roaming on foot whenever we were in safe areas.

24. In southern Indiana. I would just stop whenever and wherever it felt right to give the animals a break and find a little peace.

25. While staying the night in an old barn along Route 50 near Flora, Illinois, I put my sleeping bag on the top of an old picnic table because I could hear rodents (and other critters!) moving around on the ground. Gypsy jumped right up on the table with me.

26. Heading southwest across Missouri as we left Luxenhaus Farm near Marthasville.
*Photo by Hostkoetter Photography*

27. While taking a break after a discouraging day in the excessive heat, Good Dog Gypsy grabbed my hat to get me to play with her.

28. Rainy bravely crossed this suspension bridge in the Ozarks of Missouri.

29. Nannie Jenkins and Anthis Wright (with Anthis' son, JT) on the farm in Wheatland, Missouri, that they ran on their own.

30, 31. It was a time of worry, caring for Rainy and waiting to see what would happen with his injury. Tom Kee (shown) and his wife Barb made us feel at home in Yates Center, Kansas.

32. Minutes after the first time Rainy and Amanda met at the Kees' farm.

33. Back on the road with Amanda the mule sharing the load.

34. From an article in a Wichita paper.
Amanda took right to the traveling life.
*Photo by Bill Youmans of the* Wichita Eagle

35. A reporter's photo from windswept
western Kansas.
*Photo by Tim Stucky of* The Kingman Journal

36. At an unplanned roadside stop that offered shade trees along Route 54 in the Texas Panhandle. We stopped and rested often during each day's ride.

37. My typical view was from between Rainy's ears. Here we are crossing into Mountain Time Zone in western Texas.

38. At this stage of our journey, the animals were so used to posing for the camera, they would stand patiently as I clicked shots at landmarks.

tie
of the wagon
the solitary
ending his
re gone. At
think. But a
nton, N.Y.,
s Lunas on
e that those

big, rangy
Raindance,
the Dave
She was on
oints west
*Bulletin* for

ble young
reamed of
for a long
ight-year-
and long
nd setting
raging 20
nce made
up for a
n. That's
ined the
r needed
lissy on

ypsy, a
to ride
saddle.
bly well
are at
e but
e time

friends
spent
friends
them,
e next

**MISSY PRIBLO AND FRIENDS**   NEWS-BULLE

**39.** A news photo taken south of Albuquerque.

*Photo by Barbara Beattie of the* News-Bulletin

**40.** At first I used hobbles on Rainy to keep him from straying too far, but after a while, I knew he and Amanda would stay near our camp. This was near Prewitt, New Mexico.

## ANTELOPE

As we made our way on the road west of Dalhart, Rainy stopped and focused his ears forward on the open land to the south. I looked to see what had captured his attention. Movement caught my eye as a herd of antelope bounded over the brushland—long antlers and splashes of white on their chests. The pronghorns leapt, fast and soundless, across the high desert, graceful and delicate at the same time.

I reached forward and stroked Rainy's neck. "Thanks, Bud."

Not long after seeing the antelope we rode down a private road on the ranch where my next contacts, JD and Kim Hieman, lived and worked. A cowboy stepped out from one of the barns and reached to take the reins and Amanda's lead like it was proper manners for him to take care of my animals for me. His knowledgeable eyes appraised my horse as he patted my buckskin's neck.

"What do you call this fella?" he asked.

"Well, his *real* name is Arizona Raindance," I said proudly, "but I call him Rainy."

"Oh," he replied. "Okay." As he gathered the reins and led my horse to the barn, I heard him say quietly, "C'mon, Ol' Buck."

Several horses whinnied when Rainy and Amanda entered the barn. A young dark colt in a box stall caught my eye. He had lovely conformation but his face—most of his head, actually—was misshapen and swollen way beyond normal size.

"Oh my gosh!" I exclaimed. "What happened to this guy?"

"Snake-bit," was the succinct answer I got.

"Wow." I reached a hand over the stall door. The colt looked at me but lacked the usual energy and curiosity of a horse so young.

"Is he going to be all right?" I asked.

The cowboy shrugged. "Up to him now. We've done all we can." He swung my saddle and packs up onto a saddle rack, looked over at my face, then added, "I think he'll make it, though."

JD and Kim were a young couple with two children, Myah and Cody. Kim had a way of reaching out and making me feel like I was part of the family, too. We did the dishes together, standing shoulder to shoulder, Kim washing while I dried. I asked about the snake-bit colt, and learned that most of the big fat snakes around the ranch weren't rattlers.

"Don't worry about those king snakes," Kim said. "They're actually good; they keep the rattlers away!"

Kim told me how she met JD and wound up on a ranch in such a lonely part of the Texas Panhandle.

"I swore I wouldn't fall in love with a cowboy," she said with a sigh, shrugging as if to say, *Who can argue with the forces of love?*

I swiped a dishtowel across a plate while Kim told her children to get ready for bed. I hoped I would remember these things, the lessons about how amongst the cranky folks and the disappointments, turning down the next road could lead to a place of warmth and kindness. A place where they know there can be good snakes as well as bad. A place where they know it's worth it to nurse a sick colt back to health.

The hard experiences and the good ones can be all mixed together in the same place. It's like riding through barren lands. Look around. There may be antelope.


## WEST

We made our way onward through the brush and sage, over the rolling road, until, looking right between Rainy's ears, I read the block lettering on a roadside notice that said, "Entering Mountain Time Zone."

I'd had a sense that I could feel the rise of the land as we worked our way west. This confirmed to me that I was in touch with the land beneath our feet in a way I'd never known before.

Not long after the change in time zone, we came upon another sign. I felt a lifting inside, and I knew that the hard Texas part of our journey was finally ending. I jumped from the saddle to pose the animals for pictures near the colorful monument that announced, "WELCOME TO NEW MEXICO, LAND OF ENCHANTMENT."

JD and Kim had arranged a stop for us with George and Tink Nixon at Nara Visa, just over the line in New Mexico. When we arrived, George Nixon pumped my hand with enthusiasm, and then—unlike most people, who wanted to know all about Rainy—he lit up at the sight of Amanda. George was a mule man. Thrilled to see that I'd discovered what a mule was capable of, he expounded their virtues in a way only one who truly appreciates mules can do. He even gave me a reining demonstration on his lovely red mule, Kate.

We stayed an extra day with George and Tink, enjoying an overdue day of rest. The Nixons introduced me to the culinary plea-sure of taco pie, and George made arrangements for us in Tucum-cari and other towns to the west.

"Tink and I don't like the idea of a little gal like you riding out alone in this country," he said.

For much of the ride from the small town of Logan toward Tucumcari, a large flat-top mesa was visible in front of us. Tucum-cari Mountain broke up the horizon, its shape and colors revealed as Rainy carried me nearer, with Gypsy draped across the saddle. Originally, I'd believed the area to be spare and empty, but now I knew there were more colors and shades to rock and shadow than I'd imagined.

Winding our way past the mountain was a mark of our prog-ress, a sign that the flatlands of the Great Plains were to our backs.

There are a few explanations for the unusual name "Tucum-cari," but they sound modern and contrived. The explanation most widely accepted by historians is that the name is derived from the

Comanche language, and means something similar to "to lie in wait for something to approach." It's believed that Comanche raiders and war parties used the flat mesa top to do just that—watching for enemies and prey, and cowboys and Mexicans driving cattle along the many trails that crossed the area.

If land had a spirit, I believed that this place's spirit was represented by the mysterious mountain. If spirits were to lie in wait on the flat mountain top and watch for something to approach, on this day, they would see four travelers—horse, rider, dog, and mule—riding west together, dusty and tired, but moving in harmony.

## TUCUMCARI

The area around Tucumcari was full of connections to the past. Preserved dinosaur tracks could be found in Quay County, and the town's beginning was tied to the railroad and the colorful era thought of as the "Wild West." Route 66 eventually put Tucumcari on the map as people following the famous road from its start in Chicago found the town a welcome respite from the barren drive across the Texas Panhandle. If Tucumcari Mountain was the spirit of the town, then Route 66, "The Mother Road," was its heart. Of course, with the interstate pulling travelers away from the two-lane roads, reminders of Tucumcari's heyday had faded to just a few candy-colored neon signs, still glowing in the hope of leading travelers to mom-and-pop diners and lodgings.

West of town, Route 54 ran together with Route 66. My animals and I took a break at Stuckey's Truck Stop, where we posed for pictures and a trucker bought me lunch. I was warned that there wasn't much out the way we were riding but railroads and ghost towns.

I set up camp near the tracks at the tiny town of Montoya. It was a well-hidden spot, with old cattle pens for Rainy and Amanda. I had a dinner invitation at the Bidegan Ranch nearby, so when

Rainy and Amanda seemed settled, I walked with Gypsy up the long private road to the house.

For no particular reason, I looked down, and when I did, I stopped mid-step. Inches from my boot, marching along and about to crawl right over my foot, was a big, black tarantula.

Gypsy froze right beside me. A spider was not something that would normally catch her attention, but this one was so large she stared down at it, ears fully upright. The creature was as big as the palm of my hand. I could see every detail of its hairy body.

I looked at Gypsy and she looked at me, but other than that, we didn't move. The tarantula veered away just before it reached the toe of my boot, turning and crawling up the red dirt road ahead of us.

I mulled over the gritty land, full of beauty and hidden dangers, as we walked on. Had it really been just a few weeks before that I was walking around in my sneakers?

## HITCHHIKER

After camping and riding along the tracks, red dirt clung to everything. All four of us wore a fine coat of it as we rode along a narrow two-lane road with cracked and broken pavement.

Somewhere off to the right, Interstate 40 rolled on. Once in a while, parts of the old road and the highway would wind closer together, but mostly the sight and sound of trucks and cars were obscured by low hills as we trod a more meandering route.

At one of the points where the old and new byways were within sight of each other, we were somewhat startled to come upon a dark-haired man, standing on the opposite side of the highway fence. This was not the land of pedestrians.

The guy waved enthusiastically, then swung himself over the fence with a lively leap, jogging toward us. He carried nothing, though he wore the look of someone who'd been on the road a while. I stayed on Rainy and tried to get a read on him. He looked young. He had a few days' worth of beard going and hair in need of a trim, but there was a definite spark of life about him...as well as a winning smile.

"Hey! What's up? I can't believe you're out here!" he greeted me with enthusiasm. "Hey, good dog!" He reached down and ruffled Gypsy's fur. I rolled my eyes as she immediately sprawled tummy up at his feet.

"What are *you* doing out here?" I countered, looking at the high desert terrain around us.

"I'm John," he said, happy, it would seem, to tell his story. "I'm hitching all around the country, and it's been great, man. But here's the bummer." John paused for emphasis. "Someone stole my backpack in Dallas. Sleeping bag, clothes, everything I had. But I decided to still try to make it to California hitching and meet up with my friends there."

Dallas, Texas, was a long way from where we were. John reminded me of a half-grown pup that wandered away from home, got into a bit of trouble, but was good-natured enough to still have a lark. I wondered how he'd made it to New Mexico with no money and no food...but if anyone believed in impractical journeys, it was me. I hopped off Rainy and opened my packs.

John asked what my story was, and I filled him in, handing him my canteen. He drank greedily but briefly, leaving most of the water. I pulled out every bit of food I had and offered it—he picked carefully and ate hungrily, although he was hesitant to take much. I insisted he pocket a few packs of crackers and a candy bar for later. We talked in the way of people who have not enjoyed conversation in a while: too fast, interrupting each other, exclaiming happily at each other's tales of both incredible kindnesses and dangers narrowly averted.

We walked together a ways, me leading Rainy and Amanda so we could keep chatting. As the sun sank lower in the sky, he glanced a time or two over in the direction of the highway.

"I guess I'd better get back out there if I'm gonna get a ride," he eventually said. He gave me a friendly hug and stroked Gypsy again. Then he left us, looking over his shoulder and waving once more before he jumped the fence and disappeared into the brush, making his way toward the highway.

What must have been an hour or so later, the highway was once again running within sight of the old road. Suddenly, a sound usually reserved for rock concerts and rowdy taverns punctured the quiet heat of the day. "WOO-WOO! OW-WOO!" A green van rolled down the interstate, and there, with most of his upper body hanging out a side window, was John, yelling as loudly as he could.

"Awright! Awright, John!" I shouted back, laughing out loud at his antics. I raised my fist high in the air for him—for him getting a ride, for him having his adventure.

"GO FOR IT, BABE!" were the last words I could distinguish as the van drove on into the sun, and the wind and the road carried him away.

## CUERVO

In Eastern New Mexico, we no longer stayed in houses most nights like we had earlier in the trip. Instead, a contact usually meant I had permission to use a set of pens or camp on ranchlands.

One morning I woke to chilly air and a cold drizzle soaking everything. I started out wearing my flannel and my sweatshirt, but the dampness seeped in, no matter how I covered up.

We were traveling what remained of Route 66 where it ran together with Route 54 when we came upon the town of Cuervo. It was easy to see why the truckers called it a ghost town. We rode past a few broken-down and decaying buildings, and a feeling of lifelessness permeated the area, so I was surprised to discover a diner open on the north side of the road. I tied Rainy and Amanda nearby, and went in, Gypsy at my heels.

A man and a woman at the counter turned in mild surprise at the sound of the door opening. The place was tiny—just a counter and a half-dozen stools. A garage was attached next door. There was an awkward moment of silence as I wondered where to sit. The woman got up and wiped a spot clean at the counter, which I took as an invitation. I got the impression there wasn't a whole lot on the menu, so I kept it simple.

"I'll have a cheeseburger."

The woman stopped wiping. "We're out of cheese," she stated.

"That's okay. A plain burger is fine," I assured her, as the man got up and headed to the garage without a word.

Though it was gray and dingy in the diner, it was a comfort to hear the sizzle of the burger she threw on the grill. The scent of it mingled with a faint automotive smell of oil and gas from the garage, which might seem unpleasant but was actually the opposite. The man came back in the door at one point, stared at me for a moment, then left again. There was no sign of anyone else around. No cars passed on the road as I sat and ate, Gypsy dozing at my feet.

The woman behind the counter made small talk, and when it was time for me to pay the bill, she wouldn't take my money. I thanked her, feeling guilty for the gesture when it looked like I would probably be the only customer to wander in that day. I got the feeling that when I rode away, the man and the woman would look at each other and say, *Well, that's it. We tried.* They'd turn the sign in the window to "Closed," turn out the lights, and soon the faded diner and the garage next door would tilt and crumble and become just another ghost in this old town.

## WHAT GYPSY UNCOVERED

As we traveled, people often asked if I was scared to camp alone. I always told them no, that I found it to be peaceful. The absence of manmade noise opened my senses to the sounds of the evening: the little contented noises of the animals and the quiet of the land around us.

Deep in New Mexico, a rancher gave us permission to camp by his pens in the hills, and the night found us in lovely surroundings. The wide sky turned shades of dark gray and navy blue. I sat contentedly on the ground, and Gypsy came over, nudging me for attention. She squeezed herself right under my arm. It took me a minute to realize she seemed slightly agitated and wanted more than just petting.

She trotted back over to where she'd been scratching and nosing the dirt, worked at the spot a little more, then came back to sit by me again.

"What's the matter, gal? Having trouble with your project?" The pup looked up at me, and I scratched behind her ears. She leaned against me for a minute more, then went back to digging.

Tired as I was, it was tempting to just sit there, but I couldn't pretend Gypsy hadn't gotten herself into something. Her hind end was in the air, her front feet scrabbled furiously, and chunks of soil sprayed up from around her paws.

Curiosity got the best of me, and I stood up and brushed off my seat. Gypsy ran over with excitement, whirling in circles in front of me, obviously pleased that I was finally going to see what she'd found. Her anxious whine told me to hurry up.

The light was not good—we were in the sliver of time after dusk and before dark, when everything has a veil of gray over it. Gypsy scratched at the ground a little more, then stopped digging and looked up at me. Despite the fading light, I could see what she had just about uncovered. I froze mid-step.

It was a cowboy boot.

My heart lurched as I made out another cowboy boot next to it.

And they both appeared to be attached to something...something solid, in the shape of legs.

The loveliness of the night was forgotten. A chill ran through me. I didn't know what to do, so I just stood there, looking down in a sort of horror. Where Gypsy had been digging I could see a form that was the size and shape of only one thing—a human.

The growing darkness didn't hide the two legs spread, toes pointed down, or the narrow torso, the shape of shoulders, and the arms out to the sides, making two rows in the dirt like miniature speed bumps.

Even as my eyes registered what lay before me, my mind was denying it. I couldn't process the possibility that we were camping alone, way out in in the uninhabited hills, and that Gypsy had just uncovered what appeared to be a shallow grave. My mind just said, *NO.* My body was rooted in place.

Gypsy was grunting with her effort now, digging with her front paws and periodically stopping to run back to me. I didn't know if she was anxious or if she was trying to get me to come closer.

I let my feet move, just a small, slow inch. My hands flew up to cover most of my face.

I tried to think what to do. Then, slowly, my brain began to wonder why there was no smell—no scent of rot or decay. I looked over at Rainy and Amanda, peacefully standing at rest, undisturbed. Whenever we passed a flattened animal on the road, Rainy made an extra wide berth around it—he had a strong dislike for dead things. So why, right now, in the presence of what appeared to be a human corpse, was he so perfectly calm and relaxed?

I forced myself to move one step closer.

Something about the body now didn't look quite right. Trying to steady my nerves, I inched forward. The parts visible in the dark and the dirt were definitely dressed in a masculine fashion, and yet the figure didn't look like the right size for a grown man. But it didn't look like a child's body, either.

I went closer.

It looked...fake.

My whole posture changed. I straightened up a little and my hands dropped from my face back to my sides. I stepped more confidently toward "it," and Gypsy jumped up at me, glad we were finally checking it out together. I stared down from my closer vantage, bolder now—but I still didn't want to touch it.

I returned to our tent and came back with the flashlight, running its beam along the outline on the ground. The jeans were hiked up above the top of one boot, and I could now see that the "leg" under the clothes was a rusty metal pole. Bending closer, I glimpsed just a hint of stuffing poking out where Gypsy had dug at the edge of the tattered flannel shirt.

My breathing and heart rate began to normalize. We were not camping with a dead body, after all.

Still. I glanced around at our complete aloneness, the darkening sky and the horizon. I called Gypsy to me so she wouldn't uncover more of "him." I didn't want to turn it over and see the face. I didn't want to touch it at all, not even with the toe of my own cowboy boot.

It was a restless night. Although I wasn't scared, I was aware of the shadow the strange presence cast on our high lonesome campsite.


## GOODBYE ROAD

A pamphlet I read in a truck stop described this part of New Mexico as "where the Great Plains meets the Rockies." Mesas stood out in the miles and miles of dry, desert-like gritty soil spotted with tufts of bunch grass and sage.

The brochure described the stretch of road from Tucumcari to Albuquerque as "featureless," but whoever wrote that was missing so much. At the slow walking pace of my horse, I noticed the muted shades of rock and plant life. I felt the ever-present breeze, getting cooler by the day. We crossed paths with roadrunners and antelope. Gypsy developed a skill for flushing out jackrabbits, hidden to me until their sudden burst of movement.

We'd been traveling on a composite of three roads: old Route 40, Route 66, and Route 54—the secondary road my animals and I had been following for months. In Santa Rosa we came upon a split, marked with a collection of signs.

I jumped from the saddle and pulled out my map, laying it open against Rainy's side. Route 54 took a deep dive south, all the way to Mexico. Route 40 continued west with 66, going along with it for a while.

West was where we were going. The decision of direction should have been easy enough. Still, it felt like I was severing a tie somehow. We'd been on or near Route 54 since early summer, back in Missouri. It had taken us through farmlands, small towns, and high prairies.

I looked at the faded signs and the windswept road, then climbed back in the saddle. I twisted around, looking back and squinting a bit, as if, if I could just look hard enough, right down that center line, I might be able to see the green Flint Hills and Yates Center where Tom and Barb would be fixing supper and talking. I'd see Fort Scott, where Reid was probably wrestling an unruly calf or doctoring some horse about now. I'd see the sticky heat and colored sunsets of Missouri. I liked that we'd been on the same road for so long. It made me feel like my animals and I were still connected somehow to all the helping hands and kindness of the Midwest.

I turned back around and looked forward at Route 66, the worn old road in front of us, heading to where the sun set. I clucked to Rainy and Amanda, and we stepped onto the shoulder, saying goodbye once again.

## ▩ SKINS

The road wound upward into high, desert-like hills. If it hadn't been for the sun, I'd have worried we were getting turned around, veering from the direction I wanted to go.

The summer heat was gone, replaced by pleasant days and cool nights. The downward dip in the temperature brought out the snakes: In the mornings they sunned themselves on the pavement. Vehicles were a rarity; it was just Rainy, Gypsy, Amanda, and me, passing the rattlers carefully as they unfurled their long bodies on the road, soaking up the lingering warmth it offered. The animals and I grew used to seeing them in this sluggish state.

I spied a windmill ahead, which meant water. As we got closer, I could see a house, too—the first one in a while.

The conditions underfoot deteriorated when we turned onto the track leading toward the structures. Both appeared ancient and dry, like they'd grown there in the sand. What looked like bundles of twigs dangled along the edge of the low roof of the house. I thought they might be herbs and mesquite hung to dry. The door was open a crack.

"Hello?" I called.

No one came. No dogs barked. Abandonment hung in the air.

I turned toward the windmill. There was just enough breeze to turn the blades with a slow faint creak. It was on the other side of a barbed-wire fence, the line of posts and wire spreading far in each direction and out of sight. What appeared to be dozens and dozens of rattlesnake skins, and jackrabbit and coyote pelts, were draped along the fence, baking in the sun.

I considered our need for the water that might or might not be in the stock tank near the windmill. It was pretty unappealing to think of ducking under the skins, hanging there like a macabre laundry line, but I did it anyway, grimacing, and was relieved to find I was not unrewarded. I filled our collapsible bucket quickly.

As I got back on Rainy, the breeze picked up a little. The windmill turned lazily for a few seconds, and the skins on the fence blew in a strange dance. I sat unmoving—we all did—as if our silence was a part of the place. Then we turned back to the road and kept moving on.

## ▦ COLD NIGHT NEAR GRANTS

Our time alone together on the stretch of road that passed south of Albuquerque deepened the special connection I had with my animals. I spoke only to them, and they seemed to listen. However, the isolation wore me down a bit, making me wish for human contact and a little friendly conversation.

After several long lonely days, we arrived at a feed store outside Grants. The owner had left a bale of hay for us near the horse pens, along with a few apples and sandwiches next to the empty horse trailer where Gypsy and I were welcome to sleep that night. It was a simple thing, but it made me feel a little better that someone knew where we were.

I expected to have mail waiting for me, care of General Delivery, at the Grants Post Office. I also hoped to restock our meager supplies in town and try to find something warm to wear now that cooler temperatures had arrived—both while being very conservative with my money. I called to Gypsy and started the walk to Grants.

As luck would have it, there was a thrift shop, and I paid only twenty-five cents for a heavy wool sweater with a turtleneck to keep the wind from blowing down my shirt. With the warm sweater, a hot meal in my belly, and a pleasingly heavy sack of mail to read,

I felt a lift in my spirits as we walked back to the feed store. There was a cool, clear feeling in the air, and I put my hands in my pockets. I didn't need the autumn leaves of home to remind me that fall had arrived and change was in the air.

I threw a little more hay to Rainy and Amanda as the evening turned colder. I crawled inside my sleeping bag on the floor of the horse trailer, pulling the top of the bag over my shoulders to keep warm as I read my mail by the light of my lantern. Letters described what was happening back home: A favorite hangout was closing. Two of my close friends were getting married, and with some of my mail weeks old, the weddings were happening soon. It was a bit shocking to think of all that was going on without me. *"We wish you could be here,"* my friend Kevin wrote, knowing that I'd still be traveling when his wedding took place. I couldn't be there. I was thousands of miles away, lying on the floor of a horse trailer in the middle of the high desert.

I felt Gypsy stir beside me. A few seconds later I heard the cry of a coyote.

I saved Reid's letter for last, but it was brief and impersonal. I pushed the mail aside and laid my head down, my thoughts restless. I turned over, and through the trailer's back door, I stared at the patch of stars visible in the cold, clear sky. I listened for the coyote again, but all was quiet.

## AN OLD MAN, HIS COWBOY HAT, AND HIS SON

My feeling of separateness stayed with me as we rode out in the morning light. The wind had settled a bit and the sky was clear as we followed an old frontage road somewhere west of the town of Thoreau. I saw a figure way off in the distance, but it took some time to reach an elderly man, standing still, watching us. I reined Rainy to a stop next to the man, and my horse lowered his head, waiting in his gentle way for the man to reach out and pet him. Amanda tucked in beside Rainy, a little shy, waiting to see what took place.

"Name's Bill," the old man said. "I've seen you on the news, and I been out here, watching for you."

I smiled at him, thankful for the friendly gesture.

"How are you?" I asked.

"Fine, fine," he replied, brushing it off with a wave. "I saw you on the TV and saw how you said people are being real nice to you, so I wanted to give you this."

I noticed a cowboy hat in one hand. He held it up for me to see.

"A lot of stories are in this hat," he informed me. I could see it was well-worn, faded from days in the sun, the hat band stained dark. I didn't really want a cowboy hat, but I wanted to be gracious. When he held the hat out to me, I reached down from Rainy's back to take it.

"Thank you," I said quietly. "This is very nice of you."

He nodded his acknowledgment, looking serious. "I just want to know why you didn't do The Big One."

"Pardon me?" I replied, puzzled.

"Why aren't you riding The Big One? North to south? Canada to Mexico? Riding east to west is the easy way."

The *easy* way? I studied Bill and decided he was what my mom would kindly call "a little off."

"Well, I don't know," I ventured. "I think it's more miles from east to west, don't you?"

"My son, he might ride The Big One someday," the man said, ignoring my question. "That's what he talked about, a ride like you're doing. Only the hard way."

"Oh." I wasn't sure how to respond. "That would be nice. I hope he gets to do it."

The old man nodded, staring off into the distance as if he could see something we couldn't.

"My son can ride. I taught him to ride. He grew up on a horse."

I sensed grief or regret in the old man. I wanted to say I was sorry but didn't even know why.

"Well, I'd better be moving on," I said.

"Don't be in a hurry now," Bill insisted, looking at me intently. "Wait a bit."

Rainy and Amanda were starting to fidget, bored with standing on the side of the road. Rainy pawed a little, and I felt a small tug from Amanda on the lead rope. Gypsy sat quietly as the old man rambled on about his son and some things I couldn't quite hear or understand. I once more mentioned that we'd better go, but Bill again asked me to stay a bit longer.

The old service road had been empty all afternoon, but now a brown sedan drove into view and stopped behind our little gathering. A man got out of the car and approached us, notebook in hand—a reporter.

This intrusion bothered Bill, who interrupted the reporter's questions to tell him that his son would be doing the Big One someday. When the reporter mildly brushed him off, the old man said goodbye and turned to leave.

"Thank you for the hat!" I called to his retreating back. I wanted to think of something else to say, something kind, something that would matter to him as he walked stiffly along the dusty road, but the words failed to come.

I knew why he'd stayed talking so long, why he hadn't wanted me to ride on. He wore his loneliness like an old shirt; his aloneness far outweighed mine. I hoped maybe it was a little lighter for having found us.

## THE GREAT DIVIDE

Making our way toward Gallup, we stopped at a marker on the south side of the road. Solidly built of wood and stone, it informed us that we were crossing the Continental Divide. Even on a little-used road, crossing the backbone of America was worthy of a monument.

The Continental Divide is a line of mountain ranges, the most notable being the Rockies, that stretches all the way from Alaska into Mexico. It's sometimes referred to as "The Great Divide," and when you think of the distance and all the rugged slopes it encompasses, it is great indeed. It's the watershed line of where the continent's water goes: the creeks, streams, and rivers to the east of the Divide flow in an easterly direction and eventually end up in the Atlantic Ocean. The waters on the other side run west, to the Pacific.

In front of us rose layers of mountains, outlined against the sky. To the north, a line of red mesas marched parallel to our road. I'd seen them in the distance for a while, but they seemed closer, with shading and shadows now visible.

I tightened my collar around my neck, then sat on my hands to warm them for a minute. My goodness, we'd come so far. All those months ago, we'd stepped out of the farm driveway, and now here we were, riding across the spine of the United States. Like the drops of rain and the mountain streams, I could only hope the Divide would keep us in its westward flow.

As if to remind me of the unpredictability of where we were, the spit of the season's first snow—tight and tiny snowflakes—swirled on the wind, dancing crazily around us. They didn't seem to be falling from the sky; instead, it was like they'd just appeared, riding on the drafts of air, moving all around us and never making it to the dry ground. I studied the intricate details of each one as they landed on Amanda's dark coat, before her body heat made them vanish.

I shivered a minute and did up the last button on the neck of my sweater. I clucked to Rainy and Amanda, saying, "Okay, gal, let's go," to Gypsy, and we proudly took our first step across the Great Divide.

## LINES (CATTLE GUARD)

Things were going our way. We had the name of someone who'd offered us a place to stay for the night, and just as daylight faded, I saw a group of houses up ahead, on the other side of the new highway being built. There was an open space in the fence line that marked a cattle guard crossing.

Cattle guards are usually made of steel beams that cross a narrow pit in the ground, although some cattle guards are created by simply painting three-dimensional lines on the pavement to create the same effect. Because cattle, horses, and other livestock have less detailed vision than we do and have difficulty with depth perception, a cattle guard can create a visual barrier that prevents the animals from stepping across a fence line. This means you don't have to have a gate that needs to be opened and shut behind you.

The fence meant to keep livestock off the interstate was not built to accommodate a traveler on horseback—there was no gate that I could see. With a sigh I urged Rainy and Amanda forward toward the cattle guard, as if getting closer and staring at the problem would help me figure out a plan to get across it.

My relief was great as I looked down at the cattle guard and saw that this one was made up of lines painted on the pavement. Hallelujah! My horse and mule could walk right over it.

Rainy stopped and planted his hooves right at the "edge." I gave another little squeeze; he only extended his neck, lowering his nose to the pavement to inspect the "cattle guard" more closely. I gave him a moment, assuming my smart horse would figure out that it was not real and step forward across it. My assumption was wrong. I felt him shift his body slightly back, away from the painted lines

I dismounted and stood near Rainy and Amanda, patting each of them in turn. Reins in my hand, I stepped onto the false cattle guard in a casual manner. My horse did not step along with me.

I tugged a little, murmuring reassuringly, and again asked him to walk forward. He would not move.

I dropped the reins and walked back and forth across the lines on the road to show Rainy and Amanda that they wouldn't get their feet stuck, but they weren't buying it. I pulled Rainy's reins until they were stretched to the other side of the cattle guard and tugged again. Nothing. Neither horse nor mule would budge.

A man came out from one of the nearby houses and offered to help get my horse across, but I knew that a strange person pulling at him would just annoy Rainy. Soon the man's wife came out, too, and together, they suggested putting Amanda in front to see if she'd take the lead, but I knew better. There was no way she'd move from Rainy's side, not when he'd communicated his distrust of the situation in no uncertain terms.

I ignored my growling stomach and the growing dusk. A few lights glowed in the homes across the way. A truck stopped and the driver offered his thoughts on getting my animals across. Then, all on his own, Rainy reached his left front hoof out and laid it on the first line of the cattle guard grid. He looked down as if he was making sure, then the other hoof came forward. *Clip, clop*— slowly, lifting each hoof with care, Rainy finally walked across the painted lines.

*Hooray!* I thought. *Problem solved!*

Except it wasn't.

For the very first time since she'd joined us, Amanda decided she wasn't going to follow Rainy. She's decided that if it wasn't safe to walk across before, then it wasn't safe to walk across now. And this created an even bigger problem: Now that Rainy had crossed the painted surface and she hadn't, the rope I had casually wrapped around the saddle horn was stretched so taut a circus performer could have danced across it. The pressure of the mule's backward pull had caused Rainy to pull up short, and there we stood, more stuck than ever, with Rainy on one side not moving, and Amanda on the other…not moving.

By now, several cars and trucks had stopped on the side of the highway. Everyone seemed to have an idea of how to get us out of our predicament. One cowboy suggested blindfolding Amanda, so a helpful fellow ran to one of the nearby houses and returned with an old rag. I covered the mule's eyes, tucking the ends of the cloth in her halter straps to be sure she couldn't see. She still refused to give an inch.

Another man had a rake in his truck, which he offered to use to prod Amanda from behind. This only earned him a few kicks from her back feet that he just barely managed to dodge, along with laughter from the small crowd that had gathered.

Another guy claimed he could get any horse on a trailer. He produced a coil of rope from behind the seat of his pickup. "This always works with horses that won't load," he assured me. He asked two people from those gathered to get on either end of the rope, and then slowly had them close in, putting forward pressure on Amanda's rump. The mule didn't seem to be anywhere near changing her mind.

It was fully dark. Some people left, new ones arrived, and some offered a few unexplored ideas. Several trucks were parked along the side of the road, lighting up the scene. I was still contemplating our predicament when I noticed Amanda make an odd motion, tipping her head slightly and looking down. Before I could think about what she was cooking up, Amanda shifted her weight back a little and then leaped into the air from a complete standstill, flying over the entire width of the cattle guard and landing neatly and precisely on the other side.

A collective gasp rose from the small crowd, followed by exclamations of disbelief, and then a smattering of applause. We were past the obstacle—those simple yet immensely complicated lines painted on the road. When the last of the truck doors slammed and we were left alone in the darkness, I picked up the packs I'd taken off the animals earlier. Rainy, other than looking sort of surprised when Amanda suddenly landed beside him, appeared no worse for the delay. I loosened his girth and we all started to walk toward the houses nearby.

I cast one last look at the lines on the road. The cattle guard must have been at least ten feet across. I ran my eyes over Amanda's little body and shook my head. The mule had decided she wasn't going to step on those lines, and she hadn't. In her own time, she'd found her own spectacular way across.

## UNPLANNED

On a dirt road, we came upon a trading post. The small store looked like someone had tacked a creaky porch onto an old cabin. I jumped down and tied Rainy's neck rope and Amanda's lead to the railing out front. Gypsy sniffed about, showing interest in an old gum wrapper and other debris the wind had distributed. I let her go about her dog business while I went inside.

I was in the store only a few short minutes, but when I stepped back out, I was greeted by a horrifying sight: There was my little Gypsy, in the middle of being bred by a big, furry, black dog.

I yelled at them without thinking, and Gypsy turned her face toward me. But she remained coupled with the black dog. I did not want to believe what I was seeing.

After what felt like far too long, Gypsy and the big dog separated, and he casually ambled off, disappearing as quickly as he'd materialized. I was traumatized. I had seen no signs of my dog being in heat. I clung to the hope that Gypsy was so young, it would be an unproductive mating.

I carried Gypsy in the saddle with me for the rest of the day.

The next day, still feeling awful about the incident, I found a convenience store with an outside payphone and called Tom and Barb in Kansas. They each picked up a line so we could all talk at once. As I launched into my story about Gypsy, I could hear Tom's low chuckle; even Barb sounded like she was trying not to laugh.

"And the worst part of it is, I would *never* have chosen that dog for her!" I wailed.

This proved too much for Barb, who finally burst out laughing. "That's how parents always feel!"

"I just hope it didn't take," I said dejectedly. I heard another round of laughter from them and demanded, "What's so funny?"

"Oh, honey," Barb said. "It's just one of those things. It's… well…when you don't want it to, that's when it always takes!"

I didn't want to believe her. It was the height of irresponsible dog ownership to have Gypsy, not even a year old, impregnated with a litter of puppies when we didn't even have a home or a regular vet, or for that matter, anything normal about our lives at all. I felt just terrible about the possibility.

## FORT WINGATE

We spent a day and night with Candido ("Candy" to his friends) Garcia and his friend Barbara Dains. They helped me figure out my riding route for the days to come.

"Gallup is a wild town," Candy warned. "I wish there was another way to go, but there are no roads that don't go far out of your way. The weekends are crazy with bars and fights and all the drunks."

I was surprised a small town had such a bad reputation, and I didn't take his warnings all that seriously. Rainy, Gypsy, Amanda, and I would just pass through and be gone.

Candy presented me with three things before we set out: First was a full rain-suit cover-up—waterproof gear that would be invaluable. The second item was a pair of soft leather gloves. Every morning my fingers had been stiff and sore from the cold. Last, and perhaps most important, was a fencing tool. About the size of a pair of pliers, one end was a wire cutter, and the other part grabbed the wire, wrapped it, and pulled it tight. With it I could both cut wire and repair it. It would be invaluable the next time we encountered a cattle guard with no nearby gate. Candy and I didn't need to discuss the importance of rewrapping any wire I cut—anyone who had ever worked around livestock knew that.

Candy and Barb were both guards at Fort Wingate and had arranged for us to stay there before we reached Gallup. Since the 1940s, Fort Wingate had been used to store and demilitarize munitions for the United States Military. Its thousands of acres of land were also a refuge to herds of Mustangs, antelope, and buffalo. The area was connected to both the Zuni and Navajo cultures, and archaeological ruins existed on the land that could be traced back as far as the Anasazi—the ancient people of the Southwest whose disappearance as a society is the subject of study and debate.

Fort Wingate was a stronghold during the Apache wars, in the days of Kit Carson. It had the sad distinction of being the staging point for The Long Walk, when the Navajo were driven off their own lands. The last armed expedition the United States government ever made against Native Americans was from Fort Wingate, when the 5th Cavalry was sent to the Four Corners area after a group of Navajos in the early 1900s. It was later used as a refuge for Mexicans displaced by the Mexican Civil War and the Pancho Villa uprising in 1914.

Almost a century beyond these events, Rainy, Gypsy, Amanda, and I made our way to the fort. The guards on duty seemed to get a kick out of our arrival—my animals and I were a diversion from their regular work duties. We obligingly posed for pictures, and when the guards flirted with me, I flirted right back.

Still, I was aware that our light-hearted visit was like a slight breeze passing through, compared to all that had happened at Fort Wingate in its past. I was quietly awed by the idea that on this personal journey, our inconsequential footsteps stirred up the same dust where so many lives had been changed, and the history of this land, good and bad, was made.

## ▒▒ FEELINGS FOR NEW MEXICO

From Fort Wingate on toward Gallup the landscape around us became even more dramatic. From desert with sandy soil and prickly succulents here and there, we rode into red-rock country, the land of wind-carved mesas and mysterious rock formations.

Occasionally we crossed long dirt drives that led to small homes, miles from the nearest neighbor. I'd come to realize that the people in them were there because they were born to this land. I could imagine how hard it would be to leave the wide vistas, the swirling dust devils and the tiny orange and yellow flowers hidden low to the ground. I saw the beauty and felt the pull, too, but I understood that no one lived there because it was easy.

The wind was a presence that never left. There were times as we walked along when I thought, for a moment, *The wind's gone*. Then from somewhere across the vast openness, a breeze would come and lift Rainy's mane in front of me, rippling it up his neck, and ruffling the thick fur along Gypsy's shoulders. The wind carried a new coolness, a feeling of something distant, like the coming season or a faraway mountain. Even with the chill, the air was softer, taking the edge off a land that seemed hard and unforgiving, unless you breathed in the air fully and let it touch you.

## EAST OF GALLUP

As I rode along Route 66 near the outskirts of Gallup, we passed a group of about a dozen men, young and old, lounging under the only tree in sight. Empty glass bottles lay scattered on the ground. We were almost upon them before one of the young men looked up, and spotting us, yelled hello.

I greeted him back and as soon as my voice was heard, all the heads swiveled around in my direction.

I had to give Rainy a subtle squeeze with my legs, because he was so used to stopping when we encountered people on the road. I didn't want to be rude. I was not scared. But I knew this was not a good place to linger.

One guy said something I couldn't understand, and they all hooted with laughter. A few others chimed in, and I got the tone as they all snickered and laughed. One young man jumped up from where he was reclining, and in a ridiculous high voice intended to make his buddies laugh asked, "Where are you going?"

"Meeting some people up the road," I answered in a clipped manner.

"Stay here and have a drink!" he called. I shook my head. "We don't bite!" Then a moment later, "Hey, where you from?"

"I'm from far away," I answered, keeping Rainy moving forward, past their laughter, past their empty bottles.

Less than a half-mile down the road, I saw an odd shape, heavy and dark, lying motionless on the side of the road. Rainy raised his head and snorted as we got closer, the smell upsetting his sensitive nose. To my dismay, it was a dead horse, stiff and bloated.

Where I was from was far away indeed.

## SIDEWALKS OF GALLUP

Old 66 became the main street of Gallup, and arriving in the afternoon put us right in the middle of a mix of people and traffic in the little city. It was busier than I expected, and Rainy, Amanda, Gypsy, and I had to work our way around parked cars and wait for breaks in traffic to cross side streets. We made slow progress.

We came to a point where a concrete wall on the north side of the road shielded the commerce area from the railroad tracks, and the road narrowed and made riding on that side of the busy street difficult. We crossed over and stepped up onto the sidewalk, so we were passing just a few feet in front of the neon signs and storefronts squeezed in tight together in the downtown blocks. People stepped around to let us pass. No one seemed to mind the horse and mule downtown, and I tried to be extra careful of pedestrians.

We rode by one place where the only windows were small and set up high, about seven or eight feet off the ground. Beer signs cast colorful reflections in the glass. I always thought windows like this were meant to keep a bar dimly lit, and probably keep the patrons inside from being on view to sidewalk passersby. On Rainy, I was high enough to look in, and I did as we rode past.

A second or two later, I heard a door pushed open hard and wide enough to hit the wall and the sound of voices behind us. I turned in the saddle and looked back.

A stoutly built American Indian followed by a few other bar patrons had spilled onto the sidewalk. He had a long-neck bottle in one hand and oddly, a top hat on his head.

"OH, WHOA!" he blurted loudly. "Lady, you had me going for a minute there!"

His friends, also holding beer bottles, laughed and jostled him with their shoulders. They walked over to where my animals and I had stopped.

"Lady," he said again, looking up at me, shaking his head in disbelief. "I'm just sitting there, having my beer, right?"

I nodded to indicate I was listening. His lilting soft accent, where he rolled the Ls, made me smile and completed the comical picture of his round squat body with the incongruous hat on top of his head and the incredulous expression on his face.

"I'm having my beer," he continued, "and I look up at the window and there is the *tallest* lady on earth walking by! I thought I was dreaming or something, but then I look to the next window, and there she goes, walking by again! I said to everyone, 'Run outside! I want to see the ten-foot-tall lady that just walked by!'" Then, as if he was just figuring it out, he added, "And it's you!"

The small crowd laughed; I did, too.

"I'm only five-feet-something," I assured the man, "except when I'm sitting on this guy." I patted Rainy affectionately.

"Yeah! Yeah!" he agreed, raising his beer bottle in salute. "Man you got me going!" He and a few of the others came closer and reached out to touch Rainy and Amanda. Top Hat noticed Gypsy in the saddle, calmly observing the scene. "Look at your dog, riding the horse, too!" he marveled.

"Yep, she's something, isn't she?" I replied proudly.

"What's up? Like, what's this all about?" one of the other guys from the bar asked, tipping his bottle toward my animals and packs. "Where're you from?"

"I'm from New York."

Top Hat's mouth opened in surprise. "New York!" he exclaimed. "I didn't know they had horses in New York!"

A few more minutes passed as questions were asked and answered; it was a genial little group. Then my bar buddies realized they'd emptied their beers, and so wished us luck and headed back inside.

As I started Rainy forward again, Amanda stepping beside us, we heard the *whoop* of a siren, and the heads of the people around us turned toward the street. A police car barreled toward us, lights flashing. Vehicles on the street pulled over to the side, and the squad car came at us at an angle, stopping with one front tire up on the sidewalk, uncomfortably close to me and my animals.

There was no choice but to stay right where I was. The front doors of the police car opened simultaneously, and a uniformed officer stepped out from each side, then strode toward me.

People all around me froze in their steps, waiting to see what was going to happen, wondering what sort of crime had been committed. I was wondering the same thing.

One of the policemen stepped right up to Rainy's side and looked up at me. "You'll have to get off the sidewalk," he commanded in a deep, stern voice. "Now."

I smile nicely at him. "What?" Buying time. "Why?"

"You can't ride a horse on the sidewalk. It's unsafe," he answered. "It's a violation."

More people gathered, beckoned by the flashing lights.

I pointed across the main street to the lack of shoulder along the cement wall. "Look," I said. "It's more unsafe for us to be in the street." Rainy and Amanda stood perfectly still, as if watching the scene unfold around them, unfazed.

"You can't be on the sidewalk with a horse. This is a commerce area!"

"Okay. Just let me go up to there," I tried, pointing up ahead, not knowing but hoping there was a spot where the wall and the railroad tracks veered away and made the roadway a little wider.

Before I got a chance to argue further, my top-hat friend from the bar reappeared, stepping in quite close to the cop. "Aw, leave her alone," he said. "She ain't hurting nobody."

A murmur of agreement rippled through the curious crowd. I heard someone say, "Don't you have anything more important to do?" and someone else call out, "Leave 'em alone, they got a right to walk through town!"

It was an easy guess that the police weren't very popular with this group. I didn't know whether to laugh at the commentary or worry that the cops were really getting mad. The verbal back-and-forth got a little louder, and the two cops seemed unsure about their next step.

"It's okay," I announced. "I'll go back on the street." I looked directly at the policeman nearest to Rainy and me. I turned Rainy to the right, he stepped down over the curb, and we began to weave around parked cars. I waved goodbye to my crowd of defenders, shouting, "Thanks, you guys!" with a smile.

After watching me ride in the street for a minute, the policemen got back in their car and drove away. As soon as they were out of sight, I cued Rainy to the left, and we got back on the sidewalk to make our way through the rest of downtown, safe from the traffic. We were stopped a few more times—now by friendly passersby, offering their coats and hats. By the time we reached the western end of Gallup with the wind swirling grittily around us, I had three or four of each tied to my packs.

We'd been surprised a few times by unexpected bursts of hard rain, so when the sky got gray, I dismounted and unrolled my rain poncho, laying it across Amanda and the gear she carried. Not two minutes later, I was back on Rainy, and a blast of wind peeled the poncho back, wrapping it around the mule's hindquarters and back legs.

She exploded, bucking and kicking like crazy. Someone yelled, "YEE HAW!" from a passing pickup as Rainy twisted around to stay with her, and I tried to keep the lead from tangling around his legs. Amanda hopped and twisted in the air, tossing her head while her back end moved in a different direction. I held onto the lead rope and the reins and did all I could to stay in the saddle.

Finally, the rodeo was over. Amanda stood still again, breathing hard, with Rainy beside her, braced for more shenanigans. She was docile once more, waiting calmly for me to untangle the poncho that dragged behind her. I removed the offending article, rolled it up, and tied it behind my saddle. I'd take my chances on our stuff getting wet.

## NAVAJO WOMAN

We had crossed paths with a lot of different people as we rode through Gallup. One old Navajo woman caught my eye as we made our way because of her blouse—it was a beautiful rich velvet in a deep shade of midnight blue, and I had wondered, in passing, how she could be warm enough without a jacket on such a blustery day.

I hadn't thought of her again, but as I fixed Amanda's packs after her bronco routine, I noticed the same woman standing nearby, smiling at me. I said hello, and her smile got wider as she started to chatter, but she was speaking Navajo, and I couldn't understand her. I just smiled again.

Seeing more room on the opposite side of the main road, I looked over my shoulder to see if it was safe to cross over. The old Navajo woman was there. She crossed the street, too.

We were past the main part of town, but whenever I looked back, there she was, behind us, smiling and waving. I smiled and waved, too. Her pace was much slower than ours, and a couple times she fell quite a ways back, and I lost sight of her.

Outside of Gallup I stopped to give the animals a brief break, jumping down from the saddle and loosening Rainy and Amanda's girths. I rubbed Gypsy's belly when she rolled over, feet in the air, then reached into my saddle bag for the McDonald's hamburgers we'd been given and unwrapped one for Gypsy. I jumped when I turned and found the old woman standing right behind me.

"Oh, hi," I said, startled.

She smiled. "Hello," she said in English.

She was carrying two tote bags. I could see a few colorful skeins of yarn poking out the top of one. She was round—chubby in a solid sort of way—and neat in her pretty velvet top and long full skirt. She wore one glorious piece of turquoise-and-silver jewelry around her neck. The brown skin of her face was crinkled with age and years of sun. If she was cold, she showed no sign of it.

"How are you?" I tried. No answer, just the same big smile. I turned back to tighten the girth again, and she began to mutter something. I shook my head to show her I didn't understand.

I'd put my foot in the stirrup to pull myself up on Rainy's back when I heard, "Go with you." This, I understood. I put my foot back on the ground and turned to the woman.

"Oh, no," I said. "We're going far, very far." I made a pushing motion with my arm, palm facing west, trying to indicate a great distance.

"Go with you," she repeated.

The old woman's arms hung straight down at her sides. She was very still, making no movement at all, like she was waiting for me to mount up so we could all start walking again.

I shook my head. "Too far. Too far," I repeated. I had a brief vision of myself, knocking on someone's door down the road: *"Hi, can we camp here for the night? It's just me, my horse, my mule, my dog, and an old woman…"*

"I'm sorry." I said it a few times, trying to say no but be friendly at the same time.

Finally I got on Rainy, saying goodbye. It felt mean to walk away. But I didn't know what else to do.

The pace of a horse is somewhat faster than that of a human walking, especially a heavyset, older woman in a skirt. I thought she had only caught up with us at all because of the many times we stopped in Gallup. But I looked back and still, she was following. At first I could hear her chatter and see her smile. But as we gradually outpaced her, she got smaller in the distance behind us. I waved each time, hoping she understood my well-meaning gestures.

The last time I turned in the saddle and waved, I yelled, "Take care!" She was a short plump figure, far back in the fading light, far enough now so I couldn't be sure if she was moving or standing still. I didn't know whether to laugh or cry.

## KINDRED SPIRIT

After a windy night in the corrals at the "horse hotel" west of Gallup, we rode on in the morning sunlight. We hadn't gotten far when a police car came to a stop in front of us. *What now?* I thought. A New Mexico state trooper stepped out and walked over to where I'd brought Rainy to a halt. His eyes took us all in, pausing on Amanda, who had her long ears turned toward him as he approached.

"So it's true, then? You're riding across the country?" he asked.

"Yep, it's true," I answered. The officer reached his hand toward Amanda; she let him pet her nose.

"I've also heard that you're out prospecting for gold."

I laughed. With her small size, long ears, and the packs she carried, Amanda did bear a resemblance to every cartoonist's version of an old prospector's donkey. The trooper broke into a grin, and I shared with him some of the other rumors that had preceded or followed us. My favorite was from Ohio, where we had passed a schoolyard full of children at recess. By the time we reached the farm that was our destination that night, the family there had heard in town that I was a teen runaway with a gun and a wild fox that rode with me.

"Well, I'm glad I found you," said the trooper. "I was asked to give you something." He pulled a crumpled and worn envelope from his back pocket and handed it to me. Written in a shaky scrawl were the words: "For the lady riding across the country." I slid my finger under the flap of the envelope.

Inside was a crumpled ten dollar bill and a torn scrap of paper. In the same shaky writing, on the paper were the words, *God bless you.*

I looked up at the policeman, who had been watching me. "Who is this from?" I asked. "Is there a name so I can say thank you?"

He paused, taking his time before speaking.

"There was this guy, this really old man, who came into the police barracks," he began. "He was looking for you—said he'd heard there was a lady with a horse and a donkey, riding across the country. He figured we'd know where you were. I didn't, but I knew I'd find you sooner or later. There are only so many roads you could be on.

"The thing is, the old man walked to the barracks. He has no car or truck. One of the guys I work with sort of knows him, says he's a hermit or something and lives way out in the hills—a squatter on the land. This is the part you'll like: he came to these parts years ago on foot. I guess he walked all over with a couple of donkeys. All packed up, like yours." The trooper nodded toward Amanda. "He traveled around the reservation and all over the West, and ended up staying in these parts. That was a long time ago. He's really old now."

I imagined a young man, wandering and free, faithful little burros on the road with him. And I envisioned him now, bent and slowed by age, walking through stone and brush, on dusty roads and trails. All so he could give me ten dollars. And wish us blessings. My eyes filled as I again looked down at the money and the note.

"Good luck to you," said the policeman. "Be careful."

I thanked him, gathered up the reins, and called to Gypsy, waiting patiently at Rainy's feet. When I looked back, the officer was standing with his hand on his car door handle, watching us ride off. He touched his hat in a little salute.

Much of the time I felt like my animals and I were so alone on this journey. But we were not. We really were not.

## HERE AND NOW

It took some time in the beginning of our trip to adjust to the unstructured, fluid lifestyle on the road. I spent my energy worrying about what was up ahead, what was going on at home, what the future held. But now, each day felt like the only thing that mattered; each minute and each hour was a time in and of itself. I had to be in the moment to stay safe, and to see and feel all that was around us. There was no room for fretting about the future or the past. I didn't think about my final goal or what would happen after we reached it. Learning to live in the present was not a conscious effort; it was a natural result of our journey.

For some unexplainable reason, I became aware of the feeling of a westward pull on the far side of Gallup. Everything was flowing west: the traffic on the highway, the waters of the Rio Puerco River, and the trains on the tracks that ran together along with the roads.

On an unmarked road we passed a small sign for the Arizona line. The wind had calmed. The sky was clear and turquoise. I almost felt warm. Rainy's ears were forward as he stepped along smartly. Red rocks cast shadows on the sagebrush and brown earth.

I pulled the hat off my head and felt the breeze run through my hair. We were in Arizona! I wished I could call someone immediately and share the news. But the space was vast in front of us, hard-edged mountains rose in the distance, and I knew we wouldn't get to a phone for quite some time. I smiled to myself. That was okay. I had my three best friends right there with me. We'd share in the accomplishment together, like we shared everything, every day.

## NEAR LUPTON, ARIZONA

Just past the Arizona line, we veered back onto 66. Huge rock formations that seemed to be in the distance grew near, and the road wrapped along the foot of one great rock wall, leaving us in shadows as I rode under it.

Timing was on our side when just before dark, we came upon a small group of mobile homes. I walked Rainy and Amanda over to one of the trailers, its shell a flat white color, identical to the others around it. There were no yard decorations, no planters beside doors. Nothing twirled or chimed from the eaves. It was as if the hard wind and hard sun kept everything outside to a minimum.

I heard the sound of a light aluminum door banging open and voices. A young Navajo girl came from behind the nearest trailer. She had her eyes lowered as she walked; when she looked up and saw us, her mouth made a little "O" in surprise.

"I'm sorry!" I apologized. "I didn't mean to startle you."

She quietly waited for me to say something else. She was strikingly pretty.

"Do you live here?" I asked.

She nodded.

"Do you think I could ask your parents if I could camp near here tonight?"

She shrugged, moving closer and reaching to stroke Rainy's neck and shoulder. "He's soft," she said quietly. Then she looked at me. "You better ask them." She motioned with her chin toward the trailer.

I tied Rainy and Amanda while the young girl continued petting them. I walked to the nearest trailer door with Gypsy at my heels. I stepped up on the one thin metal step and the aluminum door opened before I could knock. A Navajo woman stood before me.

"Hi," I said. She didn't respond. She just waited, like the girl had done.

"My name is Missy. This is my dog and that's my horse and mule over there." I paused. Still no response.

"I'm riding from New York to California." Usually this got a reaction, but not this time. "Could I just tie my horse and mule here and get some water? I'd be camping just for tonight. We don't need anything else…"

"Okay," she said, unmoving in the doorway.

"It's okay?" I confirmed, unsure with so few words exchanged. She nodded, then closed the door.

I didn't know what to make of it—the woman didn't seem mad or bothered, really, but it was hard to be sure. I unpacked Rainy and Amanda. As I started to brush them, I was joined by the girl, who shyly told me her name was Frances. A few other children materialized, including one little boy named Leander who quickly became my favorite. He told me proudly that he was nine as he reached out and gently touched Rainy's neck.

The day wound down with the children and I quietly sharing the peaceful ritual of caring for Rainy and Amanda. The wind settled. The air had a softer feel and carried the faint scent of distant desert.

The next morning started the same way. Frances and Leander were up and ready to help me, long before school bus time. Leander wore a maroon jacket with "Rio Puerco Braves" printed on the upper left side.

"That's my school," he announced with pride, pointing to the logo. Then he asked, "Will you and Rainy be here when I come home?"

I'd almost finished saddling Rainy and Amanda; I shook my head apologetically as I answered, "Sorry, Leander. Rainy and I will be farther down the road." The boy nodded solemnly. All I could think to say to him before swinging onto Rainy's back was, "I hope you get a horse someday."

It earned a smile from him.

The morning sun rose behind us as we set out. We were a few miles down the road when the loud yellow school bus passed us, heading toward the highway. I raised my hand and, rising up in the stirrups, waved until the bus was gone from sight, just in case one of the round, open little faces pressed against the windows was Frances or Leander.

# A DIFFERENT VIEW

I followed dusty tracks, ranch roads, and parts of the almost abandoned Route 66. All these eventually led back to or near the new interstate. One of these forays brought us to where we could hear the hum of trucks on the highway. The trail became narrower and ended in a cluster of distinctive rocks that formed the backside of a rest stop. As we made our way around to the front, I could see a parking area and restrooms. After the solitude that had mostly filled my day, it was disconcerting to see people walking around and taking pictures of the rocks.

I unsaddled Rainy and Amanda for a break, and a few tourists came over to say hello. One couple, visiting from Japan, snapped what seemed like a hundred pictures.

Pleased at the unexpected bonus of finding this place, I hurried as I made my way toward the restrooms where there would be running water to fill my canteen and bucket. Real soap to wash my hands and face! And *maybe* even vending machines with cold soda and sweets!

Feeling fresher and cleaner than I had in a long while, I returned to my animals. It was pleasant out, with the sun at its high point in the sky. I was back to wearing just a t-shirt, the wool and flannel of previous days stashed in my saddle packs. I sat with my back against the warm rocks and watched Rainy and Amanda search for grass along the base of the red stone. It was hard to believe that we'd already seen flakes of snow and ridden through harsh, cold winds.

The colors of Rainy and Amanda and Gypsy stood out against the red rock and blue sky. I found my camera and climbed onto a nearby stone, framing Rainy in the sights. I stopped short and lowered the camera from my eye. I wasn't accustomed to seeing Rainy from this unusual vantage point. I stared at him. The smooth rounded curves of his hips were slightly, just slightly, more angular. He had lost weight.

I let the camera hang around my neck, jumped down, and went to my horse. I ran my hand along his ribcage. I felt the flesh along his neck. The difference was subtle. He had good muscle tone but…. Now that I was looking at him with a searching eye, I thought his coat was just a shade less shiny and vibrant-looking than usual. It was autumn, and back home he'd be growing his winter coat. I hoped that was all it was.

Being on the road was not an easy life, but it had seemed like Rainy was thriving. Throughout the trip, he'd looked like a healthy robust example of a Quarter Horse in his prime. I'd received quite a few compliments on his appearance. This was the first time I could see that he'd lost a little of that healthy bloom.

When I got back in the saddle, we rode into the sun, everyone in their place. Rainy's pace was steady and strong. But I chewed my lip, wondering what the change in Rainy's appearance might mean.

## ▨ DOUGLAS SKY

We traveled on through open land. Tall mesas rose here and there while hills seemed forever in the distance. As we neared a cluster of tall trees, I heard, "Hello!" and a man jumped down from the branches.

Gypsy, who'd been walking alongside Rainy, seemed the least surprised of all of us, wagging her tail and immediately trotting over to the fellow. She stopped at his feet and looked at him, waiting for him to pet her.

"Douglas Sky," he introduced himself. "I heard about your journey and was hoping to meet you."

I was amused by the idea of Douglas, waiting up in a tree, hoping we'd come along. Granted, there were not many other roads we were likely to be on, but his friendly faith that we would meet this way was endearing.

"Would you join my wife and me for a meal at our home?" Douglas asked. He assured me that my animals were expected to eat at his place, too.

I jumped off Rainy and walked alongside Douglas on a rough trail leading away from the road. We stopped at a small lean-to built into the slope of the sandy ground. Inside were two open stalls for Rainy and Amanda. Douglas poured a scoop of grain into the mangers for each of them; then we walked up to the house.

Douglas Sky's wife registered no surprise when she saw me on the doorstep with her husband. I figured I was not the only "stray" this friendly man had brought home. Mrs. Sky had a kind smile and was quiet and reserved, letting her husband do most of the talking.

They explained they were working on finishing their home themselves. It was small and very rustic, made out of juniper logs. In its two rooms, sunlight leaked in through cracks between the logs. It wasn't chilly, though; it was quite warm and homey inside.

There was no phone, no television. When Douglas asked if I'd like to wash up before eating, his wife heated a bowl of water over the flame of a gas stove. We sat down together at a small table, and when they clasped their hands and bowed their heads, I did the same. Mrs. Sky said a prayer in Navajo, adding a prayer for me and my animals, and our journey. We ate Navajo fry bread and vegetables grown in the garden I'd seen right outside the house.

As we talked during the humble and lovely meal, I began to understand Douglas' ability to empathize with me being a stranger on the reservation and in this land. He was from somewhere far away, like me. Douglas was a Lakota Sioux who had fallen in love with and married a Navajo woman.

Sharing time with the Skys showed me that there were all different ways of finding peace and a simple life. Everyone's quest for peace and simplicity was uniquely their own—whether the kind of road you traveled or the kind of home you made.

## FRIEND AMANDA

Amanda had been a trooper, carrying our load and adapting admirably to life on the road. Always a willing worker, she regularly demonstrated her allegiance to Rainy. While it felt like Rainy and Gypsy and I trusted each other implicitly, it still was different with the little mule. I would have been happy to have even a bit of that connection with Amanda.

We walked steadily, lost in the southwest wind and the beauty of the country. When we reached our place for the night, near some old cattle pens, I fixed a spot for Rainy and Amanda, checked hooves, and groomed them both. With them settled, I called to Gypsy. She ran over, darting back and forth as I walked around the area, studying the rocks and tracks in the sand.

Then I heard Amanda's unique call.

The mule used a variety of noises to express herself, and I recognized this sound as one of anxiety. I immediately turned and quickened my step to see what was wrong.

Nothing appeared to be amiss in the pens. Rainy had his nose to the ground, foraging. The only unusual thing was the way Amanda watched Gypsy and I approach, her large radar ears pointed toward us.

I went to her and scratched her neck. She gave a contented grunt or two as I pressed my hip against her and laid my arm across her withers while I scratched her shoulder.

Gypsy, sensing that our walk around camp was delayed, stretched out with a sigh and rested her head on her paws. I didn't want to do anything to disturb the moment. Even with her equine companion nearby, Amanda had called out to me.

We stood together in the last of the day's light. The air carried the fragrance of sage and the scent of the horses. I kept scratching Amanda, occasionally rubbing her ears or threading my fingers through her bristly mane. She leaned into me, ever so slightly. Actually, we both leaned a little on each other.

## SUNSETS, SEASONS

If you tried to paint the incredible sunsets we rode into in Arizona, there's no way you could make it look real. Only Mother Nature could get those colors to come together in that way. The sky before us melted into streaks of amber with violet edges, and all the colors blended into a horizon that spread flat and forever in front of us.

One sunset leading us westward was so absorbing that it was only when the light finally faded and left us riding in evening's dusk that I wondered why we were still on the road so late in the day.

No two days were exactly alike for my animals and me, but generally we managed to be near each day's end destination before darkness set upon us. That day's ride had felt easy enough, and I thought we were making good time.

I rarely ever knew the time, but *timing* mattered. I knew how many miles we could do in a day, and how many hours we should travel. My animals and my own body let me know if I pushed it. So the dark coming on before we'd reached a place to stop for the night didn't seem right.

Then I realized we weren't making bad time. My sense of mileage and pace was not off. It was something else.

The days were getting shorter.

I'd lost sight of all the markers that normally signaled that autumn was here. I'd heard no talk of "back to school" plans; I was a world away from "new fall fashion." There were no tree-covered hills turning orange, red, and gold, and my hands had not yet felt the new growth of a winter coat starting on Rainy.

I thought back to times in Illinois or Missouri when I'd be brushing Rainy, settling in for the night, and we could still see the sun, and my little radio would tell me it was past eight o'clock. I remembered being at the Kees', riding around with Reid and Gypsy when the day's chores were done, and the sun would still be sinking over the Great Plains.

It happened no matter where you were or what kind of journey you were caught up in. The planet turned slowly, making its way around the sun, and the seasons kept changing. My animals and I had gotten farther away—farther from the bright green fields of the early spring when we'd set out from home, thousands of miles behind us.

PART FIVE

———

# THE ROAD IS OURS

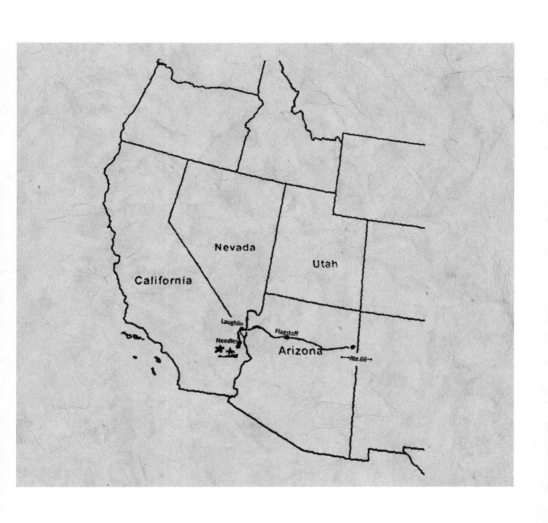

## CHAMBERS, ARIZONA

A bright moon lit our way as we reached Chambers, Arizona, in darkness. We'd made it to the only motel within miles; one lone vehicle sat in the parking lot. Inside the motel, doors and hallways looked unfinished, and tools, boards, and signs of renovations were everywhere. The clerk at the desk looked up and smiled, though, setting me at ease.

"We've been expecting you!" he said in greeting.

I had no reservations, nor had I made any type of contact with the motel. I wondered who had made the arrangements for us... Candy and Barb? Douglas Sky? A friendly stranger? The clerk started writing on a paper in front of him.

"I guess I won't ask what kind of vehicle you have!" he joked. "There's a set of pens for livestock out back." He held out a key. "How many nights will you be staying?" I opened my mouth to ask how much it would be, but before I could, he added quickly, "No charge, of course."

"Two nights," I heard myself say without thinking. Two nights in a real bed sounded grand and decadent.

I walked Rainy and Amanda around to the back of the motel's main building. There was a sturdy corral and plenty of room for them. A fresh bale of hay sat near the gate. Someone was taking care of us. Bless the rural grapevine...again!

In the darkness, Rainy stood and raised his head very slightly; his nostrils fluttered just a little. Gypsy mirrored him, her nose in the air. I called it "checking the wind," and I envied the way their noses and ears told them so much more than mine told me. I'd taken to stopping, staying still for a moment, and trying it, too. Sometimes I thought I could feel the coming weather in the air, or hear the sound of a far-off owl or a train in the distance. I stood in the moonlight in the company of my animals, still and quiet, trying to learn about the things around us. I sensed water and the smell of earth. I got a feel for the night and the big sky above me. When I looked up, I saw a blanket of stars in numbers like I'd never seen before.

## THE ONLY DIRECTION

The clerk at the front desk and I hunched over a map of Arizona, trying to plan for water stops when my animals and I continued our journey. He shook his head.

"I can't think of anything in that direction," he said, frowning.

Another motel worker and a truck driver having coffee agreed—they thought there was a rest stop to the west, but no one was sure how far it was or if I could access it without being on the highway.

When it was time to leave, no option other than the highway rest stop had presented itself. I'd been warned more than once about undesirables seeking prey at rest areas at night. I worried about being vulnerable in a tent there, but I also knew I might have to choose our need for water over a place where no one would see us.

I had no way to guess what would come next as we headed out. Even if I veered to the south or the north, I found nothing on the map to aim for. I didn't want to go north or south anyway. I rode forth with faith that something would work out, heading west, the only direction for us, and before long we were riding once again in a land forgotten by anyone who was in a hurry.

The road had a gentle rise and fall, wending around low mesas and dry arroyos. We shared the day with the occasional jackrabbit, bursting from the brush. It felt like I was the only human for miles, so I was surprised to hear a car approaching from the east.

It turned out to be a reporter and a cameraman from a television station in Phoenix who were in the area pursuing another story. Dan and Rick had heard of my journey in Chambers and decided to find us and do an interview. I enjoyed visiting with them—as did Gypsy, who got her belly rubbed. The time was brief, though, as they had their other story to finish, and while I had always said there was no hurry, I felt the pull to move on, too. Before they left, we exchanged contact information, and Dan reminded me on which channel the piece would appear, even though we all knew I was unlikely to be near a television when it aired.

When the plume of dust from the news crew's car settled, it was just the brush, the open range, me, my animals, and the slow road once again.

## REST STOP: YOU NEVER KNOW

As the breeze began to cool, signaling the coming of evening, our lonely track wound back toward the frontage road. As luck would have it, I could see the interstate and a place where a dirt parking area puffed out on each side of the highway. A few big rigs were pulled over, idling. I rode forward eagerly—this had to be the rest stop I'd discussed with the guys back at the motel. We followed a trail through the fence that led into the parking area. I looked around expectantly for a pump or fountain, then looked again more urgently. No matter how hard I searched, there was no sign of water.

I rested a hand on Rainy's neck. I couldn't let my travel companions down. I peered across to the twin of the rest area on the eastbound side of the highway. Maybe there was water there. It was a long shot, but it was the only idea I had at the moment. I tied Rainy and Amanda extra securely to a sign post, then Gypsy and I ran across the interstate and did the same fruitless hunt for water on that side.

As I was about to walk back, I was stopped short at the sight of a New York State license plate on the back of a big, dark-colored Lincoln. A man was in the reclined driver's seat, trying to doze.

I glanced around. There were a few other cars and it wasn't dark yet; there didn't seem to be much danger in talking to the driver for a minute. I walked closer to the front of the car, and the man rolled down his window and scowled at me.

"What?" he said sharply, already suspicious. I figured he thought I was looking for money or a ride.

"Hi," I started. "I just noticed your license plate. Where in New York are you from?"

"The City," he answered. In my home state, people referred to New York City as "THE City," like it was the only one.

"Ah." I nodded, knowing now we wouldn't be having one of those "we're almost neighbors" conversations. Upstate and "The City" were pretty different. I still wanted to tell him I was from New York, though.

"I just asked 'cause I'm from New York, too. Upstate," I added.

"Oh, yeah?" He seemed a little interested.

I couldn't resist telling him. "I rode here on my horse." I turned and pointed toward the other side of the highway where Rainy and Amanda were visible, tied in the dusky light.

"No way. Are you serious?"

"Yes," I answered, patting Gypsy's head.

"Well, I'll be." He shook his head. "Only a crazy New Yorker would do something like that, huh?" he asked, his pride in eccentric city-dwellers extending to the whole state now.

"Yeah," I said, to be agreeable. "Well, I better get going. I'm looking for water for my animals." I glanced around once more, discouraged, at the desolate rest area.

I turned to walk away.

"Hey, wait," my New York friend called. "How much water do you need?"

I looked back at him. "Enough to fill a bucket or two."

"Take a look at this," he said. The man opened his door and slid his large frame out of the car. He was a really big guy with salt-and-pepper hair (mostly salt) and a big bushy mustache. He walked around to the back of his vehicle, stretched stiffly, fumbled for a key, and opened the trunk.

"Look'it," he said, pointing with the key into the trunk. "They don't know how to make a good sub in L.A. You can't find a sandwich there like they make in New York. So I buy a bunch of meat, rolls, you know, the works. I keep it all cold in these coolers so I have my own food on my drive. Now the ice is all melted."

I looked in the trunk. There were two Styrofoam coolers, both about half full of water.

"You'll let my horse and mule drink from those coolers?" I asked, hope flickering inside.

"You bet. Help yourself."

"Fantastic!" I exclaimed. "Wait here—I'll be right back!" I then caught myself before running back to get Rainy and Amanda, turning to him and vigorously shaking his hand, which cracked him up. "I'm Missy, by the way."

"I'm Ron Karabatsos," he said through his laughter. "Retired New York police detective."

I felt like skipping across the highway.

I hurried my horse and mule across the double lanes and median as if the water in the trunk might disappear, like a cartoon mirage in the desert. I led them to the back of Ron's car, and after a moment, Rainy dipped his head to the white coolers and Amanda followed. They drank deeply.

"I'll be damned," Ron said with a laugh. "Wish my buddies in New York could get a load of this!"

As I watched my horse and mule, packs and all, with their muzzles buried deep in the trunk of a Lincoln Continental, I smiled and shook my head. I always knew where we were going on this journey. I just never knew where we'd find ourselves.

While Rainy and Amanda lipped at what remained of the clear, cold water, my curiosity got the best of me. "Can I ask what a New York City detective is doing out here on reservation land?" I asked.

"Ah," Ron began with a smile. "Funny story. I was a full-time detective and working a side job as a bouncer in a club."

It was easy to imagine this with his tough-guy New York accent and big burly build.

"Some producers from Hollywood were in the club," he continued, "and when they saw me, they asked if I'd do a bit part as a bodyguard in a movie. I thought they were pulling my leg, but it was for real. They got me out to L.A., and a new career was born. I've been in a couple of movies now, a television show, and a series. I'm a 'character actor,' I guess, always playing the role of 'big tough guy from New York.' But I hate flying. So when the work picked up, I started driving the whole way. I bring my food when I can. I've driven New York to L.A. and back a few times now."

As Ron and I leaned on the bumper of his car, Rainy and Amanda turned from the coolers to search for bits of grass at the edge of the turn-off. Ron rattled off some of the projects he'd worked on: a well-known soap opera, a made-for-television movie with Elizabeth Montgomery, and a new show about a wanna-be rock band with John Stamos.

"But my favorite part is on a new show set in Boston," he continued. "There's a bartender named Sam who used to be a ball player, and this waitress, and all the characters are diehard Boston

Red Sox fans. I come in, an obnoxious New York Yankees fan." He smiled and joked, "Quite a stretch for my acting abilities."

"Oh, I bet it is!" I laughed with him. "I know Yankees fans."

"Anyway, the show's called *Cheers*." He then told me the date his episode was going to air, and I repeated it back to him so I'd remember.

"I don't get near a TV very often these days," I admitted. "But you never know. I can try."

It was time to set up my camp across the highway. Ron noted he'd better get that nap I'd interrupted before he hit the road and drove through the night. He insisted I take some of his food.

"No, you need it!" I protested.

"Are you kidding? Look at me!" He placed his hands on his girth. "Besides, in a matter of an hour or two I'll be able to get more food and water. Who knows when you will?"

I accepted it gratefully, giving him a big hug.

"I'm so happy I met you," I said.

"Happy I could help," he replied.

Gypsy, Rainy, Amanda, and I walked back across the interstate. Soon it would be dark. I'd never know when the New Yorker/detective/actor pulled out into the empty night, heading east.

## ▨ REST STOP WEST: CIRCLE THE WAGONS

Things were a little more crowded back at the westbound rest stop. Several trucks had pulled in. A few big campers maneuvered into place, claiming spots for the night. Rainy and Amanda's horseshoes made a distinctive sound on the pavement, and people turned and looked.

A fit-looking older couple with white hair and matching vivacious personalities came right over. He called her Jo, she called him Brownie, and as soon as they discover how far we'd ridden, Jo made numerous trips back and forth from their RV, bringing me food. I finally stopped her, laughing, as she started to head to the camper once more.

"I have enough," I insisted. "This is a feast! Thank you!"

A few others from campers—all older, retired, outgoing—came over to visit, but I had to excuse myself.

"I really have to find a place to set up my tent so we won't be visible to traffic at night," I said, apologizing for having to leave the friendly chatter.

"Hold on a minute," one of the men said. "Wouldn't it make sense for you to camp right here, right where the vehicles park?" Looking around at the other couples and their campers parked nearby, he continued, "We could surround you. Your tent would be practically invisible from the road, and anyone who pulls in will think the tent goes with us. Who would bother this many people in a group?"

The white and gray heads around me nodded in agreement. They would circle the wagons, so to speak, and Rainy, Gypsy, Amanda, and I would be relatively safe, right in the middle.

"You're right," I acknowledged. "You guys think right here, maybe?" I pointed to a spot right beside the line of RVs. The men liked that I asked their opinion. They had plenty of advice and were happy to give it. Jo clapped her hands in delight.

"Now we can have a breakfast cookout in the morning!" she exclaimed happily.

Though I had worried about having to camp at a rest stop, there we were: Rainy and Amanda all settled, feed and forage nearby, with water now readily available from the RVs. The older folks and I roasted marshmallows on a portable grill as we visited and talked about our travels. The moon rose over the tops of the campers, making them glow in the darkness. Oceans of stars twinkled above us.

I woke only once that night, when Gypsy gave a whine and I let her out to chase a jackrabbit into the brush. Otherwise I slept in peace, knowing I was surrounded by my protectors and that we were adventurers in our own ways, all of us.

## LITERAL

I picked up a trail and skirted through part of the Navajo Reservation. The land rose from the flats on a worn path along a ridgeline with an open view to the south. The ridge was void of most everything but sagebrush and wind until we came upon an old fence and a Navajo man tightening the wire. If he felt any surprise or curiosity upon seeing us here, it did not register on his smooth brown face.

The man stopped his work and turned to face us, leaning in a casual way against the fence post. I asked Rainy and Amanda to halt and waited for the man to acknowledge us, but he stood there without saying a word.

"Hello," I offered.

After a pause, he replied: "Hello." He met my eyes but remained expressionless.

Out of habit I asked, "How are you?"

"Why?" he responded.

Having expected something along the standard, "Fine, how are you?" I was a little flustered. I couldn't think of an answer—why *did* I need to know how he was? I fidgeted in the saddle and decided to change the direction of our sort-of conversation to something more practical.

"Um, can you tell me how far it is to the next town?"

He appeared to give the question some consideration. He turned his gaze to Rainy, Gypsy, and Amanda, looking them over carefully.

"Too far," he answered.

The man went back to his fence repairs. I waited, expecting him to laugh or say, "Just kidding!" but he had apparently answered honestly and to his satisfaction.

I felt funny just riding off without saying anything else—it wasn't how I was taught to end a conversation—so I called out, "Well, okay. See you later."

The man looked up at me once more and asked, "When?"

## CANTEEN

Narrow dirt roads appeared and disappeared across the area where we traveled. Barely visible dirt tracks, hardly a lane wide, were used as ranch roads. The rough tracks would have been off-roading to a vehicle, but the lack of concrete was easy on Rainy and Amanda's feet.

As we passed a faded sign for the Painted Desert and Petrified Forest, I reached back for my canteen. My hand felt nothing where it should have been.

I jumped to the ground and dug through my saddle packs, tossing aside rolled up t-shirts and horse brushes.

The canteen was missing.

I left Rainy and Amanda ground tied, and Gypsy and I walked back down the road. My boots kicked up puffs of dust as I scuffed along, my eyes on the tan-colored ground. After a short time I gave up and headed back, climbing into the saddle, dispirited. I turned Rainy around to ride back a little farther. All three animals walked slowly; it must have seemed strange to them to be heading east after all this time.

I had to admit the search was futile. The land here was a good place for things to hide. My canteen could have been anywhere. We swung around and resumed our westward journey.

I was discouraged and lost in my thoughts when I heard the sound of a car coming up behind us. To my surprise, I saw that it was Dan and Rick, the reporters we'd met on the road near Chambers.

"Hey, I can't believe we found you!" Dan called as they get out of the car. "How are you doing?"

I smiled down at them from Rainy's back. "Great to see you guys. I'm doing okay."

The two bickered good-naturedly about whose idea it was to follow this particular road and which one had said they'd find us here. They told me about a few stories they were working on in the area and commiserated when I mentioned my lost canteen. They wished me luck, noting that we weren't far outside of the town of Holbrook before driving off.

As my animals and I walked on, I started to feel thirsty. I knew it was a trick of my mind because I didn't have the canteen, but boy, did I want a drink. Rainy's pace seemed to drag just a bit, as if he, too, felt discouraged.

Time ticked by before I saw the reflection of late sun glinting off metal. It seemed crazy to see two cars within a few hours on the old road. It took me a minute to realize that it was Dan and Rick again. My smile grew wider when they stopped and got out, and I saw they were carrying a bag from McDonald's and a big frosty Coke. The ice was melting from the drive, but it tasted so good. I stood beside Rainy and unwrapped my burger with gusto. Dan went back to their car and returned with a brand new canteen full of water. Bug spray, too.

"Oh my gosh! Thank you!" I gushed. "How did you get all this?" I clasped the canteen like it was solid gold. Rick and Dan laughed, pleased with my response to their unexpected gifts.

The two explained that Holbrook had an outdoor supply store and a McDonald's—it was funny to think that I felt such a sense of space and isolation, yet stores and takeout food weren't quite as far away as they seemed.

Dan and Rick leaned against the bumper of their car while I ate. Gypsy begged for food as we enjoyed each other's company. My whole outlook brightened.

When it came time to head out again, I got back up in the saddle and picked up the reins, feeling refreshed. Dan and Rick waved and got into their car. We started walking, but then Dan's door opened again, and he walked back to us, reaching up and rubbing Rainy's forehead before speaking.

"You said you're heading toward Flagstaff?" he asked.

I nodded. That was roughly my planned direction.

"I'm going to be up in that part of the state next week. Some friends of mine are having a big barbeque. I thought if you're in Flagstaff by then, maybe you'd like to come with me. If you want to, I mean. To this party…"

His words trailed off as he suddenly seemed unsure of himself and got flustered. It was kind of endearing. Dan was nice, but I couldn't imagine how it would work—it was hard to predict exactly where I'd be in a few days. And once in Flagstaff, I could maybe go out for a while if we had a place to stay where Rainy and Amanda were safely housed in a corral or barn. But if we were camping, I didn't see how I could do it.

"Well, thanks for asking," I smiled at Dan as he waited for my response. "But how would we get in touch? How would you know where I am, and when?"

The detail didn't concern Dan in the least. "We found you twice already, didn't we?"

I laughed and admitted he had a point. He wrote a phone number for his friend's place near Flagstaff on a piece of paper, and I tucked it into my saddlebag, knowing it was unlikely that I'd see him again.

Dan left me with a wave and a smile. "See you next week," he said.

### HIGHWAY

With the shorter days, it grew dark while we were still on the road. I was trying to guess how much farther it was to Sun Valley, where we were spending the night, when a young man named Ron drove up, looking for us.

"You're almost there," he assured me. "Got a place all set for your horses. Just follow me." He pulled ahead in front of us with his headlights on. The extra light made me feel better.

At the Stuart Ranch, Ron helped me untack Rainy and Amanda, check their feet and legs, and feed them, all in a short time. I'd forgotten how fast chores could go when you weren't doing them alone.

The animals and I left Sun Valley in the morning, and after passing through part of Holbrook, we took an unpaved road leading west. By late afternoon, we came to its end—right at the interstate. I couldn't see any other road in my line of sight or on my map for several miles. With no other option and unwilling to turn back, I rode up through an opening in the fence.

We'd been on frontage roads occasionally, but until this spot in Arizona, I'd been able to avoid being on a highway. Luckily, the ubiquitous fence that lined every interstate was quite a long way from the actual roadway, allowing for a wide stretch of grass between where we walked and the pavement. It was not the most peaceful or scenic route, but I told myself it was only for a short time.

After several miles I began to look for an opening in the fence to get us back to an old section of Route 66. Before I found one, I saw Ron's pickup, moving along slowly in the right lane. He pulled onto the shoulder ahead of us and got out carrying a covered plate—a picnic meal for us to share along the roadside. He had water in buckets in the bed of the truck for Rainy, Gypsy, and Amanda.

We sat together on the ground, enjoying lunch, while Rainy and Amanda grazed the grassy stretch. We talked about what I'd find to the west. Ron knew ranches and horse people near Winslow and beyond, and said he would call ahead for us. He also gave me a list with several additional good contacts.

When the horses suddenly stopped grazing and looked up, we followed their gaze. A state trooper had slowed his police car to a stop behind Ron's truck. The trooper got out and marched through the grass toward us. He stopped and stared at us but didn't say a word. It was unnerving.

"Hi?" I mumbled. It came out sounding like a question rather than a greeting.

"You have animals here," he stated.

The officer waited, as if he was expecting a story from Ron or from me. Somehow, this actually kept me from wanting to provide my usual explanation of our journey.

The trooper fiddled with his keys. "Horses on the interstate..." he finally said. "I think there's some kind of law about that."

He shook his head, walked back to his car, and drove away. For a few seconds, Ron and I were speechless as we watched the patrol car drive out of sight. Then we looked at each other and burst out laughing.

As soon as possible, I found our way off the interstate and rode once again on a secondary road. The sun was setting as we continued on, hoping to make it to Joseph City before dark.

## ▨ WINSLOW

Ranching families in the west may be far apart in geography, but they are close in other ways, bonded by their shared lifestyle. Meeting a ranch family was always beneficial to me because I picked up more contacts that usually helped in some way down the road.

Bud and Julie Johnson were acquaintances of Ron Stuart's family. The Johnsons raised livestock and sold feed at their place in Winslow. I rode onto their property about sunset. The barns and the house were bathed in warm light, and as I jumped off Rainy, dogs gathered around us in greeting.

As soon as I met Julie Johnson, I could tell she was a kind soul. She planned to ride with me the next day to a ranch on the other side of town. It had been quite a while since I'd had human company on the road, and it gave me something to look forward to.

In the morning, I asked Julie what she thought about Rainy's weight and condition, which still had me concerned. She thought he looked okay but suggested they send us on with as much feed as we could carry. At the Johnsons' suggestion, I also planned to leave our packs for the day so Rainy's load would be light, and Amanda and Gypsy would remain behind, too. Bud would bring my gear and my animals at the end of the day when he met us to pick up Julie and her horse.

I expected Amanda to put up a fuss when we rode away without her, but surprisingly, she only called out a time or two. Gypsy, on the other hand, had to be taken inside the house.

Julie and her bay gelding led us on trails and across open land. Riding Rainy without packs felt light and free. The concern for my animals and the touch of loneliness that had been nagging at me melted away. The horses' hooves made even footfalls and the saddles creaked in harmony. Glad for the company of another horse, Rainy stepped lightly, his ears flicking all around, showing his interest in our surroundings.

Mid-day, we detoured off the trails and went into Winslow for lunch. Unlike other places we'd ridden through, two horses walking the streets didn't attract much attention in such a Western town. We tied the horses outside the Burger King, like that was the usual thing to do, and sat inside near a window, where we could watch them as we ate and chatted companionably.

The horses' shoes rang out on the pavement as we set out again after our break, and a song played in my head as we rode past a street corner: The Eagles' *Take it Easy*. I sang my own version to Julie, and we rode out of town laughing and singing out loud: "*It's a girl, my lord, on a buckskin horse, slowin' down to take a look at me.*"

## TEEPEE ROCK RANCH/TURQUOISE RANCH

Past Winslow, I began to note changes in our environment. We were riding through tall, yellowed grass. A line of cottonwood trees stood in the distance.

Ahead of us, two cowboys rode into sight. Julie introduced me to Pete McKay and his son (also Pete), owners of the Teepee Rock Ranch. It was their land we were riding on, and it was where my animals and I would spend the night.

As all four horses walked together, the McKays told a little of the history of the ranch, which had also been known as "Turquoise Ranch" for the vein of semi-precious gemstone that could be found here.

The sight of a few trees, listening to Julie and the McKays talk of ranching life, a quick glimpse of a coyote along the trail—all this made my soul happy. My worries about Rainy's health seemed unfounded with the sprightly way he was walking along. It was the kind of ride and the kind of day I wished could go on and on.

When Bud arrived at the McKays' ranch, towing a trailer, Amanda let loose one of her crazy-loud calls. I immediately led her to Rainy. With happy grunts and squeaks, she nuzzled him along his flanks, then fell into step beside him, back in her place in the world.

Gypsy jumped and danced in circles, thrilled to have us all in the same place again. There was no mistaking the happiness swirling in the air around us. It was almost a physical feeling in my chest, how surely we belonged together.

As the McKays grilled steaks for dinner, Julie asked if she could talk to me for a minute, and we wandered side by side toward the horse corral.

"With our feed business, sometimes we let people barter items for feed," Julie began. "One older Navajo woman trades handmade jewelry for feed for her sheep. I want you to have something to remember your ride, or at least the Arizona part, and I thought one of her pieces might be right."

Julie opened her palm to me, revealing a ring, silver with turquoise stones set like a sunburst. The nuggets were organic in shape, not perfectly round or oval. The color was the same as the clear Arizona sky.

"That's a beautiful ring," I said with admiration.

Julie handed it to me. "It's an old piece," she explained. "You can tell by the silver and the style."

I turned the ring in my hands, respecting the design and craftsmanship. It was big enough that you really noticed the color but not too big. It slid onto my finger and fit perfectly.

"I love it."

Julie Johnson, in her generosity, had somehow figured out a perfect gift that symbolized the land I was beginning to love.

## MOONRISE AT TWO GUNS

Our ride west of Winslow brought us near railroad tracks once again, though we never saw a train all day. We moseyed along, watching for glimpses of deer, coyote, hawks, and reptiles that rattle, but with the weather cooler now, snake sightings had dwindled.

With no set destination for the night, I pieced together the trails beside the railroad, and late in the afternoon, we were back on an old section of Route 66. Rainy and Amanda's hoof beats made an easy sound in the quiet as we came to a sign for the turnoff to Two Guns. We followed the sign with the KOA (Kampgrounds of America) symbol down a narrow, unpaved road. It seemed strange that Two Guns was noted on the map because there clearly wasn't a town in this place.

I hopped off Rainy and looked around. Only one aluminum camper was on the grounds that I could see, and from the look of it, it had been there a while. The last rest stop I'd passed along the highway had been full and busy, yet just a few miles away, there was nobody around.

The sign on the door of the campground office was turned to OPEN, however, and a handwritten paper tacked beneath it said, "Ring bell." So I did. I waited. I looked back at Rainy and Amanda, tied to an old section of rail fence. Suddenly, the screen door to the KOA office creaked open. A young man looked out at me, disheveled in a hooded sweatshirt, unzipped and thrown over bare skin. I was sure I'd woken him up. He held the door open, and Gypsy squeezed in along with me. The guy looked over at my horse and mule but didn't say anything.

Inside, the man went around to the other side of a counter and finally asked, "Can I help you?"

"Can I rent a campsite for the night?"

"Yep," he answered.

"And my horses are okay here?"

He shrugged, then started quoting prices. The cost was more than I thought it would be. I was very conscious of how my funds had dwindled.

"Wow," I started. "Do you have anything a little cheaper?"

He looked up from the form he'd been filling out. "Well, I got a few cheaper, out back, but there's no electrical hook-up."

I stole a good look at his face to see if he was being funny. I wondered if my mention of the horse and mule had registered. I felt a bit of a giggle building, but the young man looked at me in such a humorless way, I just said, "Cheaper will do. I don't need electric hook-up."

"You don't need electric?"

"No." I shook my head. "Just a tree to camp by, maybe. That'll do."

I set up the tent, and with the horses relaxed and dozing, Gypsy and I set out for a little exploring. It was a lucky thing to be out in the cool evening air, and a big round shining disc of a moon rose right in front of us.

I stopped in my tracks and said quietly, "Look at that moon," though only a horse, a dog, and a mule could hear me. It hung in the sky with its bottom balanced at the edge of the earth. It bathed the rundown campground in a rose-gold light, and the dusty path we were camped beside was a silver ribbon, leading straight to it.

## TRUCK STOP DINER, TWIN ARROWS

Near a few low buildings were two huge arrows stuck in the ground as if shot from the bow of a giant. The paint on the arrows was old and peeling, but they still got your attention.

It had to be Twin Arrows, which I'd seen on my map.

I stopped Rainy near a store and pair of gas pumps next to a single-wide trailer that served as a diner. Several tractor-trailers were parked at the diner, nose-in like horses tied to a hitching rail.

I tied Rainy and Amanda out front, pulling off their packs and saddles. I spread my jacket on the ground nearby, and Gypsy laid down on it as I headed toward the store with my collapsible bucket.

Inside, knives and other items were displayed along the wall. Turquoise jewelry and old-looking candy bars filled glass cases that hadn't been dusted in a while. I helped myself to water and bought one of the candy bars to be courteous.

Once the animals had their water, I headed to the diner. I stepped up to the entrance, then hesitated, unsure if I should go on in. It was so narrow there were no tables—there was only a counter with stools, and each of the stools had a man sitting on it, except one. Even the person wiping the counter was a man. When the door banged shut behind me, every head turned my way.

I was not prone to self-consciousness, but the situation sure felt awkward. It was as if I'd stepped into a private men's club. I looked over at the only empty stool, and with no other seat available, I headed over to it, my boots sounding unexpectedly loud.

I assumed the men around me were the drivers of the rigs parked out front. I squeezed in between two fellows of rather large proportions, keeping my elbows close to my sides, afraid of bumping one of them. No one said a word.

The counter man placed a plastic menu in front of me. I ordered a cheeseburger, periodically turning to look out the windows and check on Rainy, Amanda, and Gypsy. I was conscious of eyes following me, conscious that they saw the animals out there, resting where I'd left them.

I was pretty uncomfortable, and when I started to eat, it got worse. I felt the burn of one big truck driver's stare. When I snuck a glance to my right, he didn't even bother to look away. I was more aware than ever that I was the only female within miles, and I wished I hadn't gone into the place.

Suddenly the Staring Man slammed his fork down on the counter.

"Miss! Excuse me!" he demanded.

I looked at him in surprise, as did everyone else.

"I drive a route from Pennsylvania all over the Midwest and the West. I been seeing you on that same damn horse for six months. WHERE THE HELL ARE YOU GOING?"

The small place erupted in laughter, thankfully breaking the tension. I laughed, too, in relief, and began to answer the questions that now filled the air. The guys cracked jokes and offered advice. They paid for my lunch and tried to give me money. They wrote names and addresses and places they knew as good rest stops on napkins and handed them to me as they prepared to leave. They patted me on the back, and outside, they stopped to admire Rainy, Amanda, and Gypsy, patting them too, wishing us all safe travels.

## NUTS...AND GRATEFUL

We began to see the outline of the San Francisco Peaks in the Flag-staff area rise ahead of us. We'd left the high, flat desert behind, the flatlands gave way to foothills, and my animals and I found our-selves working our way uphill on a winding, tree-lined road to meet the Juarez family.

The Juarez place had a nice pen for horses behind the house. It had a roof and was clean, open, and airy.

I liked the Juarez family—Nick and Linda, and especially their teenage daughter, Alicia—and when they invited me to stay over an extra day, I said yes. There was a brief flurry of excitement when a Flagstaff reporter and his cameraman showed up, asking to film footage of my animals and ask me questions about the trip.

In the morning, Alicia's parents reminded her that she'd prom-ised to collect pinyon nuts to earn the money she needed to show her horse. I asked what they were talking about.

"Ah, pinyon nuts," Nick began. "They're very tasty and people use them for cooking. There are pinyon trees all around here, and kids collect them and sell them to markets as a way to make a little money."

"They're pretty easy to get," Alicia added. "The trees aren't too tall."

"I like all kinds of nuts, but I have never heard of these," I admitted.

"They've been picked for centuries," Nick went on. "Histori-ans think the Navajo, Hopi, Zuni, and the different Pueblos may even have established their cultures here on the Colorado Plateau because they learned to use the pinyon nuts for food, like the ancients before them."

"Do you want to come with me?" Alicia asked.

I nodded eagerly. I definitely did. It was exciting to think of being amongst the trees. I'd been in farmlands, plains, and high plateau country for so long; I missed the woods.

It got even better when Alicia informed me that the best way to pick the nuts was on horseback. We headed out from the back of the property onto wooded trails with Alicia on her pretty red mare. We both rode bareback, our legs hanging loosely down the warm round sides of our horses. The sun shone down on the beautiful autumn afternoon.

As we entered the woods, everything became quieter. Soft needles coated the trail, and the nearness of the pines created a hushed, closed world. A breeze fluttered the needles and caused the branches and little cones to sway. By some tacit agreement, Alicia and I stopped our chatter. We let the woods, the soft hoof beats, the delicate piney scent, and the sound of the occasional jay and raven fill our senses.

Arizona was pretty amazing. A few days before we had been riding in the dry brushy land of red rocks. Today we were soaking in the cool evergreen forest. *This whole country is amazing,* I thought. *And it's Rainy who carried me here and showed me all of this.*

I reached forward and placed my palm on his withers, feeling each stride and his sun-warmed coat.

Alicia and I were back, doing the evening chores, when Linda came to find me, saying I had a phone call. *Who could be calling me here?* I wondered.

I didn't recognize the male voice on the other end. Then, when he asked about my canteen, I realized it was Dan, the reporter who had said he'd track me down in Flagstaff.

"Mike, the reporter who interviewed you yesterday, is a friend of mine," he explained.

Dan had been right. It was easy to find me.

He asked about Rainy, Gypsy, and Amanda, and the last hundred miles or so since I'd last seen him. Then, Dan got to the point.

"I'm meeting some friends for dinner in Flagstaff, and I wonder if you could join us—in about half an hour?"

I'd been on the road a long time, making independent decisions and being self-reliant, but, "Hold on a minute," is how I responded to Dan. Then I covered up the phone and turned to Linda and Alicia, who were watching me on the call with curiosity. "What should I do?" I whispered.

Because he was a reporter on a television station that covered the whole state, Dan was something of a familiar face—Alicia and Linda knew who he was and insisted I say I'd go, practically pushing me down the hall to Alicia's room.

"Did he say where you're going for dinner?" Linda asked. She and her daughter exchanged looks at my answer, and they started rifling through the closet, pulling out clothes for me to try on. Within seconds, a set of hot rollers was plugged in, heating on the edge of the bathroom sink. Apparently my twenty-five-cent sweater from the thrift store in Grants and my worn flannel would not do.

It felt weird after the way I'd been living to all of a sudden wonder how my hair looked and if I was wearing the appropriate thing. At the same time, it was sort of fun, too. It felt easy, in a way, because whatever happened, I'd be leaving soon, and would likely never see Dan again. It took the typical complications and expectations away.

Acting like a concerned father, Nick grilled Dan in a gruff but friendly way, and when Dan walked me to his truck, I turned back to see all three family members, and my dog, watching us from the door. I felt like I was sixteen again and almost laughed out loud.

Dan had a great sense of humor, and both of us had the "gift of gab," so the night turned into a great deal of fun. Before we headed back to the Juarez place, Dan took me to see his friend Mike, the reporter from the television station in Flagstaff. The two had a surprise: They had collected the news clips of our story from several other stations and were able to play them for me. It was really special since I rarely got to see our interviews and news clips on television.

When Dan dropped me at the Juarez home, he asked again if I could go with him to his friends' barbecue—the event he'd originally asked about when he brought me the new canteen.

"I have plans with the Juarez family tomorrow," I said apologetically, but Dan assured me his party wasn't until later in the day. "That should work, then," I said, and we agreed on a time for him to pick me up.

Before going inside the house, I walked out back to say goodnight to Rainy and Amanda. It was the perfect way to end such a pleasant day—seeing them comfortable and at peace.

## GOLD IN THE DAY

It was a beautiful fall morning. Gypsy and I rode along with the Juarez family to the Smith Ranch where Domingo, Linda's horse, was being trained to drive. The road climbed away from town and up into the hills. The tall pines cast cool shadows over our vehicle.

Domingo was a tall Appaloosa with a black coat and a striking snowflake pattern. Nick, Alicia, and I watched Linda and Mr. Smith put the horse through his paces. He trotted around the ring, the wagon wheels making long lines in the raked dust. Then we jumped from the fence and hopped on the wagon for a ride around. Mr. Smith called "Gee" and "Haw" to the horse—the traditional way to signal a driving horse to the left or the right. The moment had its own music. Bits of chain and rings from the harness jingled, mixing with the hoof beats and creak of the wagon as it rounded each turn.

Dan pulled up in his small Ford pickup late in the afternoon. In quick order he managed to do two things that assured I would hold him in high regard: First, he brought his dog Heather along and invited Gypsy to come to the party, too. Second, before we set out, he asked to see Rainy and Amanda again.

Dan and I, Gypsy, and Heather squeezed into the cab of his truck and headed south with the mountain peaks behind us, and he said we had time for a hike in Oak Creek Canyon. Rust-colored rocks lay strewn on the canyon bottom, and crystal water sparkled and reflected the perfect blue sky above us. Fingers of rock the color of maple leaves reached upward. I took pictures like crazy because it was all so fantastically pretty. Dan and I even posed for pictures together, using the self-timer on my camera.

"Isn't it weird that we're taking pictures of each other and we're practically strangers?" Dan asked.

We both laughed and took more pictures.

Somewhere during the small talk of the pleasant barbecue that followed, somewhere in the midst of answering questions about my trip, I pictured Rainy and Amanda and had an itch to be brushing Rainy's soft coat. I felt a distinct pull to get back to my animals and began to wonder what awaited west of Flagstaff. I was having fun, but it was time to get back to my animals and back on the road. I had always felt pretty comfortable socially wherever I was, but I got the fleeting notion that I might not really belong around people anymore.

## TRUST

My adventure made the connections I developed with people I met along the way happen more quickly and strongly than when meeting people in "the real world." Others who have traveled recount experiencing the same phenomenon. With every new friend, there came a hard time with goodbyes, and I felt emotional leaving the Juarez family, where I'd been so welcomed into their home.

We all hugged, and I set out with sweet memories and extra clothes from Alicia's closet. They said, "Call us when you get to California," and "You'll stop on your way back through, won't you?" The doubts and the worries about a girl alone on the road had mostly been replaced with the assumption that if I'd come this far, I was probably going to make it all the way.

It was hard for me to think too broadly. I took each day as its own time, and I never assumed anything was a given. I knew that with each step we took and each road we rode on there were many ways things could go right or wrong. I took nothing for granted. California was still somewhere else. Arizona was here and now.

In this here and now, we had the woods again. After months on the plains and the desert plateaus, I felt welcomed into the arms of trees. I rode on trails through sweet-smelling pines and stands of aspens with gold leaves flickering in the wind like a million candle flames. The air was cool in a way that was both invigorating and familiar.

Rainy seemed to feel it, too. Both he and Amanda walked with spirit in their steps. The time of rest had been good for them, and the forest paths were easy on their feet and legs after the paved roads we'd traveled for so long.

The view changed as we rode, and vistas opened up when there was a break in the trees. We seemed to be ever climbing. The view was gorgeous, but it startled me to see how high up the trail had led us. The land sloped steeply down to the south, on my left, into meadows of yellow grass, and beyond that, more evergreen forest, and it sloped up on my right. I was not particularly comfortable with heights, so I tried to focus instead on the trail in front of us.

We moved forward, climbing more. Gypsy, who had been up in the saddle with me, suddenly wanted to get down. Once there, she did none of her usual sniffing and exploring—instead, she placed herself way in the back of our little line, following Amanda.

The trail narrowed further, and Amanda shifted away from her usual position—slightly to the back but alongside Rainy—and stepped directly behind him, instead. We were now all in one straight line: Rainy in front carrying me, then Amanda, then Gypsy. It was a good thing because the trail became so narrow there was no other way we'd fit. I no longer looked at the view or admired our surroundings. I was well past my comfort level with heights.

Rainy seemed focused on keeping his head level and picking his way carefully along the path. Though we were no longer climbing, the trail had shrunk to a width I was well aware we should not be on—a thin, worn line where you had to place one foot carefully in front of the other and hug the uphill side to keep from slipping.

*What if the trail narrowed and ended?* We couldn't turn around, and I couldn't imagine all four of us backing down what we had just come up. It was so steep on the side of the mountain that now, to my left, the drop was practically vertical. Boulders jutted out in spots and tenacious scrub trees reached out from places where their roots were able to take hold. I forced myself to take a peek, and a swoop of nausea overcame me.

I was scared, but I didn't want to stop Rainy because I was afraid to break his concentration or cause him to look down or step wrong. If one of us went down the side of the mountain, we were all going, and it would be a long fall. I began to tremble and willed it to stop so Rainy wouldn't sense my fear, but I had no control over it. I could feel through the rope in my hand that Amanda was studiously keeping Rainy's exact, careful pace. I didn't let myself turn and look at her or Gypsy because I didn't want to do anything that might shift our balance even one iota. Instead, I focused on a spot on Rainy's neck. I looked at the way his black mane fell to one side and moved a little in the breeze. I watched the glide of his shoulder with each step he took. But my eyes shifted—I couldn't help it—and I looked down again. That was it for me.

Rainy, my wonderful horse, though, he didn't seem to be scared or hesitant. He wanted to keep going, so I leaned forward and slowly let the reins become a loose drape. Riders are taught that it is important to be the leader with a horse. We're supposed to be in charge at all times, but I closed my eyes and put us all in Rainy's care. Every ounce of trust and faith I had, I put in Rainy. He never faltered. He kept up his steady walk, placing each sturdy black hoof in the right place one step at a time.

After what felt like hours but could have been minutes, the trail began to widen. We kept moving forward slowly. Gradually, we descended, from the views and the cliff and my fear, until Rainy safely brought us all to a flat dirt road through the pines.

## BEAUTY LARGE AND SMALL

I rode in the shadows of ponderosa pines outside Williams, Arizona, looking for the home of Bob and Peggy Dean. We followed dirt roads past small ponds and alongside clearings of goldenrod and snakeweed.

The Deans' rustic home sat alone next to a corral. I found a note on the door, welcoming us. I brushed Rainy and Amanda and rubbed their legs with liniment. I paid extra attention to Rainy, checking to see if I could feel his ribs more than I should.

Deer skulls and antlers were tacked along the front of the Deans' house. Rough-cut rail enclosed a porch where two rocking chairs sat. The beams supporting the roof were in their natural shape: Not perfectly straight like factory-cut wood, they showed the same lines and contours they had as trees. One was even forked, adding to the natural feel of the structure. I stacked my saddles and packs carefully in the corner, and sat down on one of the rocking chairs to wait. The wind was light in the evergreens and carried the smell of mountain air. Gypsy stretched out on the porch beside me.

When they arrived, Bob and Peggy Dean hustled me inside, where Bob made a fire while Peggy made us hot toddies.

"I promise it'll take the chill out of you," she said.

We traded tales over the steamy drinks, and I learned that Bob and Peggy were both native Arizonans from old ranch families. Their home had been built by Bob's grandfather over a century before.

I shared what had happened on the high trail and told them how I'd closed my eyes and let Rainy take charge. They both nodded solemnly, and we raised our glasses to my horse.

"I truly believe," Bob announced, "that you and your animals are being watched over by the Great Trail Boss in the Sky."

The Deans let me leave Rainy and Amanda with them for a few hours the next morning, as Dan was in the area. When I'd told him the route we'd be riding after I left the Juarez family, he'd insisted I could not pass through Arizona without seeing the Grand Canyon. We'd made a loose plan for him to take me if things worked out.

Gypsy and I climbed into the cab of his truck and we headed out. Riding in a vehicle through the beautiful scenery around us felt strange, like it was all moving by too swiftly.

It was early on a fall weekday, and there were few people around as Dan, Gypsy, and I walked toward a spot along the south rim of the Grand Canyon. As we got closer, Dan said, "Close your eyes." I took his arm, shut my eyes, and let him lead the way.

"Okay, you can open them now," Dan told me, giving my arm a little squeeze. When I did, my hands covered my mouth in astonishment. There was no fence, no railing. It was just *right there*. The most spectacular sight I'd ever seen spread out inches from my toes: the canyon, carved over eons by the wild Colorado River far below.

At first glance, it seemed like just a massive display of red rock, but a longer look revealed how the sunlight, the fall season, even the very air seemed to create shadings and color variations in different directions. One direction had a protruding ledge of yellow and dark orange; across the way, it looked midnight blue and purple, and the shadows on the sides of the great chasm were deep gray. Hardy vegetation grew here and there—pinyon and juniper clinging to edges and sheer rock faces.

Dan grinned proudly, seeing my awe. Gypsy stood right at the edge, peering down, and I nervously called her to come to me. She turned, looked at me, then went right back to staring into the canyon.

As I remembered my camera and started to fiddle with it, a flash of bright blue on my finger caught my attention. I considered the beautiful turquoise in the Navajo ring I was wearing—the one Julie Johnson had given me. My gaze moved from the ring back out to the immense beauty of the canyon spread before us.

I turned to Dan, close beside me.

"Thank you," I said.

I had seen the heart and the spirit of Arizona.

## SADDLE TRAMP

I rode down from a hill trail and picked up Route 66 again somewhere near the town of Seligman. The road veered well away from the new highway and took a northerly turn into the low hills of Northwest Arizona. Here Route 66 was on its own, not demoted to a frontage road for the new interstate or paved over as part of another highway. I was too young to know much more about Route 66 than what I'd learned in songs and novels, but I had read *The Grapes of Wrath*. In that book, John Steinbeck sealed the road's place in history by depicting the struggles of the refugees of the Dust Bowl as they migrated west, and it was he who coined the term "The Mother Road."

It had surprised me to find the road mostly forgotten, but travelers had abandoned it in favor of the newer, faster interstate.

The towns along it often felt like they were on the edge of survival. Other than a few closed and crumbling roadside stops, the miles between towns were often empty and quiet, much as I imagined they would have been long ago, before railroads or road trips had any impact on the area.

I was told someone would be watching for us out past Seligman, and as I rode near a well-kept, ranch-style home, a woman stepped out along the road, holding the neck of her cardigan closed against the chill air. I greeted her, and she said, "Let me show you where you and your horses can spend the night."

My assumption that we were heading toward a barn out back was wrong. We were heading toward a row of maroon-colored boxcars, white lettering faded on the sides. I'd seen them all over the West, off the rails and sitting still, used for storage or as sheds for livestock.

I was a little surprised to be escorted to the railroad cars but also found it kind of cool. In my early childhood, my family lived in Pennsylvania in a coal-mining town with railroads running through. My mom had an uncle who would show up every now and then. When I asked where he came from, my mother explained that he rode on trains, and, as she put it, "went wherever the wind would take him." She said it like his was a sad, failed life, but I was fascinated by the idea. At five or six years old I horrified my mother by saying I wanted to grow up to be a hobo.

I pushed my packs and saddles inside one of the boxcars, and while Rainy and Amanda grazed on the nearby grass, I filled our water bucket at the side of the house. It was almost dark when I led Rainy and Amanda into the train car. They stepped right up the little ramp and in, as if they were loading onto a horse trailer. It was not bad inside: Old straw bedding covered the floor, and there were tie rings bolted to the wall. The faint aroma of horses made us feel at home.

I poured out grain from plastic bags for my horse and mule. The feed was getting low; I had to find more grain at the next town or ranch we came to. I found the sandwiches and apples I'd saved from a previous stop and sat cross-legged on the floor, the animals and I sharing our meal together.

By the light of my lantern, I penned short notes to update the growing list of people who wrote to me. I answered everyone who sent me mail on the road, even if it was just a postcard. I finished the evening with a short "hello" to Reid, although letters from him were becoming fewer and farther between.

Dawn brought cold air blowing in but no clouds in the purple sky. I knew it would get warm later, when we were on the road and the sun rose at our backs. As I hopped out of the boxcar, I could see the lights were on in the house. After saddling Rainy and preparing our packs, I walked over to ask if there was a post office or feed supply anywhere near.

I knocked on the door, and the woman who'd shown me to the boxcar answered right away. She looked surprised to see me, like she'd forgotten we were out there.

"Good morning," I said. "I wondered—"

"We're just about to finish breakfast," she interrupted. I could smell the wonderful aroma of bacon in the air. "When we're done, if we have any left, I'll put it on a plate and leave it outside for you." She shut the door before I could say anything more.

I didn't know what to think. I stepped back, rather stunned, and looked at my animals, packed and ready to conquer the road ahead. I walked over to them, patted each one of my friends, tightened Rainy's cinch, and got on.

The bacon smelled amazing. But I was not going to take leftover food off her plate. I turned Rainy west, clucked to Amanda, and called to Gypsy. Like a wandering stray dog, we silently slipped away as the sun lightened the sky.

**41.** A shot taken by a reporter along Route 66, nearing Gallup, New Mexico.
*Photo by Don Armstrong*

**42.** The intelligent face of Amanda.

**43.** Here you can see the neck rope my farrier back in New York made for me. It was attached to Rainy's halter so I had an easy way to tie him on our trip. I rarely see them used anymore. (Gypsy snuck into the picture!)

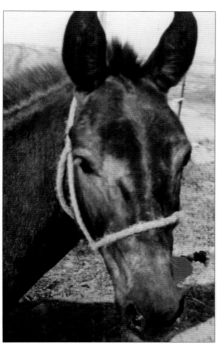

44. With the guards at Fort Wingate in western New Mexico.

45. Struggling to get moving in the stunning red rock country near the Arizona border. I think Amanda was acting up in this picture!

46. I was able to get a few pictures, like this one in Arizona, by using the timer on my camera.

47. With one of my "Rest Stop Guardians," west of Chambers, Arizona.

48. Gypsy at the edge of the Grand Canyon, staring down in awe, like all visitors do!

49. We all enjoyed the forest and meadow trails around Williams, Arizona.

50. Patrons and workers at "The Point," an old-time honky-tonk on Route 66, where I had a great night.

51. Members from the Chamber of Commerce from Bullhead City, Arizona, and Laughlin, Nevada, found us on the road and presented me with a plaque and a medal to commemorate our time in the area.

52. Nearing the summit around Union Pass as we crossed over the mountains into Nevada and California.

53. Arriving in Needles, California, our end destination.

54. With Arlene Allison during the celebration in Needles.

55. Dan surprised me in California, showing up in a helicopter, looking smart in his suit!

56. The end of the trail. My animals posed one last time at the California state boundary monument. Doesn't Gypsy look proud?

57. The final picture from the journey: Rainy, Gypsy, Amanda, and me, in Needles, California.

*Photo by Judy Browder Photography*

58. Shortly after moving to our own piece of land in New York State in 1984.

59. At home in the late nineties with Rainy, Gypsy, and Amanda.

60. With Rainy almost twenty years after our trip, in 2001.

61. My one and only selfie, taken with Amanda in our barn, thirty-five years after our trip, in 2017.

# ON THE WILD TRAIL

I had a choice between staying on an old two-lane or riding along the railroad, and almost automatically, I turned Rainy to the tracks. Amanda and Gypsy followed steadily along. Everything was quiet.

It wasn't long before we came to another split in the trail. One path stayed near the train tracks, but it was the other that intrigued me. It followed neither the tracks nor the road. Instead it made its own way, angling toward the hills in a westerly direction. Where did the trail lead? What was its reason for existing? I squeezed my calves, and Rainy walked forward.

We traveled all day on the dirt trail. We were in the rare situation where there were no signs of humans or their handiwork. I no longer knew where the road or railroad tracks were. There were no hogans—traditional Navajo dwellings; there were no ranch signs, no mailboxes. There were no inhabitants but the wild ones.

Gypsy roamed in wide circles, progressing with us but probably walking twice the miles that Rainy and Amanda did. The land rolled away from our trail in a landscape of faded gold, while the hills in the distance were cast in dark green, indicating trees were growing on their steep sides. The reins hung loosely on Rainy's neck. With no worries or distractions, it was easy to be in tune with every step and every breath of my horse, and to notice every little thing around us.

A mule deer appeared from the brush on the side of the trail, crossing the path in front of us. Rainy and Amanda watched her pass with interest. The deer didn't seem to be frightened by us, adding to the strange feeling I had that we belonged there, beneath the wide and blue sky.

Several times, Gypsy stopped and looked behind us. Rainy flicked his ears back. From the saddle, I turned and swept my gaze over the brush. I saw nothing but the squat, sharp-needled trees along the trail. But then there was a gentle tug on the lead line in my hand as Amanda, too, tried to take a look behind us. With my lesser senses, it took several minutes for me to finally spot what my friends had known for a while.

Blending in perfectly with the gray and brown landscape was a coyote. He was far enough away that it took me a minute to focus on him, but close enough that our eyes met. He seemed neither frightened nor aggressive.

I rode forward for a while, and he followed behind us. Intrigued, it occurred to me to get a picture of our new friend, and I reached into my saddlebag for the camera, turning Rainy sideways, to get the angle. But with no zoom lens and the way the coyote's color blended softly into his surroundings, I couldn't get a good shot.

Then I remembered the remains of lunch I carried in my packs. Perhaps the coyote would come closer to get food, and I could get the picture I wanted. I pulled out a square of wax paper and sandwich, and gave it a good toss, like a Frisbee. It fell loosely on the ground between us and the coyote. He cocked his ears forward and looked at the offering. He was interested! He took a step toward the bread. Slowly, I raised the camera to my eye. He crept a little closer, and I got him in the frame.

Suddenly, a flash of a different figure, low-slung and fast, ran into the camera's sights. *What the...?*

It was Gypsy. Without slowing at all, she snatched that sandwich practically from under the coyote's jaws and ran all out back to where I sat with Rainy and Amanda.

I lowered the camera, my mouth hanging open.

I felt a moment of fear that the coyote would chase Gypsy or fight her for the food, but he just stood there, looking perplexed. Then I felt a surge of affection. *She thinks I dropped the sandwich, and she's bringing it back to me!* But Gypsy ran right past me, dropped to the ground on the other side of Rainy, and quickly gobbled down the sandwich. She glanced back at the coyote with the last piece of crust hanging from between her teeth. After a surprised moment, I tipped my head back and laughed and laughed.

We continued along, and following his humiliation by Gypsy, our coyote friend wandered away. We came to a place with three evergreen trees in a half circle, and I dismounted, cleared the cones that had fallen, and spread my jacket on the ground. I took everything off Rainy and Amanda, scratched their backs, and let them relax. They munched on the wild grass along the trail.

Gypsy and I sat on my jacket and I shared my water with her. The canteen was pretty full, but I needed to keep my eyes open for water if we stayed on this trail. I removed the sandwich from my pack and looked at my dog.

"Are you going to take this, too, Gyps?" I asked, roughing the top of her head. She flopped over so I'd get her belly, as well.

I unsnapped my knife from my belt and cut up apples to share with Rainy and Amanda. A blackbird flew in, hopping from branch to branch until he was as close as he dared, keeping an eye on us and any crumbs of food we might leave. A slight breeze touched the tips of the trees and bowed the heads of the tall grass. It lifted the manes of Rainy and Amanda, and gently wrapped their tails around their hocks from time to time.

I wondered when water from my canteen had become enough, and I'd stopped craving ice-cold soda. I wondered when I'd stopped wishing I had a napkin and just happily wiped my grimy fingers, sticky from feeding apples to horses, on my jeans. I wondered when I'd begun to feel like I was a part of all this: the blackbird and the horse and the mule and the dog and the wind and the yellow grass and the tiny gravel beneath our feet.

I wondered if a person could turn wild.

# CHEERS, PEACE

The Leases' barn in Yampai had two rows of stalls with a well-swept aisle down the middle. Their horses were in when we arrived and whinnied at the newcomers. A cot with fresh sheets and a blanket was set up in the tack room for me, and Mrs. Lease invited me to join them for dinner and to use their phone to call home.

After supper, Gypsy and I returned to our little place in the barn. Lately, I'd spent so much time alone with the animals that it became necessary to sort of step back when I was around people. Roadside visits, interviews, and new acquaintances could be fun and broke up long days, but I felt more…more myself, maybe… riding alone in the company of Rainy, Gypsy, and Amanda. I was grateful for all that had been done for us by the people we had met along our road. But my soul had gotten used to solitude.

In the airy barn, I moved my cot in front of the stall doors where Rainy and Amanda were spending the night. As usual, I wrote in my journal—where we'd traveled that day, who we'd talked to, and the sights we'd seen. I looked at the date I'd inked at the top of the page. It had a familiarity…was one I'd made note of…but why?

When it came back to me, I knew I had to go back to the Leases' house and make a weird request.

At my hesitant knock, Mrs. Lease peeked out the door, then opened it wide. "Come in," she said with concern. "Is everything okay?"

I felt awkward. I'd had to ask for help many times on my journey, but I'd never asked to watch someone's television before.

"Can I watch a show on your TV?" I felt sheepish, and Mrs. Lease looked surprised. I launched into the story of Ron Karabatsos, how I'd met the actor at a highway rest stop and that he was in an episode of a new television show—and that episode was airing that night.

Mr. Lease joined us, and the couple invited me inside, amused by the story of the big tough police investigator who was afraid to fly. They warned me they only got two channels, but as luck would have it, NBC was one of them.

When the man I met at that lonely rest stop appeared on the screen, I leaned forward with excitement. "There he is! That's him!" I practically shouted. And it *was* him, playing an obnoxious Yankees fan to Ted Danson's Red Sox fan, just like he told me.

We all agreed the show was pretty good, and I said goodnight to them once again as the credits rolled up on the screen. Mr. and Mrs. Lease invited me to sleep on their couch, but I assured them the space in the barn was perfect.

Gypsy squeezed right on the narrow cot beside me. I laid my hand on her head. The horses made soft noises: They turned in their stalls and lowered their heads, blowing gently from their nostrils as they drifted to sleep. Peace was all around us.

## ▓ THE ROAD IS OURS

Route 66 was one of America's first long-distance roads to be paved. In the 1930s it carried the hopes of farmers escaping the dust storms of the Midwest. Other Americans headed west on 66 during the Depression, and the road became synonymous with new beginnings. It's credited with popularizing the American road trip in the fifties and for practically inventing the idea of roadside attractions: trading posts, souvenir shops, Wild West shows, reptile farms—any quirky idea that might entice motorists to stop. In the sixties it stood for freedom, self-exploration, and "movin' on."

There wasn't a hint of its significance where I rode—no historical markers to be seen, no monuments awaiting our discovery. Toppled signs held messages too faded to read. Weeds poked through cracks in the pavement.

We'd passed from one small town to another: Ashfork to Seligman, on through Yampai, Truxton, Peach Springs, Valentine,

Hackberry. We found water, and very occasionally, a general store to replenish supplies. The land was a series of hills, and the road climbed upward, wound around, then rolled back down again.

I'd acquired a habit of saying, "Okay, Rainy, the road is ours," when there were no cars. On this empty stretch of two-lane, my animals and I rode in the middle of the road.

As I walked alongside Rainy, stretching my tired muscles with some time out of the saddle, he stopped and raised his head, focusing his big brown eyes upward. I followed his gaze and saw a hawk circling on the wind, riding the drafts of air in easy swooping circles. The animals and I all stopped to watch. What did that hawk see, as he flew effortlessly over the land that took us days to cover? I wondered if he could easily make it to California on the wind, the place that had seemed so distant for so long.

My attention was drawn back to earth as I heard a vehicle approaching, the first I'd seen in a while. An ancient pickup came into view, slowing to pass around us. The driver gave a friendly wave. He, too, looked up, probably curious about what had us stopped and staring at the sky. He'd see it was just a hawk, nothing out of the ordinary.

The truck moved on, over a hill, and was gone from sight. I looked behind us—nothing. I got back in the saddle and listened, but the only sound was the gentle whisper of the breeze as it rustled dry grass at the edge of the pavement. We walked on in the middle of the road, undisturbed. The road was ours. Ours and the ghosts' of those who'd traveled here before.

## HUALAPAI DINER

The sun sat high overhead as we rode through the southern section of the Hualapai Reservation. I stopped at a roadside café, eager for something to eat that was not out of my saddlebags.

Inside I found a couple empty round tables and a short counter where two men sat, chatting with a young American Indian woman standing on the other side, leaning on her elbows. The conversation stopped as I stepped inside. All three stared at me. They look surprised.

I wondered if I'd done something wrong—if the establishment was for Hualapai only. But it didn't seem likely anyone would open a diner on the side of a road and then try to keep people out. I sat down at one of the small tables. The woman behind the counter said something to the two men, and they laughed.

After a long few minutes, the woman dragged herself over with a pad and pen and asked abruptly, "What do you want?"

"A grilled cheese and a Coke, please," I replied self-consciously. Mostly I wanted to get out of there, but that would be even more awkward.

The two men and the woman talked while I waited. I didn't know why, but it made me feel uncomfortable.

The woman came around the counter and dropped the sandwich on a plate in front of me with a clank.

"Thanks," I said.

She walked away without responding.

A week or so before, as my animals and I were riding on reservation land, we'd come upon a Navajo Chapter house. Knowing there was usually a payphone at these administrative buildings, I had hopped off Rainy and asked a woman at the front desk if I could use the payphone. With a tip of her head, she indicated "in there." I walked through the doors to find myself in a room where a Navajo tribal meeting was taking place.

All faces turned to stare that time, too, but with mild curiosity. Then they went back to their business. I'd made my call home, whispering that I was well and where we were, then waved silently in thanks as I tiptoed out the door.

The bigger, more heavyset of the two men at the counter turned partially toward me and said something a little louder than necessary. The woman responded and gestured toward Rainy and Amanda, visible outside the window. Mixed in with all the words I didn't understand was a phrase I did: "New York." When the woman said it, all three started laughing.

Pushing away the crusts from my sandwich, I left some money on the table and walked out the door. I untied my animals and started out on foot to clear my head. I hoped the feeling in the diner hadn't been because of something I had said or done. I recognized I was a stranger, passing through their land.

## HILLTOP HONKYTONK

We stayed on old 66 as it climbed steadily upward, looking for a place called "The Point." We found it at a bend in the road, exactly at the hill's summit.

The low-slung, older building appeared to have had several additions over the years. Part of the building was a bar, the "Open" sign lit up in the window, and four or five motel rooms faced a parking area in front. The whole structure was a faded mustard-yellow color, the paint, doors, and windows wearing a coat of dust. I tied Rainy and Amanda in the small post corral nearby.

We'd ridden past the ruins of such places before on Route 66. The difference was that although this one showed signs of age, it was clearly still alive.

The bar had only a few people in it, but I got a hearty welcome. I was continually amazed by how news had a way of getting around in these far-flung places. Everyone seemed to know I was "the girl on the horse."

"The boss says you can use the corral," the bartender said in response to my query about camping. "And you can have one of the rooms for five bucks, if you want. Dinner's on us," he added.

I couldn't believe this place—a room and dinner for five dollars.

Out at the corral, I took my time brushing Rainy and Amanda. A bale of decent-looking hay sat outside the pen. I pulled a few flakes for them and filled their water bucket, then headed back to the bar to find out about that room, Gypsy trotting beside me.

A blonde woman of indeterminate age—I thought maybe twenties, maybe thirties—was now behind the bar. When I mentioned the room the other guy had promised, she introduced herself.

"I'm Barb. I don't know about a key, but c'mon, let's find Lee, the owner." We wandered outside together, Gypsy with us, chatting as we walked.

"Hey, can you come to my birthday party?" Barb asked suddenly.

I responded the only way I could think of: "When is it?"

"Tonight!" she exclaimed. "We're gonna have a steak dinner and music and cake! I want you to come!" Her enthusiasm was almost childlike.

"Oh, you don't have to invite me," I assured her with a smile.

She looked aghast. "But I want you to come!"

I said okay, laughing a little to myself as we headed back to the bar, our search for Lee outside having been unsuccessful.

We found Lee back at the bar. He greeted me warmly and told me my room number.

"We're fixing the place up," he offered as he reached under the bar for a key. Then, with a smile: "You can have the room that has a toilet and shower that work." He slid the key across the bar to me.

"Thank you," I said gratefully, thinking of a shower, maybe flopping down on a bed for a bit. But Lee filled a beer and put it in front of me, so I took a seat and a long, slow sip.

"What do you think of Arizona?" Lee asked. "How have people been treating you?"

Barb and Lee's wife Connie pulled up stools on either side of me. "Have there been any scary parts?" Barb asked.

"Any *really good* parts?" Connie added.

I told them about the storms in Indiana and the farms in Kansas and the rattlesnake in Texas. Barb shared a story of a time she stepped right on a baby rattler...and we laughed and more beer appeared in front of us.

It was getting dark outside the bar window. Cars pulled in, wheels crunching in the gravel lot. I got up often to go out and check on Rainy and Amanda. As it got more crowded, I took Gypsy and my packs to my motel room, letting the pup settle into a tired ball on the bed. Each time I left and came back, another beer was waiting.

Most everyone who came in walked over to Barb and wished her a happy birthday. I joined her as she wiped the tables and set them for the party. Someone turned up the background music as more people streamed in the front door.

There was no easy way to describe the demographics of the crowd. There were young people, a few oldsters, women in stretch pants and teased hair. They called each other "Hon" and hugged in greeting. All the men wore cowboy hats. No one treated me like an outsider. I never got my shower, but it didn't matter; my worn jeans and dusty boots fit right in.

As steaks were brought out from the kitchen, and all of us were told to "sit and eat," I learned it was not just a party—it was Open Mic Night!

The first participant stepped up to the microphone. He was about three hundred pounds and wore the requisite cowboy hat. He opened a guitar case, tuned his instrument for a minute, then started in with "Take These Chains from My Heart," an old Hank Williams tune. Then he did Ernest Tubb and a few other songs that had their heyday forty years before. Still, everyone sang along.

The lady who followed him was in skintight pants and glasses in a style that I remembered my mom wearing when I was a little kid. People yelled out song requests—all decades old. It was like time had just passed this place by.

The singers changed and a band played next, and I got swung around the dance floor, laughing and shouting along with everyone else. It was long into the night when the main lights came on, the signal to all that it was closing time, time to go home, and in my case, time to go check on Rainy and Amanda and head to my five-dollar motel room, where Gypsy waited patiently.

Outside, pickup trucks pulled away from the parking lot. Horns tooted cheerily, and one or two drivers rolled down their windows and yelled, "Good luck!" when they saw me standing by Rainy and Amanda. I watched them all leave, mostly trucks, all older models. They had hitches in back; the beds were scratched and dented from fence posts and tools and rolls of barbed wire. They wore a coat of dust and gave off the feeling of having worked hard and come far. I could picture them, driving in from out in the hills, following the same rough roads under the same big sky that my animals and I had been riding over and beneath each day. Sometimes, out here, it looked like a land empty of inhabitants, but that wasn't the case. Whatever was needed—help, or water, or company, or even a rowdy Saturday night at a hilltop honkytonk—we all seemed to find it.

## CLOSENESS

A good relationship with a horse is a special thing, unlike anything else. There's a physical aspect: The connection of riding is like actually being a part of your horse, and vice versa. When I sat on Rainy's back, he understood the twitch of a muscle, the tightening of fingers on the reins, or a shift of weight in the saddle. And we spent other physical time together. There was grooming him, checking his legs, and cleaning his hooves. Each day I laid my ear against his side, listening to his gut sounds to make sure all systems were go. I ran my hands along his spine, his ribs, just to see how his weight was and where any soreness might be.

But our special connection also had a psychological component. It was a very positive thing in my life. I *liked* being near my horse. When I packed up in the mornings, I often stopped and leaned on his shoulder—the strength it gave me was internal. When I was cold, I held my hands against his neck, in the place where his body heat was trapped under his mane. He never moved away from these moments of affection or closeness. There was a level of communication between us that surpassed anything I've known with any other animal.

We were still where I'd come to think of as "up in the hills," riding the long, quiet road as it followed the contours of the land. When we came to a trail leading away from the road, I turned down it to find a place to take our break. Once the packs were pulled free, Rainy and Amanda stood side by side, resting. Gypsy sniffed the roots of a stunted juniper tree. After a few minutes, I noticed Rainy watching me, his big brown eyes on me in what seemed a thoughtful way. Amanda had gone back to foraging for blades of grass, but Rainy's gaze stayed steady. I walked to him and ran my hand along the slope of his shoulder.

"Hey, Bud," I murmured, scratching his withers. He leaned slightly into the scratching.

"You're such a good boy," I told him. Rainy turned his head toward me. In a deliberate yet delicate manner, he touched his muzzle to my cheekbone. Then he lowered his head and rested his chin on my chest. I leaned my forehead against his, and we stood quietly in this way for a few moments.

I treasured my horse and our connection. But this time I felt like Rainy was trying to tell me something. I stayed with him for as long as he was still.

## CAMERA-CONSCIOUS

The sun rose behind us, casting new color along the sides of the distant hills, turning them caramel, briefly, and making gray-green shadows where the pine trees stood. Though it was early, I could tell it was going to be a beautiful day. I peeled off layers of outerwear as we made our way. The air was soft and warm, and even the worn-out pavement looked like a road of gold.

I was daydreaming, lost in my thoughts, when a car came from the west and stopped near us. My animals and I waited while a woman got out of the driver's seat and strode toward us.

"You must be Missy!" she exclaimed, shielding her eyes with her hand so she could see us in the sun. I nodded. "I'm Arlene Allison, and that's my daughter Jeanine, back in the car," she offered with a friendly smile. "We couldn't wait to meet you, so we came out to find you! When you get to our feed shop in Kingman, we'll walk your horse and mule over to the fairgrounds where our horses live."

It sounded like an easy ride to Kingman, and it was nice to know the Allisons would be waiting for us. When Arlene and Jeanine drove away, it felt good to be able to enjoy the day's ride, free from worry about where we'd find water or a place to stay. But as we followed the twists and turns of the road, I felt a little twinge of sadness. The last few days had been an interesting mix of the forgotten lanes of old Route 66 and the wildness of the trails up in the hills. I'd felt separate from the busy human world and very connected with the rugged landscape.

I wasn't sure how I felt about leaving that yet.

Traffic increased as we neared town. When Rainy stopped with no cue from me, I knew why: Someone had gotten out of a car across the road and was aiming a camera at us. Rainy and Amanda waited with ears pricked forward, looking directly at the camera. Gypsy, who was riding in the saddle with me, focused forward, ears up. When they heard the distinct click of the camera shutter, the animals all relaxed and Rainy started forward again, without a cue from me.

Rainy, Gypsy, and Amanda's actions were the comical result of the many times they'd been photographed on our journey. Whenever we were in a scenic area or at a landmark, I positioned my animals, told them to stay, and took a picture. Countless others had taken our photo, too: reporters, tourists, friends. The result was my three smart animals had learned the drill. When someone pointed a camera, they posed.

Gypsy was the biggest ham of all. If only Rainy and Amanda were being photographed, she'd usually sneak into the picture. And, of course, people found it funny that she rode in the saddle. "Can I get a picture of the dog riding the horse?" was a common request. Gypsy had had her picture taken so many times, and been praised for it, that now when she saw someone with a camera, she faced the person, model-ready, head held high and proud. She wouldn't budge until she heard that click.

## DECISION

In Kingman, the whole Allison family—Arlene and husband Bob, Jeanine, and her brother Shawn—greeted me. Shawn and Jeanine walked me to the local fairgrounds where Amanda and Rainy would stay for the night.

As we sat sharing a meal, I looked around at the family's friendly faces. I recognized that strange bit of luck that happens as we travel: sometimes, things fall into place perfectly. I got the feeling that meeting up with the Allisons was one of those special connections that was meant to be.

Arlene was so intrigued by our cross-country horseback journey that she seemed to adopt it as her cause.

"New York to California," she mused over bites of dinner. "Wow. You know you're almost to California now, don't you?"

I nodded.

"So where in California are you riding to? Where are you stopping?"

I felt Gypsy, lying across my feet under the table as I took a deep breath. Maybe it was the fact that the border of California was not so far away, and I had to acknowledge it sooner or later. Maybe it was the warmth that I felt in the Allisons' home. Whatever the reason, for the first time, I said the words out loud.

"We're stopping at Needles."

Arlene looked surprised. "Needles! That's not too far away!"

I nodded again.

"This is so exciting, that we get to be part of this!" she exclaimed, clapping her hands.

It was a sweet thing to say, and I smiled at her as I explained that from studying my maps, I'd learned that Needles was the first town we would come to once we crossed the border into California. Beyond that was desert in every direction. My gambles with water—for my animals and for me—would reach a new level of danger if we continued west from Needles.

I had other reasons, too, but for now, just saying the decision out loud was enough.

## KINGMAN

Arlene was a planner, and she took my haphazard approach of dealing with things as they came as a personal challenge. She and I, along with Bob, sat at their kitchen table with maps, a list, and the phone.

"From here," Bob explained, "there's no way to get to California without crossing the Colorado River. You're probably going to have to cross at Davis Dam."

Arlene shook her head. "I don't know if a horse can go that way," she said.

"Who's going to stop her?" Bob exclaimed with a shrug. "And it's not that bad. The road is wide across the dam, and this time of year, on a weekday, there's not much traffic. It's the only way. I don't think they'll have a problem riding across."

"What about the mountains?" Arlene worried.

Bob looked at me.

"To get into Nevada and California, you have to go over mountains that border the Colorado River. Then you start the downhill ride to the desert floor on the other side. I think your best bet is to stay on 68 after Golden Valley, and climb up through Union Pass." Bob paused. "It's a rough road, steep and winding, but there's little traffic up that way. You guys should be all right."

There was no way to prepare for everything, but knowing a little of what to expect was a good thing. I appreciated that the Allisons were making arrangements for places to stay, and it was touching to see how much it all worried Arlene.

I had learned on my journey that riding through a town could be either stressful or fun, and seeing the rest of Kingman on our way out the next day was enjoyable. We walked down Main Street through the downtown business area. I wanted to slow things down a little, now that I knew California was not too far ahead, and every time we got stopped to answer questions or pose for a picture, I took my time and visited with the people who wished us well.

Gypsy rode in the saddle as we headed toward the outskirts of town and the road to Golden Valley. As we passed through the last of the business area, I pondered what it was that made small Western cities like Kingman so likable. Was it the way they maintained strong ties to their heritage, with the rodeo or fairgrounds right in the middle of town? Was it because you were more likely to encounter people who were glad to see a horse and mule in town than those who would grumble about livestock not belonging on city streets?

The storefronts in Kingman were right up against the sidewalk, so I looked into the windows from my perch in the saddle. We passed one outdoor gear store where the lights were off. I stopped Rainy and Amanda and leaned over to read the handwritten note tacked on the shop door.

*Gone fishin'. Be back Thursday.*

I smiled as we rode out of town.

## HAUNTED

South and west of Kingman, the land revealed itself as true desert. It was open and flat, but in every direction, hard jagged mountains were visible. The sun dipped behind the giant hills of rock, draining the light from the day before it should.

I reached Golden Valley and located Dennis and Sandy, contacts through the Allisons. Dennis explained that, at the moment, they lived in a small camper while they poured their resources into finding old buildings throughout the West. They moved the structures to their land and restored them to their original state, hoping to eventually recreate a Western town that they would open as a tourist stop. I could see past their camper where a couple old structures stood: one made with clay walls and wooden beams, and another, a small cabin-like shack. A red-and-white horse dozed in a nearby corral.

"Our camper is really small," Sandy said apologetically. "We thought you'd probably be more comfortable in one of the other buildings."

We walked to the structure closest to the corral.

"We think this might have been a miner or prospector's cabin," said Dennis, tapping the wooden floor with his boot. "It's in pretty good shape."

The place was maybe twelve by twelve feet, empty but for a piece of plywood, leaning against the wall. The one window had no glass in it, but it looked like they'd swept the room, and it was clean and dry.

"This will be fine," I assured them.

After Dennis and Sandy grilled burgers for dinner, I walked with Gypsy to the little building by the corral. No moon lit the night, and it was very dark inside the cabin. I dragged my packs in and looked around with the beam of my flashlight. I set up my sleeping bag near the window so I could look out at Rainy and Amanda, then peeled off my jeans and crawled into my sleeping bag. Gypsy thumped down beside me. My lantern cast a small circle of light onto my journal, and my small radio played quietly.

Most of my life I had dealt with insomnia, even as a child, but this trip had cured it. I supposed it was because I was out in the wind and the sun all day. Whatever the reason, even in the unusual places we often found ourselves, sleep came to me pretty quickly.

My head got heavy. I turned off the lantern and turned the radio down to a low murmur. I slept a while before a weird sound jarred me awake. It was the radio—it sounded like it was losing its station. It sounded like English, then gibberish, as signals from different stations came and went. It faded then got loud, as if some invisible thumb was twirling the dials.

Gypsy raised her head and looked at me as I picked up the radio and shook it. I turned it off and lay back down.

I wasn't sure how much time had passed when I was awakened again. I stayed very still, waiting for some sense of what it was that had brought me to wakefulness.

Something was scratching at the side of the cabin.

What could be making the noise? The scratching sounded like a branch when the wind causes it to scrape against a building. But there was no wind blowing. There were no trees around.

I tightened my grip on the edge of my sleeping bag. Gypsy unwound herself from her curled-up position and sat upright. *It must be some kind of desert rat or something*, I told myself. Of all people, I shouldn't be bothered by nature noises at night.

Suddenly, I sat up, pulling the sleeping bag up to my neck. *Knock knock*. A new sound. Then, louder: *KNOCK KNOCK*.

It continued: A couple knocks, followed by silence, then scratching again. Then there was a rattle—not like a rattlesnake but like the outside door clattering.

Gypsy jumped to her feet. She cocked her head sideways, listening, then tipped her nose in the air like she was checking a scent. She began pacing. I was more frightened when she moved away from my side.

"Gypsy!" I whispered frantically. "Gypsy!"

I wanted my dog next to me, but for some reason, I was afraid to make any noise. She came to me and sat on the edge of the sleeping bag, but whined nervously. I slid my hand out of the bag and laid it on her. My breathing was shallow and fast.

Suddenly Gypsy darted over to one of the empty corners of the cabin. The hair along her back stood on end. She growled and snapped her teeth while looking at the corner *as if something was there.*

I squeezed my eyes shut—*I didn't want to see.* I was afraid to move, paralyzed with fear, terrified of something I couldn't see or understand.

Gypsy came back to me, but she was agitated, turning back to the same corner and growling. I didn't know what to do.

I heard the scraping noise again. Then *the plywood sheet leaning against the wall came crashing down on top of me!*

I screeched without meaning to, shoving the wood off and leaping to my feet. I was shaking, and my legs felt like they wouldn't hold me up. Holding the sleeping bag in front of me, I bolted across the room and out the door.

I didn't know what might be outside but *nothing* would keep me in that old cabin a moment longer. I ran the few steps to the corral where Rainy and Amanda were. They were spooked, too, snorting and trotting from end to end of their enclosure. Rainy came over to me, Amanda right behind him, both of them restless and jumpy, unlike most nights—they were usually tired and took advantage of the opportunity to rest.

I climbed onto the top rail and wrapped the sleeping bag around my shoulders. Gypsy stayed right near my feet, and Rainy and Amanda stood close by. We all drew comfort from each other, feeling safer together. We remained in our huddle for a long time, until the sun came up over the desert, turning everything red and casting shadows around the old cabin.

I was packed and ready to leave when the morning brightened enough to see well. Dennis asked me how I slept, and not wanting to be impolite, I said, "Okay." In the light of day, I didn't know how to explain the night's events and not sound crazy.

Dennis saddled up the pinto to ride with us for a ways. I was quiet and distracted, my rational, logical side busy trying to come up with an explanation for the strange happenings inside the cabin. I decided to bring it up cautiously with Dennis.

"What did you say that cabin I slept in was used for?" I asked, trying to sound casual.

"Well, we were told it was an old miner's cabin," he replied. "But I was going to ask you. I thought maybe you'd know more about it than me."

I stared at him. What did *that* mean? Had he had a weird experience in the cabin, too? Had he expected something to happen out there?

"Why would I know anything about the history of the cabin?"

I tried to gauge his reaction, looking for clues, but he just shrugged and said, "I don't know." It seemed Dennis was done talking, as he was quiet for a minute before suddenly reining his horse around and announcing, "Well, time to head back. Hope it all goes well for you."

Then he rode away, east, back to his place.

## BLACK MOUNTAINS

The road leaving Golden Valley was straight and flat and pretty easy going for Rainy and Amanda. But in my line of vision rose the rough-looking Black Mountain Range, looming up in front of us. We were riding right toward those mountains.

The Black Mountain Range was what had Arlene Allison worried for us: The narrow road over the mountains, the continual steep climb until we reached the summit, and the tough walk down the western side.

It felt like I'd ridden several miles when the road started to rise, and we found ourselves in rough territory of rocks and jagged formations. We worked our way upward without the bother of traffic, though this added to a sense of isolation in the rugged, lonely place.

I got off and walked—it was enough of an effort for Rainy and Amanda to work at the steep ascent, carrying the packs and saddles. When at last it seemed we'd reached the highest point, there was a wide spot of gravel off to one side of the road, and I led the animals over to take a look at the view.

From the height of the pass I could see for miles and miles. It took my breath away. Slivers of the Colorado River wound through the valley below, and imposing peaks rose all around, the grays and blacks of the stone mountains contrasting with startlingly blue glimpses of water and sky. It was a picture of stark but incredible beauty.

I inhaled sharply. I knew the mountains on the other side of the water were in Nevada. And beyond that? The farther peaks? Could they be in California?

I thought of the Mojave Indians who must have worn the first footpaths over this pass, then later the miners and prospectors, climbing their way through, working toward their dreams. I kept one arm slung over Rainy's neck while his breathing slowed back to normal. A deep wave of emotion rose in me at seeing the land we'd been chasing for so many months.

Rainy, Gypsy, Amanda, and I had found our way here. Now we were connected in our own way to this place, to the footsteps of a thousand other journeys, to the dreams of other dreamers, and to the land, harsh and stunning, that lay below us and before us.

## WILD WATCHERS

I mounted up, and we began our long and careful downhill trek. Surrounded by peaks and cliffs and odd-shaped rocks, distance was hard to judge. We followed the road, trusting it would take us where we needed to go. I avoided the edges, which were high and open to a long, steep drop. It felt desolate in the barren, craggy cliffs, as if we were the only creatures around.

Observant, sensitive Rainy was usually the first to notice anything out of the ordinary, catching the slightest movement or change in our surroundings. But this time, it was Amanda who gave a little tug on her lead rope as we walked the narrow roadway. I turned to see what had caused her to pull on the lead, but my eyes caught nothing other than rocks and mountains.

A few steps later, Amanda stopped. Again, she was looking toward the peaks to the south of the road. This time I waited, watching her watch the ridge. The stillness and patience I'd learned from the animals paid off.

Up above us, four wild burros looked over the side of their rocky perch. The sight of the long donkey faces crowned with impressive ears pleased my spirit. I'd heard that wild Mustangs and burros roamed this unpopulated area of the desert Southwest, but I'd figured it was too much to hope for that we'd ever catch a glimpse of them. A moment with the wild burros felt like a gift, and it was thanks to Amanda.

"Those're your cousins up there, 'Manda," I whispered. She kept her gaze on the four burros, her own lovely ears pointing their way. I was happy to remain still for as long as the wild equines and my domestic ones remained curious about each other. I hoped to let the moment go on as long as possible.

## DAVIS DAM

The same two-lane road that wound over the mountain pass led us to the impressive structure of Davis Dam, one of two that harnessed the Colorado River, creating Lake Mead and Lake Mohave. To get any farther, my animals and I had to walk across the top of the massive wall that made up the dam.

I assessed the situation. The size and magnitude of Davis Dam were impressive. It was big and intimidating. On our side I could see a power station, a parking area, and a car with a security logo on it. I didn't spot anyone on foot, though cars and trucks were driving across. They slowed down when they saw our little caravan, and the drivers and passengers stared and waved.

The road across the dam looked wide with some shoulder lane, just as Bob Allison had promised. There was a sturdy barrier along the edge, which made me feel a little better about riding along the top of a high wall. My animals had crossed many bridges: high, low, wide, and narrow. I didn't think what was below mattered to Rainy and Amanda. As long as they didn't sense danger, they would treat the dam like any other part of the road, if I asked them to. Such was our faith in each other.

I looked back over my shoulder at the road behind us, then ahead again. When no cars were coming from either direction, I gave a little squeeze with my legs, and we began our long, high walk.

Some surprising incongruities were to be found in Arizona, and now it seemed ironic to think of how much time I had spent searching for and worrying about water. The same road that had led us through sandy desert devoid of water took us to this place where we could literally stand above billions of gallons of it.

If I'd read my map right, the state line between Arizona and Nevada was partway across the Colorado River. With no vehicles in sight, I stopped and took it all in: The road across the giant dam and the water below. The sharp-edged mountains, surrounding everything. I fixed the way it looked and felt in my mind.

"Okay, guys," I said, patting Rainy's neck, laying my hand on Gypsy's back. We stepped forward and into Nevada.

## CASINO NIGHT, LAUGHLIN

In Kingman, people had described Laughlin as "a mini Las Vegas, but with a river." It was accurate, as long as the emphasis was on the "mini" part. The Colorado River was a presence in Laughlin, flowing along one side of the "strip," which held only a few casinos. Other than that, it didn't really even look like a city.

I rode in on a quiet road in open desert—no houses, schools, or stores in sight. Then suddenly we were in the mini-sprawl near the casinos and hotels, with the accompanying lights and neon. Bright signs enticed people to come inside. Cars passed up and down the street. *Where did they come from?* I wondered. My animals and I dodged in and out of traffic.

In the middle of Laughlin's bustling strip was a casino called the Crystal Palace. I had to laugh when I saw the marquee out front, which read: "Welcome Missy, Raindance, Gypsy, and Amanda."

I turned Rainy in at the place, pleased to have the nice welcome but unsure what to do. It didn't look like accommodation for a horse and mule.

I didn't stand outside feeling unsure for long. A man hurried toward us, saying, "Come on out back!" I jumped off and followed him around the side of the casino. We stopped at a pen, built right in the parking area. There were shavings thick on the ground for Rainy and Amanda's tired feet. The hastily built enclosure was not far from the kitchen door where several women in waitress outfits were standing, smoking. They came to say hi to Rainy and Amanda, and cooed and fussed over Gypsy.

"There's a room inside for you," the man who greeted us told me. "Everything you need while here is compliments of the Crystal Palace. Enjoy your stay."

In the evening, Bob and Arlene Allison drove over and joined me for dinner, admitting they were the force behind the wonderful welcome. As we enjoyed our meal together in the hotel restaurant, I was paged over the loudspeaker to take a call from the Chamber of Commerce; then, paged again for another call from the radio station KBAS, who arranged an interview over at the Colorado Belle. People approached our table throughout the evening to say hello and offer good wishes, and the hotel picked up our tab.

When the Allisons had headed back to Kingman, I retrieved Gypsy from my hotel room for an evening ramble. We went out to Rainy and Amanda's pen where they were working on some hay. Both of them raised their heads in greeting as I stroked their necks. I heard cars passing on the street out front, the hum of electricity, and the muffled sound of voices. For the first time in a long while, I felt a touch of moisture in the night air from the nearby river.

I couldn't really see the stars—there were too many competing lights from the little strip. In Laughlin, there were wheelers and dealers, people who rode the Colorado and docked their boats, and others who drove in with campers and RVs. And there stood Rainy and Amanda, having arrived the old-fashioned way, as if stepping in from a different time. We'd had evenings by railroad tracks, in barns, boxcars, and backyards, but behind the casino was perhaps the oddest place yet that my horse and mule had spent a night.

A security guard came over to talk. "Don't worry about them," he said, gesturing toward Rainy and Amanda. "There's security at the back door all night. We'll keep an eye on them."

"Thanks." I smiled at him in appreciation. "That's good to know."

Suddenly, I realized I didn't see Gypsy.

"Where's my dog?" I interrupted the guard, who was telling me about Laughlin. "Where's my dog?"

The man took his foot off the bottom rung of the pen where he'd been leaning and stepped back, looking around.

"She can't be far. Probably right around here."

I hurried toward the front of the casino, panicked at the thought of the busy street. I broke into a run, calling, "Gypsy! Gypsy!" There was no sign of her out front, no sense of disruption in the street. I ran around the back again. The guard was shining his flashlight around some parked cars, looking for her.

Gypsy never let me out of her sight. I fought a sinking feeling, jogging to the back entrance to ask if anyone had seen her.

As soon as I stepped into the kitchen, I stopped short. In one corner, the waitresses had made a pile of soft tablecloths. Sprawled like a canine queen in the middle was my dog. Her belly looked distinctly more round than it had twenty minutes before.

With relief, I said her name out loud: "Gypsy!" The pup lifted her head and looked at me, thumping her tail a time or two, then let her head fall back onto the bed of tablecloths.

With her extended belly and lethargic reaction, I worried for a second that she had eaten something bad that had made her sick. I knelt to pet her, and as usual, she rolled over so I could scratch her stomach. One waitress looked at me, commenting, "She's so sweet! We love her!"

I nodded my head, still rubbing Gypsy's belly. "She's the best. I don't know what I'd do without her."

"And she sure likes prime rib, doesn't she?"

That solved the fat-belly-and-lethargy mystery.

"So, she's had some prime rib, has she?" I asked.

"She came in the back door all by herself and sat down and watched us. We gave her all kinds of stuff. She doesn't grab at it or bite your hand; she just waits nicely until you hand it to her. She's so sweet and smart, too."

"She's definitely smart," I agreed.

Gypsy raised her head again, making sure I was still there. She wagged her tail against the tablecloths as she once more let her head fall back down. I swear if she could have, she would have winked at me.

## NEVADA SILVER

On our second day's ride in Nevada's brushy, sandy terrain, a worn and battered pickup slowed to a stop and a young guy hopped out. In dusty boots and faded jeans, he strode over to where we stood on the side of the road.

"I heard your interview on the radio," he said as a way of introduction. "I think it's great what you're doing."

"Thanks," I answered. "It means a lot to hear things like that."

He nodded in acknowledgment. "I own a silver mine, up between Jean and Searchlight."

"Wow, that's cool."

"Not getting much yet." He shrugged. "But who knows." The guy paused, and then: "I want to give you something to welcome you to the state of Nevada." He handed me a small, red velvet bag. The pouch was heavy, substantial. Inside were four silver coins.

"Nevada is the Silver State," he went on. "Now you have silver to remember it by. Who knows...maybe you'll give them to your kids someday."

I was struck by the gesture, made even more meaningful that he'd given me *four* coins. Four was my lucky number. Four winds, four seasons, four directions. I was one of four children. My little traveling troupe numbered four friends.

I'd received a lot of good luck charms and tokens from people on my trip—so many, in fact, that I couldn't carry them all. I had mailed some things home along the way. The four silver coins, though, had a special meaning. I'd keep them right in my saddlebag.

## SIGN IN THE DESERT

The last few days had brought remarkable changes in the environment, from the imposing mountains where I bundled in flannel, to a drop in elevation of several thousand feet, back down to the heat of the desert floor. My cold-weather clothes were rolled up and stashed in the saddle packs once again. The vegetation was sparse, spread in clusters on the sand. Our two-lane road through the southernmost part of Nevada was paved, but little traveled and usually empty of vehicles.

We headed out early in the morning. We were in our zone, steady and quiet as we walked. Among the ridges of sand and the clusters of spiky succulents, I noticed a shape that stood out, the lines too straight to be made in nature. The vertical column was set away from the road, and a faint trail led to it. The column looked like it was made of metal, though oxidation had turned it a dark burnished shade. Words were carved on its side.

I jumped down onto the sand. Rainy and Amanda stood where I dropped the reins; Gypsy was at my feet. I reached my hand to the monument, which jutted out from a concrete base and was taller than me, now that I was on foot.

On one side, carved in large block letters, was the word "NEVADA." I stepped around the base to the other side, squinting in the sun.

It said, "CALIFORNIA."

I traced the letters with my fingers, then let my hand drop to Gypsy's head beside me. I stepped back to rub Rainy's forehead, then Amanda's.

I looked around the state boundary monument, as if I might be able to make out a real line or something else of significance. But there was only the desert. The very air was bright, quiet, and golden.

There was not another soul around for miles.

Rainy, Gypsy, Amanda, and I stood together.

After all the news reporters and photographs, the attention, and all the people who had helped us, wished us well, and wondered if we'd make it, it was just us four, out in this place, alone. It felt somehow fitting that an unobtrusive marker on the desert floor showed where the final state line was being crossed. Despite that occasional excitement to indicate progress, for all the months and all the miles we'd traveled, it had really just been us four, out here, making our footprints on the earth together.

I got my camera from the packs and took pictures of my friends near the California side of the marker. They stood patiently, like they always did when a camera was pointed at them. I hugged each of them.

"We did it, guys," I said.

I put my foot back in the stirrup and climbed into the saddle. I looked at the desert all around us, the mountains in the distance.

The breezes that had been our constant companions were still. It was just me and my dearest friends, the land we stood upon, the desert stillness, and the sky we rode under.

We were in California.

## ■ NEAR

The long road from the Nevada-California line veered close again to the Colorado River, changing the foliage and the scent in the air. I followed trails near the west bank, which rolled along to our left as we now traveled on the California side.

The trails brought us near unexpected strips of vegetation. Gnats and other insects suddenly filled the air. The oasis of green tempted Rainy and Amanda. Any time we stopped, they lowered their heads immediately to taste the shoots of grass.

For the better part of a year now, people had seen Rainy and Amanda all packed up and asked, "Where are you going?" My response—"California"—had invariably gotten a surprised or skeptical reaction. I was not sure what I would say if someone stopped and asked that question now. We were *in* California. Needles, the town I had chosen as our final destination, was not far away. I didn't have the words to describe what I was feeling with the end of our journey so near. A California morning began like all the other days: I got up early and thanked the Deasons, the family who'd let us stay at their place for the night. I fed and brushed and saddled Rainy and then Amanda. I balanced the saddle packs. Then I mounted up and we rode out, heading west. The morning sun shone down on us. Gypsy ran free, as the road was ours in the quiet morning hours. Yes, it was just like other mornings on the trip, yet different.

I had a sense of heightened awareness—of feeling things more deeply than ever. The sky seemed more intensely blue, the few feathery clouds a purer white. A desert bird flitted behind a cactus, startled by us, and I noticed the light speckles of its wing feathers and how small and delicate it looked in contrast to its surroundings.

The desert was a quiet place to ride. It was a much quieter natural place than the woods, where streams gurgled and leaves rustled and birds chirped. The life in the desert was hidden and required stillness and silence to observe.

Rainy's solid clip-clop and Amanda's more delicate tap-tap and the creak of the saddle leather formed the music I lived by; it matched the beat of my heart. I'd felt connected to our surroundings for a while now, but the last few days had also brought a sense of peace and belonging, as if the land and the sky and the road we traveled were all a part of us, and we were now a part of all that *was*. It was us alone out here, yet not alone. After all that we'd experienced, how could I not feel that all of us were weavings from the same cloth?

Far ahead of us, I thought I saw a distant shape, but with the lay of the land and the tricks of the light, it didn't last. Then I registered the out-of-place noise of a helicopter, although the sound was very distant. Not long after, a lone car approached from the west. My eyes noted the black-and-white paint and lights on top—a police car.

My imagination ran wild with possibilities: Was a search on for someone missing in the desert? Was a posse out looking for a criminal on the run?

When the squad car was at last near us, it pulled to the road-side, careful to keep two wheels on the pavement. A young police-man stepped out.

"Hey there!" he called. "They're looking for you up ahead."

"They are? Who?" I asked, puzzled.

"Local saddle club. They're riding out to escort you into town."

I squinted into the distance ahead but didn't see anything.

"Okay," I acknowledged with a nod, unsure of what else to say.

"I'll meet you that way," he replied, pointing down the road. The policeman got into his car, made a U-turn, and headed back the way he'd come.

Rainy started to walk again. Town was just up ahead? I felt a whirl of emotion. The winds of change had just blown through the quiet morning.

When I saw what I now knew were the figures of horses and riders, still small in the distance, I stopped Rainy and covered my mouth with the palm of my hand, as if that could contain or hold back all that I was feeling. Gypsy, who'd been roaming around, came and sat beside Rainy, looking up at me, her eyes asking, *What should we do? Are we ready for this?*

I didn't know.

When I finally squeezed my legs slightly, as always, Rainy stepped forward, Amanda fell into her place beside us, and Gypsy trotted along at their heels. We moved on. We rode forward toward whatever was waiting on the road ahead of us, like we always did.

## NEEDLES, CALIFORNIA

On the outskirts of the little town of Needles, California, I met up with the policeman and a small group of horses and their riders. I heard a friendly cheer as we rode into view.

I had only a moment to bury my emotions. Then I greeted everyone and smiled while they offered congratulations and peppered me with questions.

"We're going to escort you as you ride into town!" one young rider excitedly informed me.

Another asked if I would ride to the local radio station for an interview. I said yes—I had no other plan in place, no real idea what I would do when I reached Needles.

The policeman turned on his lights but no siren, and the saddle club and I fell into a loose formation behind him as he drove slowly toward the edge of town.

Cars were pulled over to watch us parade by. To my utter amazement, the children of the elementary school had been let out to greet us, and they lined the side of the road, waving and cheering as we rode in. The horses of the saddle club members, many of them Arabians, snorted and pranced nervously in all the excitement. Rainy and Amanda walked on calmly. Crowds? Cars? Noise? No big deal. I reached to pat them both, immensely proud of them for the millionth time.

Of the many miles we'd traveled, most of them had been just Rainy, Gypsy, Amanda, and me, alone together. And yet this was how we walked the last miles of our journey: with a police and mounted escort, and a large noisy group of people and horses. Overhead, I heard the helicopter again.

I pushed back at the overwhelming feeling inside of an ending taking place, and I let all the other things I was feeling rise to the surface: pride, happiness, a sense of accomplishment, the excitement at seeing all the different people who had come to cheer us on through the last steps of making my dream come true. I smiled and waved, let people take pictures, and tried to call out answers to all the questions being shouted at me.

We rode up to the radio station in our dusty glory. I was delighted to spy the grinning faces of the Allisons—of course, these wonderful people had planned most of this. Several reporters stood by with notebooks, microphones, and cameras. A crowd of well-wishers waited for me to jump down off Rainy.

I hesitated to move from the saddle. I was suddenly hit again by the enormity of it ending. I fought back tears.

Then I dismounted.

I hugged Rainy's neck, hiding my face for a moment. Then I hugged Amanda, too, and Gypsy. Everyone laughed and clapped and cameras clicked.

But this was what I did with my animals all the time.

Leading Rainy, I walked over to a table that had been set out for the occasion. On it was a sheet cake, decorated with a trail of hoof prints and words that read, "New York to California.

Congratulations Missy, Rainy, Gypsy, and Amanda." There was also a bottle of champagne with my name on it, two silver buckets full of grain, and a big dog bone.

I threw my arms around Bob and Arlene Allison, and Shawn and Jeanine, too, overwhelmed by all that they had done.

There was a wild gust of wind and a thumping sound, and we all watched as the helicopter landed, right in the parking lot, the familiar logo of ABC on its side. The door opened, and out stepped Dan, microphone ready, looking great in a suit. Rick followed with his camera. I hugged both of them, too, laughing and crying at the same time.

I suddenly knew it was time to call my family and tell them we'd made it—we were in California. The radio station disc jockey, Pete, was orchestrating interviews and a local broadcast of the event. He arranged for my call home to feed live on-air.

With the time difference, I would just catch my mom at the end of her workday back East. She taught at the elementary school I had attended as a child. Since I'd started my journey in the spring, the school had displayed a map of the United States, and the kids had tracked my progress with pushpins. Classes talked a little about the geography and history related to each part of the country I'd traveled through. In this way, everyone at my old school had followed our progress all these months.

I called the principal's office, and after offering his own congratulations, he hooked his phone up to the public-address system so the whole school could hear as my mom got on the phone.

"Hello? Missy?" She sounded tentative and worried, as she had always sounded throughout this trip, unsure what a call from me might mean.

"Mom? It's me. I'm calling to tell you…well, guess where we are." Then I blurted it out: "*WE DID IT! WE'RE IN CALIFORNIA!*"

Over the phone, across thousands of miles, I heard the voices of the school children at Horace Mann Elementary rise up in one giant unified cheer.

That's when I started to really cry. I put my face in my hands and wept. I couldn't help it.

When I got ahold of myself, I looked up to see I'd made everyone else cry, too: Pete the DJ had turned off his microphone, tears were streaming down Arlene's cheeks, and even Dan had turned away and was pretending to fiddle with some wires.

Pete, knowing it was time to lighten the mood, announced: "Here's a song for Missy and the horse that walked across the United States!" On came "Celebrate" by Kool and the Gang, and everyone relaxed and started laughing and talking again.

Throughout a celebratory luncheon, speeches, and toasts, I kept going over to check on my animals. I was antsy to get back to them.

Arrangements had been made with Judy Browder, a photographer in town, who offered her barn and pens for Rainy and Amanda. Gypsy and I had a room at the Best Western for as long as we needed it. I would forever be grateful to all those who had planned and attended the celebration. It meant the world to me that my animals and I had been so honored by the day's festivities. But I needed some time alone with my traveling companions. I was a little overwhelmed.

I took a lead rope in each hand and called to Gypsy, and we walked. The familiar sound of hooves on pavement and the nearness of my best friends restored the natural balance in me. I knew that a place just outside town had a monument honoring the early pioneers who crossed the country and came to this part of California. We headed in that direction.

A carved bear, the California state symbol, was at the top of the plaque embedded in stone. For the last time, I said to Rainy, Gypsy, and Amanda, "Go stand by that monument; I'll take your picture."

Through the viewfinder of the camera, I saw the small monument. There was brush and sand and desert behind it. Beside that stood a little mule, still carrying our packs, still feeling that all was right as long as she was beside Rainy. I saw my mixed-breed dog, my constant companion who slept in my sleeping bag and cheered me when I felt lonely. It was not my imagination that she looked proud as could be.

And there with them stood the greatest horse that ever lived. The horse who never faltered, never hesitated. The horse who led us all on an arduous journey across this great and vast land. The horse who gave me stories to tell and who carried me and my dream, and made it come true.

I saw my most beloved friends.

It didn't seem possible for one heart to hold so much love and happiness, and sadness, too, all at the same time.

I took the picture. At the click of the shutter, my friends all moved toward me.

## ▰▰▰ ABOUT ENDING...

Needles, California, was where my animals and I stopped our westward wandering. But it's not where our story ended.

I chose Needles as our final destination for several reasons. The Mojave Desert was to the west, where I knew our struggles with water would reach a new level. We'd also been on the road almost seven months, and it had been a time filled with joy, but some of it had been really hard. Traveling in the way we had could be scary and dangerous and very lonely. It was a fair price to pay for the freedom we found, the days in the wild, the feeling of the road unrolling before us, and getting to know the wide expanse of country as viewed from the back of a wonderful horse.

Once in a while, I daydreamed about resting a while, then doing another trip with my companions. Then I got the feeling that maybe I'd be pushing our luck to try. Luck and fate had been on our side for so long, I felt almost superstitious about it—like it would be too much to ask for more.

And there was Rainy. The weight-loss and lack of gleam in his coat had worried me all through Arizona. I had the veterinarian in Needles check the animals over and was relieved to hear there was nothing wrong with my horse; he was okay. He'd suffered no real ill effects from the many miles he'd walked and the adventures he'd been a part of. But I knew there was more to good horse care than him just being "okay." The vet agreed that Rainy would benefit from time off, some easy trail riding, and a steady diet that wasn't changing all the time.

Rainy had proven over and over again that he was incredibly willing and full of heart. He would have kept going, I was sure, if I'd asked it of him. But that evening, up in the Arizona hills, when he laid his head on my chest, I knew he was telling me something. That very night I looked at my map, judging the distance to California, and tried to figure out the first town we'd come to in the state. All I had to do was pick a place and say we did it—we rode from New York to California. Needles was "California enough" for us.

Amanda, of course, looked about the same as the day she screeched and ran toward Rainy in the Kees' pasture back in Kansas. I had no doubt that if the rest of us were up to it, she would easily have gone on, crossed the desert, traversed the West Coast, and trod on in her steady way to Oregon and Washington, up to Alaska, and right through to the Yukon.

And as for Gypsy—the vet confirmed what I'd suspected for weeks, more news that meant our journey was ending at the right time. My little dog was, indeed, pregnant.

"Don't worry," he said after palpating her belly. "A dog's gestation is a little more than two months. Sometimes animals will wait if they can and have their babies in a place that feels safe and comfortable to them—like home."

I thought about the unplanned mating at the trading post and wondered how much time we had.

As we rested in Needles, I hopped on Rainy bareback for short, easy jaunts into the desert surrounding the Browders' home. It was a good way to spend time with him and help me deal with my uneasy feelings about re-entering "the real world." I made a lot of phone calls and wrote a lot of letters, too. Many people had helped us get to California, and I wanted them all to share in the joy of our success. I was reminded by many in reply that we had a place to stay or a trailer ride for part of the way back if we needed it.

I was blessed. I knew this. I felt that for a while, Rainy, Gypsy, Amanda, and I were truly America's children.

During all the excitement when we first rode into town, reporters had asked me, "How are you going to get back home?" When I replied, "I have absolutely no idea," it produced a wave of laughter—they thought I was kidding. I wasn't. I believed the right thing would present itself, and sure enough, after our little time of respite, things came together.

I wish I could write another book about us piecing our way home across the country. Believe it or not, there are more tales to tell. We got a ride in a truck with chickens, goats, and some jolly pot-smoking hippies who drove us to the Route 66 town of Valentine on their way to a commune. Dan borrowed a trailer and met us there, then took us south to Phoenix, where a Quarter Horse trainer was hauling a rig to the Quarter Horse World Show in Oklahoma City, and he had space for Rainy and Amanda on his truck. (A woman screamed, "What the hell is that?" when Amanda stepped off the trailer amongst the world's top Quarter Horses.) A kind person in Oklahoma, Dave Jolly, boarded Rainy and Amanda at his place until we got a trailer ride from the World Show to Ohio.

Butch and Nancy Goodman met us there…and took us all the way home to New York.

The "chain of people" that helped us get to California was the same support system that got us home to New York. Such an abundance of help and kindness was a lesson to me and will color the way I treat others for the rest of my life.

## AT "HOME," IN KANSAS

While we waited for our trailer ride from Oklahoma City, Reid met us and took Gypsy and me to visit Tom and Barb Kee in Yates Center, Kansas. On the second day of our visit, Gypsy made a nest of clothes on the closet floor, plunked down, and started to breathe heavily. I grabbed the phone and called Reid at work.

"Reid! I think Gypsy's starting to have her puppies! What should I do?"

I heard a somewhat annoying chuckle on the other end of the phone.

"Here's what I want you to do," Reid said seriously.

I listened intently.

Then, sounding amused, he said, "Leave her alone." He laughed, this time without trying to hide it. "Missy, I'm serious. Dogs have been having puppies for many years without you."

By the time I hung up, the first pup was out. Soon another came, then another, and another. I watched in wonder at how perfectly it all worked. Reid was right: My dog knew just what to do, and so did the pups. When she finally seemed finished, a calm, relaxed Gypsy had delivered a total of *ten* puppies.

I could hardly tear my eyes away. I watched Gypsy wash them and nudge them, and how the babies squeaked and nursed. Barb joined me, and the two of us sat together, enjoying the little miracle.

"Mercy," Barb whispered. "I hope she's done!"

We laughed together, a relieved, joyful laugh. Gypsy looked up and wagged her tail.

Well into the night I sat on the floor near the closet, watching my dog and her babies. It occurred to me I had better call my parents and make sure they still wanted us to come home. I'd left in the spring with a horse and a dog. Now I was heading home with a horse, a dog, a mule, and *ten puppies*!

# PART SIX

---

# AFTER

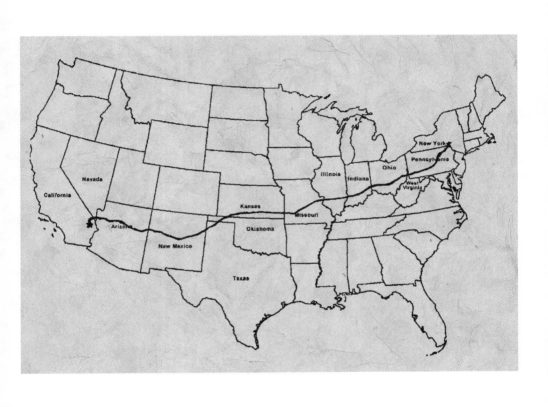

## LOVE GOES ON

Rainy, Gypsy, and Amanda are responsible for the life that I live, even now, years past our journey. After our adventure, I was asked to speak and do presentations many times, and every time I got paid for that, I saved the money. Two years after returning to my hometown, I was able to put a down payment on a little piece of land from that savings—acreage with grazing, a stream, and trees for shade. I built a lean-to barn and moved Rainy and Amanda to the land they helped pay for.

A few years after that, I met a guy who asked me, "Aren't you the girl who rode the horse across the country?" That man became my husband, John. We built a house on the land where my horses lived, and we raised four children together.

Most of what I have and what I love is related to what those three animals did for me. In this way, Rainy, Amanda, Gypsy, and the journey itself keep on giving. I carry the lessons and the memories from that time with me always.

The four of us remained inseparable. Gypsy amused people well into old age, jumping up in the saddle and riding when asked, and posing for cameras until they clicked. She lived to be sixteen years old.

Rainy lived to see the new millennium. We rode out together every day for more than a quarter of a century, so the miles and the moments I cherish with him are beyond measure. I lost him to old age near the twenty-year anniversary of our journey. I think of

Rainy and Gypsy all the time and miss them every day. But I find solace in the knowledge of what a gift they were and how blessed I am, having had them in my life for so long.

And Amanda? That little Kansas mule is waiting for me by the gate right now. At almost forty years old, she still puts love and laughter into my life every day. Before I sent out the very last pages of this, our story, to my publisher, I went out and hugged her, and ran my hand along the delicate curve of those long, beautiful ears, just for luck.

When I told people in my life I was writing about the cross-country journey the animals and I took all those years ago, they asked me: "Is it an adventure story? A travel story? A horse story?" It could be any of those, I suppose.

In the end, though, I realized it's a love story. It's about the love of this country, especially the back roads and small towns, and the places where the trees grow wild and grasses sway and rain falls and soaks into the earth and into streams that flow onward. It's about the love that people give when they hand a tired traveler a cold drink on a hot day. It's about the love of people who welcome you, and the people who let you go. It's about the love that grows when you open your heart to it. And it's about the love for three great animals that gave all they had to give in a partnership with a human. That love goes on, always.

Sometimes you hear people refer to outdoor traveling, hiking, and solo adventures as being "out there." I think often about the days when my animals and I were "out there." It may be fanciful, but I like to think there is still a little of the spirit of our journey "out there." Maybe there's an old fence wire that I unwrapped then rewrapped at a cattle guard. Or a trail with a low spot that started from a hoof print of Rainy's. Or we might have left some road dust sprinkled along the land we traveled across, like stardust.

I believe that real love stays. And thanks to Rainy, Gypsy, and Amanda, there is a lot of love, and a little piece of "out there," in me still.

From a poem written by Reid, about me, my animals,
and our journey, sent to us on the road:


*Someday I'll return to a normal life,*
*Have a job, be a mother and wife.*
*But I'll always remember in my mind's eyes,*
*Those old horizons*
*And distant skies.*

# ACKNOWLEDGMENTS

———————

Years ago, when Rainy, Gypsy, and I started out on our journey, I quickly realized that I was in over my head. I felt overwhelmed and very vulnerable. The kindness of the people we met along the way was a big part of what kept me going and helped me grow strong. Although I was able to write about some of my experiences in this book, there were many other times strangers stopped to see if we needed anything, offered meals or lodging or something for the animals, wrote to or called my parents, or offered to keep us in their prayers. I kept extensive journals as we traveled, and they are filled with pages listing every caring person we met and every moment that someone took time out of their day to help us. In this way, many people became part of our journey. So many people helped us and showed us kindness that including a "thank you" to all of them would greatly increase the size of this book. I may not be able to fit them all in these pages, but every person who touched our journey is a special memory to me. I will never forget them.

Over the years, as I lived life and raised my children, I worked on writing down the stories from the journey I made across the country with my animals. While writing is mostly a solitary pursuit, there are always people involved in the process of improving what you wrote and turning your writing into something others may like to read. The following people helped me on the way to turning my tales into the book in your hands, and I'd like to acknowledge them: The members of the Wednesday-night writers' group at Barnes & Noble in Vestal, New York, who heard many of my stories, and were a lot of fun to hang out with, especially Mark Levy, a writer, friend, and intellectual property lawyer extraordinaire. Audrey Pavia, who started as an editor and became a friend. Becky Smith, who not only proofread but encouraged me greatly, and Kate Karlson, who did a last-minute check of the final manuscript. In addition, I've been blessed with more than my fair share of good friends, neighbors, and relatives who believed in me and believed these stories were book-worthy. I thank you all, from my oldest school friends, to friends I've made through a shared love of animals, to the people who are dear to me in my family's community.

I'd like to mention a horseman from way back before the trip, Larry Reed, who did a lot to help send us on our way. Also, Jack and Nadine Betti, for coming to Needles and giving Gypsy and me a "temporary home" in California, and Casey Betti, for driving many hours across the state for us.

An extra thank you to Dr. Reid Scifers for the title *Distant Skies*.

I could not write this without going back to the time before the book or the trip and acknowledging my parents, John and Marie Priblo. It was my mother who taught me the love of books and my father who knew how to tell a story. I honor them with heartfelt appreciation. It was their love and influence that built the foundation that enabled me to go out in the world with an open mind and an open heart.

To the Priblo clan, my wonderful siblings, my sister, Jan, and my brothers, Jack and Vince—I thank you and your families for your unwavering support, your humor and love, and for believing in me. You all enrich my life.

A big thank you to my husband John who built our barn and helped build the life we have. When a non-horse guy marries a horse girl, I don't know if he realizes he'll be doing things like hauling bales of hay and fixing fence for the rest of his life. But you do all that and more. I thank you for your love and for sharing space in my heart with the animals that have been a part of our lives.

A special thank you to my four children, who each in their own way kept me going, helping me continue writing this book at times when I almost gave up. Jack, who was the first to read some stories early on and encouraged me to keep chasing the dream of a book. Maura, the one I called during a time of despair, who said exactly the right words to keep me on the right path. Kellyn, who read a story about Gypsy and said simply, "I really like it," at a time when I needed to hear that. Sam, who asked many questions about the journey and stayed up late into the night to be there when I wrote the very last word. Thank you. All of you are my everything.

And I would really like to say to you, the reader, that if you've ever had a deep connection with a dog or a horse, or if the back roads, small towns, and wide-open spaces call to you, then this book was for you, too. Being able to share stories about Rainy and Gypsy and Amanda, our adventures, and the people that touched our lives helps to keep them alive for me, and for that I thank you.

I also would like to extend a very fond thank you to Rebecca Didier, Martha Cook, and Caroline Robbins at Trafalgar Square Books. From the first time I spoke with Rebecca, every interaction with them has been a pleasure. Rebecca, Martha, and Caroline believed in this story enough to give it a chance, and for that, I am forever grateful.

Lastly, I must acknowledge once again Rainy, Gypsy, and Amanda, who will be always remembered and always loved. Thank you for carrying my dreams.

# ABOUT THE AUTHOR

Melissa A. Priblo Chapman is a freelance writer who has had work published in magazines including *The Western Horse*, *Good Dog!*, and *Doggone*. Her story "Gypsy, Cross-Country Dog" appears in the book *Traveler's Tales: A Dog's World* alongside the work of such renowned authors as John Steinbeck and Gary Paulson. Chapman has been a paid speaker to over 100 organizations in regard to her solo cross-country trip and is a member of the Long Riders Guild, a worldwide league of equestrian adventurers. Chapman is a married mother of four and lives in Upstate New York. She rides every day and continues to share life with her horses and dogs.